The Supper of The Lord

The New Testament, Ecumenical Dialogues, and Faith and Order on Eucharist

John Reumann

FORTRESS PRESS   PHILADELPHIA

to
Wittenberg University, Springfield, Ohio
President William A. Kinnison
faculty, board, students, alumni, and friends
as a token of appreciation
for the degree of Doctor of Divinity
conferred *honoris causa,* 11 June 1983

Grateful acknowledgment is given for permission to quote from:

Baptism, Eucharist and Ministry (1982), *One Baptism, One Eucharist and a Mutually Recognized Ministry,* and other papers of the Faith and Order commission of the World Council of Churches, Geneva, to its director, Dr. Günther Gassman;

Lutheran-Episcopal Dialogue: A Progress Report and *The Report of the Lutheran-Episcopal Dialogue Second Series 1976–80* to Forward Movement Publications, 412 Sycamore Street, Cincinnati, Ohio 45202;

Theologische Realenzyklopädie to Walter de Gruyter, Berlin and New York.

Biblical quotations, unless otherwise noted, are from the Revised Standard Version of the Bible, copyright 1946, 1952, © 1971, 1973 by the Division of Christian Education of the National Council of the Churches of Christ in the U.S.A. and are used by permission.

Library of Congress Cataloging in Publication Data

Reumann, John Henry Paul.
The Supper of the Lord.

Includes bibliographies and index.
1. Lord's Supper.   2. Lord's Supper and Christian union.   I. Title.
BV825.2.R47 1984   264'.36   84–47932
ISBN 0–8006–1816–5

K902E84   Printed in the United States of America   1–1816

Contents

Abbreviations

ALC	The American Lutheran Church
ALERC	Anglican-Lutheran European Regional Commission
ARC, ARCIC	Anglican–Roman Catholic (International Commission)
au. trans.	author's translation
BEM	*Baptism, Eucharist and Ministry*
DS	Denzinger-Schönmetzer, *Enchiridion Symbolorum,* 34th ed. (1967)
IDB, IDBS	*Interpreter's Dictionary of the Bible* and Supplementary Volume (Nashville: Abingdon Press, 1962 and 1976)
Jenson, *Visible Words*	Robert W. Jenson, *Visible Words: The Interpretation and Practice of Christian Sacraments* (Philadelphia: Fortress Press, 1978)
Jeremias, *Eucharistic Words*	J. Jeremias, *The Eucharistic Words of Jesus,* trans. Norman Perrin (New York: Charles Scribner's Sons, 1966; Philadelphia: Fortress Press, 1978)
JES	*Journal of Ecumenical Studies*
LCA	Lutheran Church in America
LCMS	The Lutheran Church—Missouri Synod
LED I, II	Lutheran-Episcopal Dialogue (U.S.), First and Second Series
Lehmann, *Meaning*	Helmut T. Lehmann, ed., *Meaning and Practice of the Lord's Supper* (Philadelphia: Muhlenberg Press, 1961)
LW	*Luther's Works* (St. Louis: Concordia Publishing House; Philadelphia: Fortress Press)

LWF	Lutheran World Federation
NIDNTT	*New International Dictionary of New Testament Theology* (Grand Rapids: Zondervan Publishing House, 1975–78)
par.	parallels in the Synoptic Gospels
RCLJC	Roman Catholic/Lutheran Joint Commission
RGG	*Die Religion in Geschichte und Gegenwart* (Tübingen: Mohr-Siebeck, 1957–65)
Tappert ed.	*The Book of Concord,* ed. and trans. T. G. Tappert et al. (Philadelphia: Muhlenberg Press, 1959)
TDNT	*Theological Dictionary of the New Testament* (Grand Rapids: Wm. B. Eerdmans, 1964–76)
TRE	*Theologische Realenzklopädie* (Berlin: Walter de Gruyter, 1977–)
WARC	World Alliance of Reformed Churches
WCC	World Council of Churches

Introduction

IN HOLLAND it was said among Roman Catholics in the late 1960s, "Everything changes except the elements in the eucharist." This was a way of asserting, amid the ferment of the years after the Second Vatican Council, particularly following publication of the *Dutch Catechism*, that all sorts of changes were taking place in theology, ethics, and Christian life, but above all that there were some new views about the Lord's Supper. These varied from the traditional Catholic, medieval view of "transubstantiation," that in the Eucharist the bread and wine are changed into the substance of the body and blood of Christ, though the accidents of bread and wine may still appear.

The turbulent 1960s, the no-less-confusing 1970s, and now the 1980s have indeed seen many changes in Christendom. This applies ecumenically; it applies in various denominations or confessional groups, as well as in the rise of new forces and movements inside the churches (like Neo-Pentecostalism) and outside (such as the Unification Church and Eastern religions). In few areas, however, has there been so much change in theory and practice as with the Lord's Supper, that meal in which all Christians participate who name the name of Christ. To give it some of its many names, it is variously called the Mass, the Eucharist, Holy Communion, and the Table of the Lord.

Christians of almost every denomination have experienced a bewildering variety of new liturgies or forms of service, as well as new practices, for Holy Communion in recent years. They are vaguely or sometimes keenly aware that other denominations have also changed. Probably they have heard of some of the ecumenical discussions or read of proposals, such as the statement from the World Council of Churches' Faith and Order Commission in 1982, which offers a statement of actual agreement by representatives from dozens of churches on such traditionally divisive issues as the Eucharist, ministry, and baptism. Christians of almost every denomination are less likely to know as much about what biblical scholarship has been saying in recent years about the Lord's Supper in the New Testament and in its Old Testament background, but here too momentous changes in outlook have taken place.

The purpose of this book is to describe some of the trends and proposals concerning the Lord's Supper that have emerged in the last twenty to thirty years. The focus is particularly on the motifs that have emerged in the study of the Bible and through ecumenical dialogue, because these are certainly the most significant areas for explaining present changes and for contemplating future developments. Brief attention will be paid to some significant turning points through the centuries, especially so that we may more clearly understand the current ecumenical discussion of the issues that have emerged since biblical times and that have seemed divisive.

It is appropriate to attempt such a description at this time, first, because it is always helpful to examine periodically the road traveled. With regard to the Sacrament of the Altar some will want to ask whether the general direction has been the right one in the last few decades and whether at this twist or that turn the proper course has been taken. Others will affirm the direction but wonder about the implications for the last decade or so of this century. Still others will see the recent trends as real breakthroughs and the year 2000 precisely as a *kairos,* the right time for attaining new goals.

A second reason to attempt such a description at this point in the 1980s is because there is now some semblance of order, some new consensus after several decades of intense change. That is so in Roman Catholicism, with the pontificate of Pope John Paul II, for here it seems the emphasis is on solidifying advances made in recent years, and on stabilizing things (sometimes in accord with older patterns) rather than on further changes. Ecumenically, certain important agreements have been reached, especially in bilateral dialogues. Although not always put into effect, especially on the local level, they are likely to be the sum and substance of proposals which the future must work out. We refer to the outcomes in the Anglican–Roman Catholic conversations, Anglican-Lutheran and Lutheran-Reformed agreements (particularly the Leuenberg Agreement), and the Lutheran–Roman Catholic dialogue. These are trendsetting, and we are reaping first fruits from such bilateral discussions.

Moreover, many churches have recently produced new worship books, hymnals, and lectionaries, for example the *Lutheran Book of Worship* in North America or, among many post–Vatican II Roman Catholic reforms, the *Ordo Lectionum Missae* which is used by many churches throughout the world. One senses an approaching period of greater stability and less of the wild profusion of loose-leaf booklets and weekly sheets of inserts for parish Sunday services! It should be added that a great deal of commonality in these liturgical revisions has resulted from consultation among the major denominations, as on English translations of traditional texts. However, some might feel that, though we have moved toward a new uniformity here, the results are too bland or (others say) too daring, and are subject to criticism for losing long-cherished denominational forms. Unity and/or uniformity?

A third reason for taking up the topic now is the appearance of the Faith and Order statement *Baptism, Eucharist and Ministry* in 1982. This document is simply unparalleled in its attempt to state agreements and convergences by theologians of most major churches, which were arrived at after more than a decade of intense discussion. In a manner that has never happened before, *BEM* offers a draft proposal on which all churches are asked to respond, specifically by December 1984, so that further work can then be done for further convergence on these and other topics, perhaps leading to a new but common expression of the apostolic faith by the end of this century.

Our survey will not, as already stated, try to touch on the whole history of the sacrament, but only upon aspects of obvious import in recent discussion and practice and, as far as we can tell, of impending import.

Some attention must therefore be given, first of all, in chapter 1 to the biblical basis of the Lord's Supper. This is necessary because biblical studies have not stood still in the past twenty years but have made considerable strides or at least come up with new suggestions regarding the New Testament meanings of such themes as "covenant," the Words of Institution, the roots of the Last Supper in Judaism and the Old Testament, and even the dating and type of meal in the Upper Room. We shall try to keep our eye on what is pertinent for current applications and not detail every last exegetical debate. But we shall not limit our comments only to the New Testament, for it is increasingly realized that the Old Testament–Jewish and Greco-Roman settings of the early church were not without influence on the development of the sacrament. Perhaps the most profound impact from biblical studies is the growing realization that we cannot today with surety ascertain exactly what Jesus did, said, or intended, historically; rather, we must be content with biblical perimeters or limits and guiding directions. It may also be that some ecumenical views today are based upon understandings of the biblical materials no longer as widely held as they were twenty or thirty years ago.

Chapter 2 briefly follows up on historical developments between New Testament times and modern ecumenical discussions. That there has been change over the centuries is shown charmingly (and almost unintentionally, for Professor Shepherd's aim is to show that "the service remains throughout the ages essentially the same as that which the apostles received from the Lord Jesus at the Last Supper," p. vii) in Massey H. Shepherd, Jr.'s 'At all Times and in all Places' (Greenwich, Conn.: Seabury Press, 1947, rev. ed. 1953). The imprint of each age appears as eucharistic celebrations are reconstructed by the author for A.D. 150, 500, 1400, 1665, 1830, and (at that time a forecast of the future) 1960. Our chapter seeks to give not a complete account of these centuries but just enough information about some crucial changes, disagreements, and developments to make subsequent discussion intelligible. Most of the material included has been chosen to show how the New Testament data led to various lines of development, under later historical and theological circumstances. Some see these developments almost as important as the biblical material itself, indeed more so in some instances, so far as shaping understanding of the Eucharist in a church is concerned.

Chapter 3 takes up first the discussions of the Eucharist since about 1960 in dialogues between two churches or communions or traditions. Within an overview of all such bilateral discussions, we have focused on four as most important: Lutheran-Reformed, Lutheran–Roman Catholic, Anglican–Roman Catholic, and Lutheran-Episcopal. Others are noted in passing and a brief critique of each major one is offered.

Second, this chapter gives attention to the Faith and Order statement on Eucharist, in light of its historical genesis and within the context of *BEM* as a whole. Again there is an evaluation of this document as a whole and part by part.

The brief concluding chapter 4 seeks to draw together some conclusions, with occasional personal comments, especially as the biblical and ecumenical findings are juxtaposed.

Some of this material was in draft form as early as 1980. The *BEM* document has proven a catalyst for revision and expansion so as to cover the topics indicated. It would be foolish to claim completeness in two such demanding areas as biblical studies and ecumenism. The juxtaposition of the two and their interrelation account for some of the choices as to what to include and what to exclude.

I am by profession a student of the New Testament. For almost twenty years I have also been a participant in the U.S. Lutheran–Roman Catholic dialogue. These two facts have encouraged the attempt to integrate work in the twin areas of Bible and ecumenics, while giving attention to several pertinent dialogues and especially to the work of Faith and Order. But it is not easy to claim competence in all these areas, to say nothing of nineteen or so centuries of intervening history. Where there are errors of fact or judgment, others can correct them, to the benefit of all. I have, in order not to overstress the significance of the dialogue in which I have had a part, probably deliberately underplayed its importance. But I have allowed such experience to guide me in discussion of the other dialogues. One is struck again and again by the absence of firsthand accounts of how dialogues work and how statements are arrived at by participants.

The chapters are written without the paraphernalia of footnotes. Where references, especially for quotations, are needed, the method has been followed of including date within parentheses in the sentence itself. Where books are cited several times, full publication data is usually given at the first occurrence and in a bibliography for further reading at the end of each chapter. The system of abbreviated references will probably be obvious, for example, "Paper Number" for a Faith and Order publication and *BEM* for *Baptism, Eucharist and Ministry*. The brief bibliographies list chiefly works quoted or representative of varying points of view which the reader may wish to consult. There is no attempt at completeness, especially for titles not available in English. The statements under study vary considerably in the matter of capitalizing terms like Holy Communion, Eucharist, church, Mass, and so forth. I have cited documents as published and have tried to reflect their style when paraphrasing.

Most of those who turn to the topic of this book, I suppose, and certainly all who receive or officiate at the sacrament of Holy Communion are committed to the truth of the good news of Jesus Christ and the crucial need for its continued gracing of human lives. Because the Lord's Supper is so tangible and specific an expression of this gospel, people treasure its position in the life of the church and seek ever to assert our need for it and

God's goodness in the Eucharist. But the church has no doubt made mistakes before in its sacramental theory and praxis and could again. Hence so many views and controversies. That is why it is important periodically to assess what has been happening, as we set our hopes for a deepened faith and life in Christ in the future. Of a pamphlet by F. C. Burkitt in the 1920s on the Lord's Supper, someone commented, "A wealth of wisdom for six pence." Prices for books and pamphlets have risen. But the need for discerning wisdom among God's people, even at the altar, remains always.

I suppose it is emblematic of our day that I am completing these words of introduction at a Roman Catholic retreat center run by the Redemptorist Order in Arizona, while lecturing to a workshop for Lutherans, and our companions have been during the week an Episcopal retreat group plus visitors of various traditions of faith. There is no common Eucharist, but as I write, even while posing all sorts of questions, I sense in many quarters a certain common optimism that all who have love for Jesus as Lord and pray for his coming feel a call to one day come together at the table that belongs to the Lord, not to us.

My thanks must be recorded to Norman Hjelm of Fortress Press, for encouragement to finish this manuscript; to Paula Gravelle, a student at the Lutheran Theological Seminary, Philadelphia, for deciphering and typing much of it; and to my wife Martha and daughter Miriam for patience at my time away from family life but with whom together as family we commune in our home congregation and discuss sometimes at home the meaning of Holy Communion.

Picture Rocks, Tucson, Arizona
5 February 1984

1
Biblical Motifs as Foundations: Jesus, the Hebrew Scriptures, and Early Church Developments

THE LORD'S SUPPER is one of many names for that gospel-sacrament which repeatedly brings new life from God to Christians of all sorts. Because of the variety in terminology, it is necessary to keep some of the nuances of those terms in mind as we use them.

A Note on Terms

"The Last Supper" is a term we use for the final meal that Jesus ate with his disciples in Jerusalem "on the night in which he was betrayed" (1 Cor. 11:23; cf. Mark 14:17–25). From this evening setting for the meal comes the German word *das Abendmahl*, employed in Luther's Bible translation for that meal as well as for subsequent celebrations of *das Herrenmahl* (the Lord's Meal or Supper).

"The Lord's Supper" refers to the rite involving bread and wine, which the early church developed, originally in the context of a proper meal, according to 1 Corinthians 11, at the Lord's command. It is the term for the sacrament that has clearest New Testament warrant: it is "the Lord's Supper," Paul insists that you celebrate, not your own (1 Cor. 11:20), "the Supper of the Lord" (R. F. Weymouth, *The New Testament in Modern Speech,* 1903).

Other terms that reflect Scripture and are obvious in meaning include "the Table of the Lord" (1 Cor. 10:16), "Communion" (cf. 1 Cor. 10:16, often with the adjective "Holy" added), "the Meal" (cf. 1 Cor. 11:25; Mark 14:18, 22), and, a later development, "the Sacrament of the Altar" (cf. 1 Cor. 10:18; Heb. 13:10).

Jewish and therefore early Christian meals regularly included a "blessing" where God was praised for his goodness (in Hebrew, a *berakah*). One Greek term for such a blessing was *eulogia*, as in 1 Cor. 10:16, but a

1

more Greek expression was *eucharistia,* "thanksgiving" (1 Cor. 10:30). The corresponding verbs could be used almost interchangeably, as in the story of the Feeding of the Five Thousand:

> Mark 6:41, Jesus "looked up to heaven and blessed [God] *(eulogein),* and broke the loaves, and gave them to the disciples";
> John 6:11, Jesus, "after he had given thanks [to God] *(eucharistein),* distributed" the loaves.

Never in the New Testament, and only later in the second century, does *eucharistein* ("to say a thanksgiving") become a technical term for "celebrate 'Eucharist.'" But by the second century the Eucharist had been separated from "the meal," and in the second century other significant developments, as we shall see, took place.

As a term "Eucharist" runs the danger of concentrating attention on *our* offering thanks to God and even of slipping over into the sense of "offer a thankoffering," instead of *God's* serving us (on this sense of "the Service" and of *Gottesdienst,* cf. Ferdinand Hahn, *The Worship of the Early Church,* trans. David E. Green [Philadelphia: Fortress Press, 1973], pp. 105 and xv–xvii). On the other hand, "Eucharist" yields a convenient adjective, "eucharistic"—something which none of the other terms for Holy Communion do.

We shall employ all of these terms, at times synonymously, with an awareness of their nuances.

BACKGROUNDS: JESUS AND THE LAST SUPPER

The Upper Room

To many people the obvious starting point in considering the Lord's Supper lies in what Jesus said and did in a large guest chamber in Jerusalem at Passover "on the night in which he was betrayed." Yet one of the ironies resulting from all the intense modern study of the Gospels is that scholars are more and more certain that *we do not know exactly what Jesus said that night.*

Beginning in 1953 a "new quest for the historical Jesus" was launched. Many "lives" and other studies on the man from Nazareth have been generated in the past thirty years. A "National Seminar on the Sayings of Jesus" was even announced for the 1980s to determine by scholarly vote which of Jesus' words are authentic. But the new quest, it must be said, has fragmented without yielding conclusive, agreed-upon results.

There is a parallel with regard to Jesus' words in the Upper Room. The lifelong endeavor of the late Professor Joachim Jeremias to recover what Jesus said in Aramaic over the bread and wine (in his justly famous book, *The Eucharistic Words of Jesus* [New York: Charles Scribner's Sons, rev. ed. 1966]) represents a highwater mark of such efforts. However, scholars are generally not persuaded that "This (is) my body" and "This (is) my blood of the covenant for you" stand as the only possible recovery operation from the varied New Testament evidence. Even in 1961 Robert P. Roth wrote, "the *ipsissima verba* cannot be recovered" *(Meaning and Practice of the Lord's Supper* [Philadelphia: Muhlenberg Press], p. 15; hereafter cited as *Meaning).* Since then there has been a growing awareness that we do not know the precise words of Jesus.

For example, the few pages about this final meal in Günther Bornkamm's *Jesus of Nazareth* (New York: Harper & Brothers, 1960; pp. 160–62), no doubt the oustanding "life" to emerge from the new quest, wrestle primarily with the chronological problem of the meal and Jesus' eschatological expectation of approaching death and the coming kingdom (Mark 14:25). Bornkamm doubts the supper was a Passover meal (p. 161). The more optimistic survey *Jesus in Contemporary Historical Research*, written by the late Swedish nonagenarian Gustav Aulén (Philadelphia: Fortress Press, 1976; pp. 79–81, cf. 21), states that it was a Passover meal for Jesus but allows that the texts "cause questions which have no categorical answers" (p. 81). Herbert Braun's more radical *Jesus of Nazareth: The Man and His Time* (Philadelphia: Fortress Press, 1979; pp. 34, 56–57, 113, 39) maintains that the Passover meal references are "secondary" and that "the last supper (Mark 14:22–24) might be a reading back into Jesus' last days of the Lord's supper celebrated in Hellenistic Christian congregations."

Such results come about because the biblical texts themselves are not uniform. A good example is the question of the type of final supper Jesus held before his death. John's Gospel says that it was not a Passover meal (18:28), for Jesus died before Jerusalemites ate the Passover lamb. The Synoptics identify the meal in the Upper Room as the Passover (Mark 14:12, 14, 16), though the accounts of the meal themselves do not (14:18–25 par.). Jeremias argued for the Passover date. Other excellent scholars believe John is right. The proposal put forth in the 1950s, notably by Annie Jaubert, to solve the matter by appealing to *two* calendars— so that John is correct by the official Jerusalem calendar, and the accounts that say it was a Passover meal for Jesus are correct in terms of the calen-

dar used at Qumran and perhaps in Galilee—has not commanded wide
assent.

We can only say that Jesus' last meal before he died was "at Passover
time," but about the exact type of meal or what he said over the loaf and
the cup we cannot be sure (see further, pp. 6–7, below).

Jesus' Frequent Fellowship at Meals

If all the historical-Jesus study of recent years has not made us certain
about details in the Upper Room, it has nonetheless decisively underscored Jesus' wider practice of table-fellowship with disciples and others. We now recognize in this practice a root for the meal-fellowship of
early Christianity, which we have come to know as the Lord's Supper.

Not only was Jesus often a guest at meals and receptions (Luke
5:29–32; 7:36–50; Mark 14:3; John 2:1–11), but sometimes he was the
host (Mark 2:15; cf. 2:1). Surprisingly, in spite of Jewish rules about
kosher customs and about not defiling oneself by eating with "unclean"
people, Jesus received "sinners"—including tax collectors in the service
of the hated Romans, prostitutes, and outcasts—and actually ate with
them (Matt. 11:19). Mark 2:15–20 is a typical reflection of this practice,
which Luke has idealized in a number of "table-talk" scenes.

This *fellowship by Jesus with sinners at meals* has been emphasized as
bedrock historical fact by the new quest. We see here in such meals a
glimpse of what the kingdom will be like (cf. Matt. 8:11). Moreover, a
strong note of forgiveness runs through this table-fellowship: Jesus gives
assurance of God's grace by eating as a friend with sinners (Luke
19:1–10; Matt. 11:19). Some see here, in embryonic form, the good
news of justification by grace as later expressed in the Lord's Supper. The
motif may also be related to the idea of *koinonia* (fellowship/participa-
tion) in the early church (see pp. 41–46, below).

There has also been a growing awareness that *Jesus' feeding miracles,
told as they are with eucharistic terminology intertwined, point toward
the great "eschatological banquet" envisioned in the Old Testament,*
when the kingdom is fulfilled (cf. Isa. 25:6–12; 65:13).

The Feeding of the Five Thousand (Mark 6:31–44) and the Feeding of
the Four Thousand (8:1–11) contain many of the same terms found in the
account about the Upper Room (14:22): took, blessed, broke, gave
(6:41; 8:6). Of course, much of this is what a good Jew would do on *any*
eating occasion, including the recitation of a *berakah* (as noted above, p.

1), and what a Greek Thracian householder customarily did (Xenophon's *Anabasis* 7.3.22, "He took up the loaves of bread which lay beside him, broke them into little pieces and tossed them to those whom it pleased him, likewise also the meat"). To ask whether the feeding-miracle stories have been retold under the influence of eucharistic terminology or whether the Upper Room account reflects earlier meals of Jesus is a bit like the question "Which came first, the chicken or the egg?" Most likely, *all* the stories simply reflect what was everyday practice; for religious people a meal included blessing God, with those present joining in at least with their "amen."

Some of Jesus' *parables* likewise reflect this theme of the joyous banquet where the host or king (the Lord) accepts the poor and outcast, even apparently non-Jews (Luke 14:15-24; Matt. 22:1-14, certainly so in the parables' present form).

Attention has also been drawn to *meals shared by the risen Jesus with his disciples,* in Luke's writings. Peter's sermon in Acts 10:41 speaks of "witnesses, who ate and drank with him after he rose from the dead" (cf. Acts 1:4, RSV note). Luke 24:13-32 has been interpreted as an Easter story about how Jesus henceforth will be present with his disciples, namely, through exposition of the scriptures (vv. 27, 32) and in "the breaking of bread" (v. 30; note the verbs: took, blessed, broke, gave). Elsewhere, however, only Jesus eats (24:43, to prove he is not just a spirit).

Oscar Cullmann has probably exaggerated the importance of these scenes in Luke-Acts, when compared with the New Testament evidence as a whole, as a source for the church's Supper. It is pressing too hard to fit such evidence into a distinction, drawn from the history of religions, between "eating *with* God" convivially (cf. Luke-Acts and Exod. 24:9-11) and "eating *God*" or "from what God provides" as "communion." (Cf. Cullmann and F. J. Leenhardt, *Essays on the Lord's Supper* [Richmond: John Knox Press, 1958], pp. 5-23; Åke V. Ström in *Theologische Realenzyklopädie* [hereafter *TRE*], Vol. 1, p. 44; and Helmer Ringgren and Åke V. Ström, *Religions of Mankind: Today and Yesterday* [Philadelphia: Fortress Press, 1967], pp. xxxvii, 147.)

In any case, what is now said about the special meal with the disciples in the Upper Room can be placed within a sequence of fellowship-meal experiences during Jesus' ministry (and after the resurrection, according to Luke-Acts), as background for the Lord's Supper of the early church.

The Long and Short of Luke's Text

For the Upper Room scene in the Gospel According to Luke there is a well-known variation in the Greek manuscripts and ancient versions. Most of these sources contain a longer text, which includes vv. 19b–20 in Chapter 22. This reading yields a sequence where Jesus gave the "apostles" at the table a *cup* of wine to divide among themselves (22:14–18). Then he took *bread,* gave thanks, broke it, and gave it to them, saying, "This is my body" (v. 19a). Then follows the familiar "which is given for you. Do this in remembrance of me" (19b) and a *second cup* after supper, with the words, "This cup which is poured out for you is the new covenant in my blood" (v. 20). However, the Western text, as represented in a Greek-Latin manuscript of the sixth century and the Old Latin version, preserves a shorter account which omits vv. 19b–20. Here the order is cup-bread.

In the Revised Standard Version (New Testament, 1946) and the New English Bible (New Testament, 1961) the shorter text is preferred. There 22:19b–20 is placed in smaller type as a footnote. By 1960 or so the scholarly consensus on the textual question had already shown a preference for the longer text as what Luke truly wrote. Hence the New American Bible, Today's English Version (the Good News Bible), Living Bible, and New International Version all follow the fuller account. Text critics assume the Western sources dropped vv. 19b–20 either by accident or to avoid the awkwardness of two cups.

More recently the view has found favor that Luke has two cups because he was reflecting a kind of "Christian Passover" service with which he was familiar, perhaps an annual rite with several cups of wine, as in Jewish practice.

The Words of Institution

At the heart of all four accounts in the New Testament concerning what Jesus said and did in the Upper Room are a set of interpretative sayings, indicating the significance of the bread and wine. As he institutes what becomes the church's sacrament of Holy Communion, Jesus gives a new meaning to the customary food and drink which were not only a part of the Passover meal but also a mainstay of any other festive board. Paul's account was the first of the four versions to be written down, about A.D. 55 in a letter to Corinth. The Synoptics followed in writing, A.D. 70–95; we need not worry here about their sequence chronologically. John's

Gospel lacks any such words in the Upper Room and must be considered separately (see pp. 17–21, below).

The four versions can be grouped into *two main types:*

Paul (1 Cor. 11:23–26) and Luke (22:19–20, 27–30)	Mark (14:22–25) and Matthew (26:26–29)
"This is my body which (is) for you" (11:24) "This is my body which is given for you" (22:19ab)	"Take, (eat), This is my body" (14:22; 26:26)
"This cup is the new covenant in my blood" (11:25) "This cup (is) the new covenant in my blood which is being poured out for you" (22:20)	"This is my blood of the covenant which is being poured out for many" (14:24; 26:28) Matthew adds, "for forgiveness of sins"
"Do this for my remembrance" is added twice by Paul (1 Cor. 11:24, 25) and once in Luke (22:19b).	

Simply to exhibit these texts side by side shows the problems in recovering the "original" version. Detailed examination strengthens the likelihood, advanced by form criticism, that each account reflects *liturgical* usage in early Christian communities. In other words, we are dealing with formulations employed in the early church not just as rubrics for conducting services but as actual narratives recited at the worship services in Corinth and elsewhere and for proclamation and catechetical instruction about Jesus—his death and its meaning and how subsequent believers may appropriate the blessings provided at Calvary.

A corollary is that we have apparent a variety of emphases associated with the bread and especially the cup in the Last Supper and the Lord's Supper.

DEVELOPMENT OF THE LORD'S SUPPER

If we cannot recover exactly what Jesus said in the Upper Room, we can attempt to sketch *how the Lord's Supper developed in earliest Christianity* on the basis of what these liturgical accounts say about its institution. There had, of course, been meals of fellowship during Jesus' ministry and, all accounts agree, an especially significant, solemn meal with bread and wine singled out to bear a new meaning—"on the night in which Jesus was betrayed." The verb usually translated "was betrayed" in 1 Cor. 11:23 can in connection with the Passion also mean "was handed over" (to his enemies) and may even imply "was handed over" (to death) by God "for us all" (cf. Rom. 8:32; 4:25). After Easter, Christians saw a plan of God for the salvation of humankind being unfolded in these events. They saw the results of what the cross of Jesus had wrought being now imparted in a supper of and with their risen Lord.

Post-Easter Stages and Theories

All efforts to reconstruct the history of this supper in the earliest church are precarious, but there is considerable consensus on the following stages.

1. At first what Christians experienced through the bread and cup took place *in the context of a real meal* of food to satisfy daily needs and hunger. First Corinthians 11:25 makes this clear. It also states that the one interpretative saying over the bread occurred *before* the meal and the other (over the wine) afterward: Jesus "said, 'This is my body which (is) for you. Do this in remembrance of me.' In the same way also the cup, *after supper,* saying, 'This cup is the new covenant in my blood. Do this, as often as you drink it, in remembrance of me' " (11:24–25).

Casual readers may not note how in three little Greek words, literally "after the dining," a meal is assumed. The fact that a meal separated the two interpretative sayings may explain why the sayings need not have been precisely parallel and implies that each saying carried with it the full meaning of the whole meal.

2. What was happening in Corinth before the year A.D. 55—and indeed the occasion for Paul to cite these words in his letter—pointed to a problem leading to *abuses in the meal-sacrament*. Some members of the congregation arrived early and devoured all the food. Others went hungry. (Perhaps class distinctions were involved here: servants who had to work late were thus excluded from the meal, while wealthier members who were free to come on time ate, drank, and "humiliate[d] those who have nothing.") Some Christians got drunk. And—completely contrary to what should have been an occasion for unity—each went ahead with his or her individual meal, ignoring others (see 1 Cor. 11:17–22). Individualism controlled the supper, not the Lord!

3. The solution was to encourage the people to eat first at home, as Paul suggests (11:22, 34). The result of such an action was to separate the Lord's Supper from its context in a meal for satisfying hunger. Another result was to *have the bread and cup*, each connected with an interpretative saying of Jesus, *come together,* the one directly following the other, *after the supper* or as they were finishing the meal. This latter arrangement we can see in the early church's account now found in the Synoptic Gospels:

> And as they were eating, he took bread . . . and said, "Take, this is my body." And he took a cup, and . . . said to them, "This is my blood of the covenant, which is poured out for many." (Mark 14:22–24; Matthew and Luke similarly)

Here where there is no reference to a meal between the two sayings the tendency will be more and more to parallel the two sayings or to let the second one interpret the first.

In a recent sociologically oriented interpretation Gerd Theissen, then of Bonn University in Germany, reads the situation at Corinth somewhat differently, stressing even more than the majority of interpreters reflected in our reconstruction above the socioeconomic divisions in the congregation. It is assumed that the practice had grown up in the Corinthian church, as in many Greek clubs and at religious festivals, of having a group meal including meat. Such meals would be at the homes of the wealthier members, who could boast of both house and fine cuisine. People like that were part of the Corinthian Christian community (cf. 1:26, some were "powerful" and "of noble birth"; one, Erastus, mentioned in Rom. 16:23, had been supervisor of city meat-markets for a year in his rise to the top of the political structure and was perhaps now a quaestor, one of the four most powerful officials in Corinth). These rich people were evidently willing to share bread and wine with the whole congregation, but the private meal that they had put within the framework of the Lord's Supper reflected, as in pagan banquets, the social status of those attending through the quality and quantity of food offered.

Faced with such a situation, Paul, according to Theissen, not only upbraided these factions (11:17–22) but sought to ameliorate the problem by placing the private meal between the bread and wine as a common meal (v. 25, thus seemingly making "after dinner" Paul's own phrase) and by emphasizing three particular features. One is Christ's vicarious death "for you" (v. 24), so that the scapegoat theme humbles the aggressiveness of the Corinthians toward each other. Another is the judgment-to-come (vv. 31–32) as a sanction to enforce the obligation of all Christians to the community. The third is emphasis on the elements of bread and wine—they have a "numinous" quality about them (perhaps as meat did for "the weak" or poor, who seldom otherwise saw meat), in this case binding together those who share them. For Theissen, there may even be a contrast between "the body of Christ" which is to be discerned at the Lord's Supper (11:29, taken to refer to the bread) and the animal "bodies" eaten at pagan sacrifices and the meals of the well-to-do.

Theissen's interpretation (notably in an article in *Novum Testamentum* 16 [1974]: 179–206; trans. J. H. Schütz, *The Social Setting of Pauline Christianity* [Philadelphia: Fortress Press, 1982], pp. 145–74) pushes back to a quite early date the emphasis on the "elements" and makes the Lord's Supper for Paul a means toward social integration: in this zone of time and space at the sacrament, socioeconomic differences do not hold. But many details in this analysis are questionable, and the overall approach is too new to be thoroughly evaluated as yet.

4. In any case, *"the meal" and "the sacrament" of bread and wine were separated.* The former, called in Greek the *agape,* or "love feast," survived for a while on its own, though not without difficulties (cf. Jude, v. 23, where "ungodly persons" are mentioned as "carousing" there, "looking after themselves"—the old selfishness). In the patristic period the agape became a banquet for the poor or widows. Moravians, Mennonites, and others have subsequently revived the love feast in one form or another. In the last few decades some Catholics and Protestants, even together at times, have held "home agapes," the quasi-sacramental meaning of which is by no means clear. The early step, however, of separating Eucharist from agape has been termed "perhaps the greatest change in the whole history of the mass" by J. A. Jungmann *(La liturgie des premiers siècles,* Lex orandi 33 [Paris, 1962], p. 66, as cited by J. J. von Allmen, *The Lord's Supper,* Ecumenical Studies in Worship 19 [Richmond: John Knox Press, 1969], p. 64, who disagrees).

5. The shift within the New Testament period from meal-setting to "sacrament of bread and wine" brought about significant consequences. One was a tendency to parallel the two interpretative sayings (so that Justin Martyr, ca. A.D. 155, has an absolute symmetry, "This is my body, This is my blood"). Another result was an *increasing emphasis on the "elements."* This concentration on the bread and cup to convey the cruci-

fied and risen Lord in his totality, instead of the setting of a whole meal and its fellowship, is not, then, a medieval or patristic development, but occurred as early as Mark's Gospel or possibly even 1 Corinthians (cf. Willi Marxsen, *The Lord's Supper as a Christological Problem*, trans. Lorenz Nieting, Facet Books 25 [Philadelphia: Fortress Press, 1970], pp. 11, 25 = *The Beginnings of Christology* [Philadelphia: Fortress Press, 1979], pp. 97, 110). Still another result was that the Lord's Supper, which was originally observed in a meal-setting at evening (cf. 1 Cor. 11:23), was now shifted to the morning hour, without any meal of food. The development of Sunday as the day for Christian worship, rather than the evening of the sabbath (Friday) or Saturday night, was also a factor here.

Liturgical Fragments

Here and there in early Christian writings scholars have felt they can detect bits of *primitive Christian liturgy* at the Eucharist, in addition to forms of the Words of Institution.

The closing verses of 1 Corinthians have been claimed as the conclusion not only of Paul's letter but also of a congregational gathering, followed directly by "a distinct Supper" (so, for example, Robert Jenson, *Visible Words* [Philadelphia: Fortress Press, 1978], pp. 66-67, reflecting a number of New Testament scholars):

"Greet one another with a holy kiss" (1 Cor. 16:20; cf. 2 Cor. 13:12).

"If any one has no love for the Lord, let him be accursed" (16:22). This formula from sacral law has been described as a ban upon non-Christians at the Eucharist; Bornkamm's claim that unbaptized persons were not thereby excluded remains unconvincing (H. Conzelmann, *1 Corinthians* [Philadelphia: Fortress Press, 1975], p. 300, n. 32).

"Our Lord, come!" (Aramaic, *Marana tha!*) Though likened to an epiclesis or invocation of the Lord to be present at the Eucharist, this eschatological plea probably originally referred to the Second Coming and may here reinforce the ban or anathema in v. 22.

"The grace of the Lord Jesus be with you" (16:23; cf. 2 Cor. 13:14). A benediction.

There is little doubt that Paul's letters were to be read to an assembled congregation, but was the meeting a eucharistic one? (First Corinthians is rather long to be read as the homily!) Against the theory that Paul's closing verses were designed to lead into the Communion service is the presence of his greetings at this point (16:21; cf. 2 Cor. 13:13) and a personal blessing (16:24). Caution is therefore in order (Conzelmann, *1 Corinthians*, p. 300, nn. 26 and 35; p. 301). More likely, we have here liturgical phrases blended into the letter.

In the *Didache*—an early Christian instructional manual, parts of which may date from the mid–first century A.D. and other parts of which come from the second century—we have what may be part of a dialogue between the worship leader and the congregation at 10.6, including the admonition (Jenson, *Visible Words*, p. 66): "If anyone is holy, let him come; if anyone is not, let him repent." But the text goes on about "the prophets" giving thanks *(eucharistein)* as long as they wish, and some versions add at this point a prayer of thanks "for the precious ointment" (perhaps used in an anointing).

The *Didache* is also esteemed for the prayers it contains "concerning the cup" and "concerning the broken loaf" and for giving thanks "after you have been filled" (9.2–4; 10.1–5).

A difficulty lies precisely in the sequence: these "eucharistic prayers" come *before* the dialogue noted above, and only later in Chapter 14 is there reference to the community's "sacrifice" (to be preceded by confession of transgressions and reconciliation with friends with whom there has been a quarrel, so that the "sacrifice"—whatever it is—may be "pure," as Malachi 1:11 enjoins). No doubt what we have in the *Didache* is a developing and expanding collection of ideas, diverse doctrinally and liturgically. While it has been common to compare these passages to the Eucharist, others see here a love feast (especially because there is no reference to the body or blood of Jesus or to "remembering" him), and still others sense reflections of an annual service of baptism, confirmation, and Communion at Eastertime (cf. Robert A. Kraft, *The Apostolic Fathers*, Vol. 3, *Barnabas and Didache* [New York: Thomas Nelson, 1965], pp. 59–65, 66, 165–69, 173–74).

Hebrews 13:10–16 may also contain liturgical phraseology, especially in v. 15, "*Let us* then *keep on offering up a 'sacrifice of praise'* continually *to God*" (the italicized words come from Ps. 50:14, 23). When brought into connection with the Eucharist and the notion of a special class of Christian ministers thought of as Jewish or pagan priests, these words were to have great influence in developing the concept of the Mass as a sacrifice to God.

It is important therefore to note that the author of Hebrews has made clear that our "offering" is "through him" whom he has described in v. 12 as Jesus in his death upon the cross "outside the gate" of Jerusalem.

He has also employed language characteristic of Israel in exile, when there was no Temple with its sacrificial altar, and of Qumran and the type of Judaism which stressed *spiritual* sacrifices.

Moreover the *auctor ad Hebraeos* makes clear what the constant Christian sacrifices are: namely, praise to God (a metaphorical use of the term "sacrifice")—that is, "the *fruit of lips* that acknowledge his name" (this phrase from Hos. 14:3), in the sense of confession, witness, and proclamation—and such everyday things in the world as "doing good" and "sharing what you have" (13:16). If brought into connection with Christ's sacrifice, these verses speak at most of our entering into and appropriating its benefits (for example, at the Lord's Supper, though the sacrament is not mentioned) and responding thereafter in the world with sacrificial service to others. (Cf. C. F. D. Moule, *Worship in the New Testament*, Ecumenical Studies in Worship 9 [Richmond: John Knox Press, 1961], pp. 37–41.)

In light of such passages as 1 Cor. 16:22; *Didache* 10.6; Heb. 13:10; plus 1 Cor. 11:27–28 (on eating and drinking "unworthily" at the Lord's Supper) and other references, Günther Bornkamm has posited a liturgical formula of "warning and exclusion" in the early church at the Lord's Supper. Perhaps Judas, in Luke's Gospel (where, unlike Mark's or Matthew's account, he is present for the bread and cups), is intended as an example of one who is "guilty of the body and blood of the Lord." The admonitions to self-examination in these passages are backed up with divine threats about the coming of Christ who is also Judge (cf. Rev. 22:17, 20, 12, 15; *Marana tha!*). Ignatius, fighting gnosticizing movements, directs his warnings specifically against those who minimized the "flesh" and "blood" of Christ in the Lord's Supper.

For the apostles like Paul, faith was the issue, and the "anathema" excluded unbelievers; in the *Didache* (9.5, perhaps a later view; cf. 10.6) the dividing line was baptism (so Bornkamm, *Early Christian Experience* [New York: Harper & Row, 1969], pp. 169–79, esp. 171). Still later, some churches made confirmation the criterion, and today there is debate on the age for "first Communion." But from the outset we can see a Christian concern about the seriousness of this sacrament and why it was termed "*Holy* Communion."

Given this relative paucity of liturgical material from the first century or so, one can readily comprehend why persons constructing liturgies for modern use have been especially attracted to later documents, above all the *Church Order* of Hippolytus. Materials from this church father's writings provide the earliest "full text" outlining the Communion service as performed in Rome in the first part of the third century. Through it, moderns have sought to vault back over later divisions on worship matters and return to the third century. Hippolytus has thus provided the "norm" for much recent liturgical work.

Here is perhaps the place to note the criticism, often voiced in much liturgical renewal today, that the Sunday service which most Protestants, many liturgical Lutherans and Anglicans among them, participate in "is but a *torso* of the Mass." The charge is that "the Service" without Holy Communion is like a body without the head. This criticism is based on the view that, at least since Hippolytus, the Sunday norm was a full eucharistic service. In light of recent New Testament analysis, one must go further, however, and observe that what emerges in Hippolytus and the patristic-medieval church, with its concentration on the bread-and-wine sacrament, can be called a "torso" in terms of what had preceded it, namely, a meal during which or at the end of which the bread and cup were singled out to bear special meaning. Since the sixth decade of the first century or so Christians have been having a "head without the body," that is, elements but not a meal.

All this raises the question of precisely *where*, in the long history of the Lord's Supper, we wish to say *the norm and goal* for our practice today lies—in Hippolytus, in a Eucharist with separately held agapes, in a Markanlike meal with sacrament at the end, in a meal with bread before and cup afterward (pre-Pauline), in some further development, or in a variety of services. The meal-setting is probably not possible to restore, though Arthur Cochrane has proposed doing just that in *Eating and Drinking with Jesus: An Ethical and Biblical Inquiry* (Philadelphia: Westminster Press, 1974). The meal-setting fell away for good reasons, but "fellowship" with one another remains a eucharistic desideratum, along with all the other facets of early Christian emphasis.

Development in the Words of Institution

The *sequence of development* in the New Testament texts implied above for the Words of Institution likely flows therefore from the earliest, pre-Pauline form as found in 1 Cor. 11:23–25 and recoverable in 10:16,

The bread which we break is a participation (or fellowship, *koinōnia)* in the body of Christ,

The cup of blessing *(eulogia)* which we bless *(eulogoumen,* i.e., over which we say a thanksgiving to God) is a participation/fellowship in the blood of Christ. (au. trans.)

(arranged in reverse order in the existing text of 10:16–17 so that Paul can make a comment on the "one bread" and the "one body of Christ" as the church) to that in Mark (really the tradition he employs), and then on to developments in the other evangelists.

This sort of analysis by modern scholarship implies that the phrase so emphasized in Reformation theology "for the forgiveness of sins," found only in Matt. 26:28, is probably an emphasis of Matthew's church or an even later redaction from the first evangelist's own hand. The adjective "new" in Paul before the noun "covenant" points to Jer. 31:31–34 as background; the absence of the adjective in Mark and Matthew (only later manuscripts of those Gospels have it) allows a different Old Testament background (cf. Exod. 24:8, "the blood of the covenant which the Lord has made," and Zech. 9:11). Thus the word "covenant" may, against its Old Testament backgrounds, suggest more than one train of thought (see pp. 34–41, below). The words "for you" or "for many," perhaps reflecting Isa. 53:12 (God's servant "bore the sin of many"), may or may not appear.

Particularly difficult to explain are the words "Do this in remembrance of me," found only in Paul (twice) and in Luke once (see pp. 6–7 and 8–9, above). Mark and Matthew lack this command. The standard explanation for its absence there is that the words amount to a "rubric," and "on ne récite pas une rubrique, on l'exécute" ("one does not recite it, one performs a rubric," Père Pierre Benoit). But the rubric, where we have it, is put on the lips of Jesus, ". . . in memory *of me."* That could be akin to the way Paul's command about Christ, "For as often as you eat this bread and drink this cup, you proclaim *the Lord's death* until *he* comes" (11:26), has been put into Jesus' mouth in the Apostolic Constitutions (fourth century). "You proclaim *my* death until *I* come."

There have been many theories on the "Do this in remembrance of me" clause. Lietzmann proposed that Paul added it himself on the basis of a special revelation; this view is not widely accepted. Others think Mark and Matthew felt fit to omit it because they were describing what was church practice anyway; one need not command what is already being done. The "mandate" to "keep on doing 'this' " is, in either case, a

less common feature in our texts and surely an ambiguous starting point
for analysis. (On the most difficult part of the phraseology to interpret,
"remembrance," see p. 27, below.)

Of course, all the emphases noted above do occur somewhere in the
New Testament and with one degree of frequency or another. Each has
proven precious later on in some time or place. Should we today stress the
motifs occurring most widely in the New Testament, seek a place for all
of them, or emphasize those which meet current needs? Before examining what seem to be the prominent themes by any standard of measure-
ment, we must look at two other areas of disputed biblical evidence.

The Acts of the Apostles

The Book of Acts has often been used to fill in a gap from the time of
Jesus to the oldest traditions cited by Paul, for instance, 1 Cor. 11:23–25.
Seemingly the Acts of the Apostles provides a window into earliest
Jewish-Christianity at Jerusalem. But is it an accurate picture, resting on
primitive sources, or does Luke's account reflect his own day and his own
interests? On just such questions Acts has been called "a storm center" in
recent years, to use a phrase from the Dutch scholar Willem C. van
Unnik.

Characteristic is the debate over reference to "the breaking of bread"
as a feature of community life in the Jerusalem church (2:42; cf. 20:7,
11; 27:35; and Luke 24:35). This has been taken to refer to a Eucharist—
an abbreviated phrase denoting the whole rite, or a "communion in one
kind" (just bread), without wine or even water (cf. A. Vööbus, in *Meaning,* pp. 42–43). Since there is no reference in these passages to the death
of Jesus (though the sermons in Acts are full of it) but considerable
emphasis upon apocalyptic gladness and enthusiasm (2:46), a kind of
agape-meal has also been conjectured, a meal marked by eschatological
joy of the new age; any emphasis on the cross or on penitential sobriety is
then taken to be something imposed later by Paul and others. So Hans
Lietzmann, who tried to draw a direct line from the fellowship meals
during Jesus' lifetime to this "breaking of the bread" and the descriptions
in the *Didache,* in contrast to what—emphasizing the Upper Room,
Paul's words on the death of Christ, and Hippolytus—became the Western Mass.

This variety of interpretations for Acts has continued in recent years.
James D. Dunn *(Unity and Diversity in the New Testament: An Inquiry*

into the Character of Earliest Christianity [Philadelphia: Westminster Press, 1977], p. 163) believes that "the breaking of bread" refers to ordinary meals, without wine, continuing Jesus' practice of table-fellowship but marked now by a sense of his presence and an eschatological enthusiasm. That these meals of food to satisfy hunger were conducted "daily" (2:46) may be in contrast to an annual celebration of the Lord's Supper at Passover time. Gerhard Delling, on the other hand, sees reference in "the breaking of bread" to a Lord's Supper celebrated within a meal context, marked by especial jubilation *(Worship in the New Testament*, trans. Percy Scott [Philadelphia: Westminster Press, 1962], p. 145; *TRE,* pp. 56–57).

Only if Acts is taken as our primary source and as an accurate one for the earliest church and then is interpreted in a particular way is it possible to conjecture an original "meal of joy," later amalgamated with a "cross-centered Lord's Supper." But it is extremely implausible that two types of meals developed and then combined within the space of only ten to fifteen years after Jesus died. If, on the contrary, the texts are read "as they stand," the Passion emphasis was there originally, from the Upper Room on, and the (pre-)Pauline formulas echo it. If one is hesitant, with the critics, on the one hand, about recovering what Jesus himself emphasized on the night before he died, then it is likely the Pauline account (1 Cor. 11:23–25 and the eschatological thought of v. 26) "is the more or less genuine report," and Luke 22:15–18, 24–30 originated from a later eschatological tradition which influenced the final working of Mark 14:25 (E. Schweizer, *The Lord's Supper According to the New Testament,* trans. James M. Davis [Philadelphia: Fortress Press, 1967], p. 28, as revised from his original position in the 1956 *RGG* article on which the Facet Book cited is based). But this complex matter remains under debate.

The Gospel of John

The Fourth Gospel has always presented peculiar problems in the discussion of the Lord's Supper. Communion between the Vine (Jesus Christ) and the branches (his disciples) is prominent. John 6 attaches a discourse of Jesus on himself as the life-giving bread to the story about five thousand persons being fed. Yet the scene in the Upper Room (Chaps. 13—17) has no Words of Institution, indeed no reference to bread and wine "during supper" (13:2), but makes prominent instead the foot washing (13:3–20), the "new commandment" to "love one another" (13:34), and Jesus' words of promise and warning. The very attitude of the Fourth Gospel toward "sacraments" has been interpreted in ways poles apart—from one extreme that it is antisacramental to the other extreme that it is an ultrasacramental approach (cf. Dunn, *Unity and Diversity,* pp. 168–69, for examples in recent discussion and his own judgment that the answer lies somewhere between the nonsacramental and "modified sacramental" views).

Lutherans have long had a further problem of perceiving any reference to the Lord's Supper in the one obvious passage in John, namely, Chapter 6. Their emphasis on truly receiving the body and blood of Christ in the Lord's Supper, polemically stressed against left-wing opponents in the Reformation, caused these opponents, especially the Swiss like Zwingli and Oecolampadius, to caricature the Lutherans as "rending the flesh of Christ with their teeth and digesting it along with other food" in almost a "cannibalistic" way. The language derives ultimately from John 6:52, where "the Jews" of Capernaum responded to Jesus' discourse about his "flesh" as "bread of life" by asking, "How can this man give us his flesh to eat?" (Jesus' reply talks of "gnawing" his flesh and—in a phrase abhorrent to Jews, in light of Lev. 7:27—"drinking his blood.") Accordingly the Formula of Concord in 1577 asserted against these opponents:

> We believe, teach, and confess that with the bread and wine the body and blood of Christ are received not only spiritually, by faith, but also orally [that is, in the mouth, traditionally termed "manducation"]—however, not in a Capernaitic manner but, because of the sacramental union [of body and blood with bread and wine], in a supernatural and heavenly manner. (Epitome, Article VII, section 6; cf. Solid Declaration, Article VII, 64)

Traditional Lutheran exegesis therefore interpreted John 6 as applying to "spiritual eating," that is, faith, which indeed is necessary for worthy reception of the sacrament but which does not render superfluous the "sacramental eating" of the body of Christ which is really present in the Supper. But eating and drinking in 6:51ff. were taken as metaphorical, referring to belief in Christ. It may be added that the chapter also had an attraction as a proof text for communion in both kinds by the laity. For Luther's views on the passage, especially 6:63 ("the spirit gives life, the flesh is of no avail"; he took it to mean the self-centered person cannot gain life), see D. C. Steinmetz and G. Krodel in *Interpretation* (37 [1983]: 257–58, 283–88).

In recent times, Lutherans have come more readily to grant that John 6 is eucharistic (cf. Jenson, *Visible Words*, p. 84; Krodel, *Interpretation* 37, p. 288)—though among the church fathers in the early centuries there was no unanimity and even the Council of Trent did not so designate it. Luther's Swiss opponents agreed John 6 referred to faith. Since Vatican II, Roman Catholic practice has permitted the cup to lay persons, and cheerful guitar ditties enjoin us to "eat his body, drink his blood."

Nonetheless the sense of John 6 remains under dispute, in part precisely because of its contents and structure. We may outline it thus:

6:1–15, the multiplication of the five barley loaves and two fish to feed a multitude by the Sea of Galilee at Passover;

6:16–21, Jesus and his disciples make their way across the Sea to Capernaum (they by boat, he "walking on the sea" and then in their ship);

6:22–51b, next day to the crowds in Capernaum (in the synagogue, v. 59) Jesus discourses on "the bread of life" or "of God" which "comes down from heaven and gives life to the world," that is, himself—in spite of murmurings against him from the Jews (41–47);

6:51c–58, in a further discourse and dispute, Jesus identifies this bread as his *flesh* which one "gnaws" (the verb is stronger than "eats") and speaks the offensive words about drinking his blood, so as to "live for ever";

6:59–71, reactions by disciples, who either take offense and go away or confess him, as Simon Peter does, to have "the words of eternal life."

All would agree the chapter is christological: Jesus' coming and words mean life, when responded to in faith, or lead to offense, unfaith, and ultimately judgment. But is the chapter eucharistic?

Rudolf Bultmann's commentary (1941, Eng. trans., *The Gospel of John* [Philadelphia: Westminster Press, 1971]) argued that 6:51c–58 is *a later addition*, by an "ecclesiastically-minded redactor" to bring the otherwise nonsacramentalist outlook of the book into conformity with emerging Christian orthodoxy. If Bultmann is correct, John 6 was originally only indirectly sacramental, if at all. In recent years the trend, however, has been to emphasize more strongly than Bultmann did the likelihood that 6:51c–58 was integral to the evangelist's thought, though exegesis still reckons with sources behind John 6, chiefly of a midrashic sort expounding the manna theme of Exodus 16 typologically.

Another approach is therefore to take the disputed verses as a genuine part of the whole chapter but to conclude, in light of its entirety, that John's overall position is a *protest against extreme sacramentalism* present in the church of his day (cf. Dunn, *Unity and Diversity,* pp. 170–71). If the language is almost crudely rigorous in vv. 51c–58, that is part of a polemic against Docetists (who denied that Jesus had really come "in the flesh," 1 John 4:2). But John, on this reading, really means to stress *faith*—believing in Jesus runs through the whole chapter as a leitmotif (vv. 35, 40, 47, 69, for example). We may add that what vv. 51c–58 then do is to focus this belief on the actual eating and drinking. But on this view, the closing emphasis in John, along with faith, is in v. 63: "The Spirit is what gives life, the *flesh* is of no use in any way at all, the *words* which I have spoken to you are Spirit and are life" (au. trans.). Of course, if 6:63 stood at the conclusion to the discourse without vv. 51c–58, it could simply be the familiar New Testament contrast between God's Spirit (or even the human spirit enlivened by it) in contrast to the human being as he or she is by nature without God. But the minute the disputed verses are regarded as part of the whole, the "flesh" in 6:63 becomes related to the "flesh" (of the Son of man) in vv. 51–55; hence the conclusion of some that John's overall perspective is a warning against those who misunderstood "the flesh of Christ" in the Lord's Supper as a magical "medicine of immortality" in the sense of the mystery religions.

A *mediating position* is well represented in the Anchor Bible commentary by Raymond E. Brown *(The Gospel According to John I–XII* [Garden City, N.Y.: Doubleday & Co., 1968], pp. cxi–cxiv and the exegesis of Chapter 6). He allows here two different discourses on the bread of life, the earlier in vv. 35–50, employing wisdom themes, the latter (clearly eucharistic) in vv. 51–58. But this second, radical rethinking of the theme in 51–58 contains material originally "located in the Last Supper scene" and put into Chapter 6 at the "final redaction" by the evangelist (not by some later hand, as in Bultmann). "Flesh" in 6:63 then "has nothing to do with the Eucharist" (p. 300).

Brown's later work, however, on the Johannine literature *(The Community of the Beloved Disciple: The Life, Loves, and Hates of an Individual Church in New Testament Times* [New York: Paulist Press, 1979]) sketches a picture of the various parties reflected in the Fourth Gospel and three Johannine epistles in the late first century, each of which can be characterized by certain doctrinal views and distinctive practices. They range from the Jews and "crypto-Christians" on the right to "secessionist Johannine Christians" on the left. As regards the sacrament of Communion in the life of the three groups that can be reckoned "Christian" in between these extremes, Brown suggests (pp. 169, 74, 78-79, 88, 158) that:

> Jewish-Christians did *not* understand the Eucharist as the true flesh and blood of Jesus (a "low" sacramentology);
>
> "Christians of the apostolic churches" looked on Jesus as the institutor of this sacrament (a "high" view);
>
> Johannine Christians, with an extremely high Christology, so stressed their unity with Jesus that they had a low concept of the church (almost as a "conventicle") and of the ministry; sacraments were for them a continuation of Jesus' own actions during his ministry, for example, feeding the multitude.

By separating the Eucharist from the context of the Last Supper, John "launched Christianity on the road to a distinctive sacramental theology whereby visible elements are signs of communicating divine realities" (n. 145). (The left-wing group that had moved even further away from apostolic Christianity and from the Johannine Christians emphasized Spirit—not flesh or sacraments—even more.)

Brown's analysis, even if it compounds our difficulty in precisely determining the mix of views in John 6, is valuable in order to call attention to the variety which probably existed in Christianity at the end of the first century and in order to pose the ecumenical question then and today about how much pluralism is possible in recognizing allowable positions and practices in the church.

All in all, examination of Acts and John shows how controverted is the question of sacramental understandings at the start of the post-Easter development and at the end of the first century, compared with the (pre-) Pauline and (pre-)Synoptic material. One insight to ponder, however, is the considerable role of the Spirit with regard to the Lord's Supper that thus emerges, a role greater than that to which some traditions have been accustomed.

The History of Religions and the
Old Testament as Influences

Given these lacunae in our sources for Christian sacramental development, some scholars have invoked the history of world religions *(Religionsgeschichte)* in a search for clarity.

Since Jews had no sacraments, some have pointed to rites among Gentiles where people banqueted at the table of the god in his temple or even "partook of the deity" by eating food from a sacrifice. Such influences were no doubt present in a place like Corinth (cf. 1 Corinthians 8 and 10, esp. 10:20–21). The Hellenistic world must have affected some of Paul's converts, if not Paul himself, but these analogies and possible influences do not suffice to explain origins or key steps of development.

Jews did have, if not sacraments, the annual Passover meal, ceremonial meals of societies (as when a teacher and disciples ate together, the so-called *haburah),* and at Qumran a certain protocol for (daily) meals. As we have seen at points above, all these have been invoked, but no totally convincing background has been worked out for the New Testament accounts from any of them, even Passover. We have also seen certain influences from *the Old Testament*—Mal. 1:11 (see p. 12, above), the hope for a messianic banquet (see p. 4, above), covenant passages (see pp. 6 and 14–16, above), "sacrifice" (see on Hebrews, p. 12, above), and the manna (see pp. 19–20, above). All of these references in the Hebrew scriptures are at points related to the emerging Christian sacrament; however, no one of them or even all of them together account for it.

One of the most interesting recent theories, based on the Old Testament backgrounds, has been propounded by Hartmut Gese of Tübingen. He points to Psalm 22 (so much reflected in Jesus' Passion) and other Psalms (51, 69) which are laments or thanksgivings (116) or both, as used in Israel. In Psalm 22 the righteous sufferer—who once so despaired as to cry, "My God, my God, why hast thou forsaken me?" (22:1)—would, after Yahweh delivered him, gather with friends to praise the Lord and celebrate his deliverance in a *todah,* or "thanksgiving ceremony." This rite included prayer, sacrifice, eating, and an account of what should be "remembered" by future generations (cf. 22:22–31). Psalm 69:30–31 emphasizes the praise of God as the proper thanksgiving; 51:18–19 shows how such praise from the lips replaced ancient animal sacrifice; 116:13–14, 17–18 parallels elevation of "the cup of salvation," when God's deeds are proclaimed, with the sacrifice itself.

Gese suggests that Jesus' disciples gathered at meals after Easter, with their risen Lord regarded as present, to recall and celebrate what God had done in Jesus and to thank God. From this practice would have arisen the church's Eucharist. In Gese's opinion there were never two types of meals which coalesced; for joy in God's saving action (Acts 2:46) and remembrance of the death of Jesus (1 Corinthians 11) were together from the beginning (as in Psalm 22 both motifs occur). Moreover, word and meal, prayer and proclamation go together in this service of worship. There are difficulties with the hypothesis, however, and it has not yet attracted much support from New Testament and liturgics scholars as an explanation of the origins of the Lord's Supper. (Cf. J. Reumann, "Psalm 22 at the Cross," *Interpretation* 28 [1974]: 43–48, 54–55, 58; H. Gese, "The Origin of the Lord's Supper," *Essays on Biblical Theology* [Minneapolis: Augsburg Publishing House, 1981], pp. 117–40.)

SOME KEY THEMES IN THE LORD'S SUPPER

Our report on recent investigations into the development from meals of the historical Jesus, including the Last Supper, to the Lord's Supper of the first-century church has brought to light a host of emphases that to one degree or another are part of the biblical picture of Holy Communion. A great number of such "meanings" can be listed (Roth gives seven in *Meaning*, pp. 23–26; *BEM* cites five).

It is presumptuous to claim to catch all that the New Testament says in any list, but recent exegetical work on the subject and biblical theology certainly agree in lifting up for attention the four major themes discussed below. No subsequent understanding can claim to be biblically Christian if it ignores them. All these themes of course center in Christ, so that the Gospel of Philip, a document found in Egypt in a Gnostic collection, expressed a biblical truism when it said, "The eucharist is Jesus" (II, 63, line 21, as translated in *The Nag Hammadi Library in English,* ed. James M. Robinson [New York: Harper & Row, 1977], p. 138).

The Eschatological Perspective

Ever since Albert Schweitzer's work on *das Abendmahlsproblem* at the start of the present century (now translated, see p. 76, below), New Testament scholars have been unable to overlook the constant emphasis in the Gospels on "the last things"—such as death, destiny, resurrection, judgment, and "life of the new age"—as imminent or already breaking into human existence. Schweitzer's studies on the quest of the historical Jesus and his own eschatological reconstruction of the heroic Nazarene messiah arose, in fact, out of his initial analysis of the scene in the Upper Room. According to Schweitzer, who accepted Mark's story as the oldest and authentic account, there was no command from Jesus to "Do this in remembrance of me." The key lies elsewhere—not only in his references to his approaching sacrificial death but also in his expectation of an imminent reunion with the disciples in the new kingdom of God (Mark 14:25).

No one in biblical studies has since been able to ignore this eschatological note. However, all too often "the last things" have been kept last (and touched upon only if time permits), especially in some systematic theologies. Or the *future* tone of eschatology has been transmuted primarily or exclusively into the idea of "already realized eschatology" (C. H. Dodd especially), so that "the present" is already regarded as the new age.

With regard to the Lord's Supper, there has unquestionably been widespread agreement on the high importance of the eschatological perspective, and specifically one of future fulfillment seen as impinging on the present moment. Roth calls it "expectation" of Jesus' return and of the judgment, and a "foretaste of the eternal Messianic banquet in heaven" *(Meaning, p. 36, last in his listing). Eduard Schweizer fits it into a past-present-future scheme of Jesus' death, new confirmation of the covenant at each celebration of the Lord's Supper, and anticipation of the messianic banquet, even though he sees that eschatology has had its ups and downs of emphasis in various New Testament sources *(Lord's Supper, pp. 3, 18–22). Jeremias, in his last major book, refers to "gathering with Jesus at table" as "an actualization of the time of salvation" and prefers to call it not "anticipation" but "an *antedonation* of the consummation" *(New Testament Theology, Vol. 1 [New York: Charles Scribner's Sons, 1971], p. 290). Jenson *(Visible Words, pp. 65, 78) follows those exegetes like Eduard Schweizer who treat the eschatological promises in the Upper Room as originally distinct statements and, coming from Jesus himself, perhaps the primary ones (cf. Albert Schweitzer's view of Jesus). In modern liturgies, such as the *Lutheran Book of Worship* (1978), the note is struck by such congregational responses as "Christ has died, Christ is risen, *Christ will come again"* (futurist eschatology) or "This *is the feast of victory* for our God . . ." (realized eschatology).

The future-eschatological perspective is strongest in the closing words of Jesus in the Upper Room (Mark 14:25 par.): "I shall not drink again of the fruit of the vine until that day when I drink it new in the kingdom of God." Luke has it more pronouncedly *before* the Words of Institution (22:15–18) as well as afterward (cf. 28–30), though the exact age of these verses is debated. Paul has the note in his words, ". . . until he comes" again, a reference to Jesus' Parousia, as was the *Marana tha* originally (1 Cor. 11:26, 16:22; cf. p. 11, above); however, these are part of Paul's comments (11:26–34), not of the formula he quotes. Does that mean that eucharistic formulas of institution occurred in the early church without a future-eschatological perspective? Perhaps this is true when present joy overwhelmed the qualification that full realization of what is promised would come only in God's good time. But even then the whole celebration was characterized by the eschatological bliss of the future, now regarded as present. It is a mark of all Paul's theology and practice that Christians, even at the Eucharist, have not yet attained to all God's promises. Even at the moment when God gives them a foretaste, there is a note of reserve. Christians must still live and struggle in "this age," even when "the end of the ages has come" upon them (cf. 1 Cor. 10:1–13 as a warning against presumptions about the power of "sacraments," as ancient Israel's story vividly illustrates).

The New Testament writing that has the strongest strand of "realized eschatology" is, of course, the Fourth Gospel. Even the resurrection of believers is there regarded as already past, and they are in the new age, partaking of eternal life (5:24–27, especially if Bultmann is right that the futuristic statements of 5:28–29 were added by a churchly interpolater!). In John, therefore, we might particularly expect the Lord's Supper to become a sacrament focused entirely upon the present. But as we have seen, the Fourth Gospel, perhaps just because it emphasizes eternal life through union with Christ and by the Spirit, does not concentrate on the Lord's Supper as the means to this. Precisely in those verses which we noted as most overtly eucharistic, 6:51c–58 (see pp. 17–21, above), the "future reserve" is most manifest (for example, 6:54, "he who eats my flesh and drinks my blood has eternal life [a thought repeated from v. 47], and *I will raise him up at the last day*"; cf. 5:28–29). Thus even in John, when the thought is eucharistic, it maintains the future as well as the present perspective.

We must conclude from these observations that the early Christian Supper always stood in a horizon of eschatological hope, that is, of future fulfillment as well as present experience. Even at the Lord's Table, all is not yet complete and cannot be in this age. Indeed, because the sacrament fulfills past promises over and over again, it also spawns future promises. Eschatological hope always accompanies the celebration of the Lord's Supper.

Proclamation of the Death of Jesus

This theme of Jesus' death is also part, one might say the main point, of Paul's interpretation of the Lord's Supper at 1 Cor. 11:26, "As often as you eat this bread and drink this cup, you *proclaim* the Lord's *death.*" For Paul the risen Lord is Jesus who was crucified (1 Cor. 1:23; Gal. 3:1).

The emphasis is also found in the formula Paul cites, however, in the reference to Jesus being "betrayed" (by Judas) or "handed over" (by God) to die and in the interpretation of the cup as "the new covenant *in my blood.*" "Blood" represents life poured out in self-sacrifice on all of these texts (Mark 14:24 par.). The phrases added to describe his body ("given for you" [Luke 22:19], "broken for you" [1 Cor. 11:24 in some manuscripts and translations]) and his blood ("poured out for many" [Mark 14:24 par.]) point in the same direction—toward the death of Jesus as an atonement for human sin.

The passion context of the narrative about the Last Supper heightens the connection. The Gospels as a whole, as "passion narratives with extended introductions" (M. Kähler), are proclamations about Jesus, centering on his cross. Even in the Gospel of Philip, the reference to Jesus as "the eucharist" reflects his crucifixion (and perhaps a criticism of eucharistic practices in the "donkey-church" of the day, cf. R. McL. Wilson, *The Gospel of Philip* [London: A. R. Mowbray & Co., 1962], pp. 112–13).

Eduard Schweizer describes proclamation of the death of Jesus as the first of three theological motifs at work in the Lord's Supper texts of the New Testament *(Lord's Supper,* pp. 1–2, 12–13). Jeremias favors the atonement motif of a redeeming death "for many" as the core of Jesus' own words in the Upper Room *(Eucharistic Words,* pp. 220–31). Roth makes separate points of "proclamation" and "sacrifice (atonement)" *(Meaning,* pp. 25–27, 31–32). Jenson seems to find it especially in Paul, Mark, and Matthew, but not in Luke-Acts *(Visible Words,* pp. 65–66, 80–83); however, neither theme—"proclamation" or "Jesus' death"—is prominent (cf. index but also pp. 68, 70–71).

Denominational and ecumenical statements usually accord a high place to this theme, as in the 1974 Faith and Order statement *One Baptism, One Eucharist and a Mutually Recognized Ministry* (Geneva: WCC, 1975):

> 4. This meal of bread and wine is the sacrament, the effective sign and assurance of the presence of Christ himself, who sacrificed his life for all men. . . . 8. Christ instituted the eucharist, sacrament of his body and blood with its focus upon the cross and resurrection, as the *anamnesis* of the whole of God's reconciling acts in him. . . . It is the Church's proclamation of God's mighty acts. (pp. 20–21)

The Greek word *(anamnēsis)* employed here leads us to the related topic of the "remembrance" of Jesus, a topic that is of immense importance in modern ecumenical discussion.

"Do this in *remembrance of* me" (1 Cor. 11:24–25; Luke 22:19) has already been discussed as a command to repeat what is being done in connection with the bread and cup (see p. 15, above). Opinion remains divided, however, over precisely what "this" refers to in the sentence. Obviously it means share this bread and cup, as Matthew enjoins and Mark describes. Leonhard Goppelt *(Theology of the New Testament,* Vol. I [Grand Rapids: Wm. B. Eerdmans, 1981], p. 222) refers "this" to "the presentation of the bread and the cup under the words of institution." But Jenson further suggests that this "gloss" (does he mean added by Paul?) may refer to "the ceremonies of thanksgiving before and after the meal" *(Visible Words,* p. 67). Conzelmann takes in "the whole administration" as referent *(1 Corinthians,* p. 198). Delling *(TRE,* Vol. 1, pp. 52–53) appeals to the Old Testament for the somewhat different sense of "keep" or "observe" the Passover, festival, or ordinance (Num. 9:2–4; Deut. 16:1, 10; Exod. 12:47; 13:5).

The sense depends in the final analysis on the next phrase, usually rendered as "in memory *(anamnesis)* of me," from which developed the influential theme of "Christ-anamnesis" in the patristic church. At times in Christian history it has been taken to refer merely to the remembrance of Jesus by the congregation during Holy Communion. The sacrament thus becomes a sort of *aide mémoire* for Christians. There are those who argue that "because Jesus knew that the disciples might forget him and all that he signified, he instituted the meal of the New Covenant" (so A. R. Millard in *Apostolic History and the Gospel* [Grand Rapids: Wm. B. Eerdmans, 1970], pp. 242–48). In support of this view, Millard has appealed to the fact that covenants in the Old Testament often included devices for helping vassals of the ruler, or suzerain, to remember their obligations to him (p. 45). But this application of "covenant" is somewhat wide of the mark for the New Testament, as we shall see (p. 39, below).

While this "memorial" theme must be part of our thinking about the Lord's Supper (cf. Roth, *Meaning,* pp. 32–34), biblical theology in the last sixty years has emphasized that in the *Old Testament* (and hence here in the New) the term "remember" suggests not so much *our* calling something to mind as an action where *God* as subject makes concretely present something out of the past so that it speaks afresh to the contemporary situation. To ask Yahweh to "remember" his mercy or his covenant is to expect him to apply it to things now. To ask God to "remember me and visit me," as Jeremiah did (15:15; cf. 14:21), means for God to make operative again his old relationship. In this interpretation, "in memory of me" would involve a "re-presentation" or "being present" of Jesus Christ at the sacramental celebration.

The biblical-theological view thus sketched is well represented by Nils Dahl's inaugural lecture at Oslo University in 1946 (in English as "Anamnesis: Memory and Commemoration in Early Christianity," in *Jesus in the Memory of the Early Church* [Minneapolis: Augsburg Publishing House, 1976], pp. 11–29). "To remember" (Hebrew *zakār*) means that an event "is called forth in the soul" of a person which then assists in determining direction and action in life. For God to remember (his covenant, for example, Luke 1:72) means he intervenes and acts in conformity with his past deeds of mercy; for him "no longer to 'remember' sins" means "to forgive" (Jer. 31:34 = Heb. 8:12). Cultic commemoration, as of the Exodus at Passover, involved Israel remembering Yahweh and also led to the result that "past salvation became again an actual and present reality" (p. 14). At the New Testament remembrance of Jesus "the commemoration was not something that took place essentially within individual believers, in their subjective memory"; rather the commemoration was "an *anamnēsis* of the death and resurrection of Jesus where the history of salvation was re-presented by the sacramental commemoration" (p. 21, citing especially Odo Casel).

"Re-presentation" has become in recent years a kind of jargon word in biblical and liturgical theology, but warnings are in order about misunderstandings of it which confuse "God's act with ours" and falsely suggest that human actions, by a priest or minister for instance, can by their "intrinsic power" bring Christ to be effectively present (Jenson, *Visible Words*, pp. 73–74, against Casel). Some understanding is required that falls between these extremes of mere human recollection and an ontological process which borders on the magical.

A view which has attracted considerable attention is the contention of Jeremias that the New Testament phrase should be rendered, "Do this, that *God* may remember me." Jeremias took it as part of an "eschatological program": as often as the Lord's Supper proclaims Jesus' atoning death and the *Marana tha* arises heavenward, God is reminded of the as-yet-unfulfilled climax of his work of salvation, "until Christ comes" *(Eucharistic Words*, pp. 249–55). A strength of this interpretation is that the future aspect of fulfillment (see pp. 24f., above) is clearly retained. A weakness is that it seems to make the Lord's Supper primarily an enacted prayer for the Parousia. Dropping that sort of eschatology but keeping Jeremias's sense of God's remembering, Jenson would stress both what God has done in Jesus (above all at the cross) and his promise to fulfill what he has pledged, but he would also make every Lord's Supper into an "acted-out . . . dramatically performed remembering," so that when we do it "an event occurs to which eschatological promises 'come,' to create a sacrament" *(Visible Words*, pp. 72–74).

The Jeremias interpretation, however, "has not been universally endorsed," to say the least (cf. K. H. Bartels, "Remember," in *The New International Dictionary of the New Testament Theology* [Grand Rapids: Zondervan Publishing House], Vol. 3 [1978], p. 245, who thinks the command means "Do this by eating the bread and drinking the cup . . . , by preaching the word [1 Cor. 11:26] and the singing of praise"). Conzelmann concludes that the Jeremias interpretation contradicts "the plain wording." The theory is "regretfully" dismissed by von Allmen *(The Lord's Supper*, pp. 28–29), especially because "it has no support in the ancient liturgical tradition."

One wishes, if such is the sense, that the New Testament formula had made it clearer that "God" is to be supplied as the subject of the remembering, perhaps by adding to the words "for remembering of me" a phrase such as "before God," which Acts 10:4 actually uses. A recent, detailed examination of the Old Testament usage of the verb "remember" leads to the conclusion that, when God is the subject, the point is made clear by some specific phrase such as "before the Lord" (Exod. 28:29; Num. 10:10) or by context, as in Sirach 45:9, 11 (cf. W. Schottroff, *"Gedenken" im Alten Orient und im Alten Testament* [Neukirchen-

Vluyn, 1964; 2d ed. 1967], discussed in Millard, *Apostolic History,* pp. 245–47).

There is a considerable, recent literature on the topic of "remember-ing," literature about which, one fears, a good deal of ecumenical discus-sion on *anamnesis* (see chap. 3 below, especially the section on Eucharist in *BEM)* simply does not seem aware. For a survey of research (though admittedly from a viewpoint that opposes the positions of "the Benedic-tine School" of Dom Odo Casel and those "Lutherans" and others who stress "re-presentation") see C. Brown's discussion in *NIDNTT* (3:234–39, cf. 232). Brevard S. Childs's *Memory and Tradition in Israel* (Studies in Biblical Theology 37; London: SCM Press, 1962) is one standard work on the topic; it emphasizes memory quite apart from cult, for "to remember" is "faithful response to the claims of the covenant" (p. 54). Schottroff sums up his findings with regard to the term "memo-rial" *(zikkārōn)* thus: even in cultic passages it does not deal with sharing in a "cult-dramatic actualization" but with entering by remembrance into a complex of happenings, "with events of the past made actual through proclamation or signs" (cf. also his article *"zkr* gedenken," in the *Theologisches Handwörterbuch zum Alten Testament*, ed. E. Jenni and C. Westermann [Munich: Chr. Kaiser, 1971], Vol. 1, col. 517). In another wordbook article on *zkr* in vol. 4 of the *Theological Dictionary of the Old Testament* (Grand Rapids: Wm. B. Eerdmans, 1980), H. Eising cites Schottroff's views (no cultic realization of the past, "instead a moral motivation for obedience to the commandments based on recollection of God's blessings in the past") but balances them with the earlier views of, for example, H. Gross: "feasts established by God himself" do actualize "the gift of salvation . . . by virtue of an immanent dynamic implanted by God in the memory itself" (p. 81). Eising inclines to the latter view and to a position that in cult "the worshipper would offer sacrifices . . . in which was given . . . the experience of actual sacrificial communion with the deity" (p. 82).

No discussion would be at all complete without reference to Gerhard von Rad's famous statement, "the cult brings Israel to the remembrance of Jahweh" *(Old Testament Theology* [New York: Harper & Row], Vol. 1 [1962], p. 242). Later he speaks of Israel at Passover, entering into the saving event of the Exodus, "participating in it in a quite 'actual' way" (Vol. 2 [1965], p. 104). But how shall "this day" marking Passover be for Israel in later generations "a memorial day" (Exod. 12:14, *lᵉzikkārōn*)? Von Rad suggests that two possibilities existed (Vol. 2, pp. 108–12). One was cultic and came from Israel's environment, for other nations of the ancient Near East also commonly assumed that their religious festivals "actualized"—by liturgy and sacred mime—events from the past, such as a creation-battle victory by its god over the forces of chaos. Within a cyclical view of history, cultic celebration annually made present the past victory and assured its benefits for the coming year. The other possibility assumed a linear view of time. It sought to make present to subsequent generations a past event of history—the Exodus—by the words of the preacher actualizing the past scene, above all by a call to remember and the use of devices such as the terms "today" or "this day" in Deuteronomy. Indeed, von Rad suggests, there was a "crisis in the cultic actualisation of Jahweh's saving acts" that the Deuteronomist School addressed by using such passages as "Not with our fathers did the Lord make this covenant, but with us, who are all of us here alive this day" (Deut. 5:3) or "You stand this day all of you before the Lord your God" (29:10).

In these two views, are we faced with a "theology of the word" through proclamation versus a view of "cultic event on the basis of the rhythm of the fixed orders of nature"? There was, according to von Rad, "a radical division between Israel and her environment" over the idea of history, and how *zikkārōn* or "memory" is conceived enters into the picture. (Cf. also Schottroff, *"Gedenken,"* pp. 123–26, 315–17.)

Schottroff argues, among other things, that the Hebrew root *zkr* can mean "proclaim" and that Israel's view was that at great festivals, when the people of God were called upon to "remember," the God who did great deeds in the past was regarded as speaking again to them in the present. That would in 1 Corinthians make the words "Keep on doing this that I may be remembered" (11:24, 25) a parallel to "proclaim the Lord's death . . ." (11:26), and v. 26 is obviously commentary on the debated sentence in v. 25, introduced by the same words "as often as. . . ." "Remember" is then synonymous with "proclaim" and "confess" (Goppelt, *Theology of the New Testament,* Vol. 1, p. 222; similarly G. D. Kilpatrick in *Liturgical Review* 51 [1975]: 35–40). The community, in carrying out the celebration, relates itself "to the event to which Jesus bound himself at the Last Supper and lets itself on its side be determined by this event," namely Jesus' death (Delling, *TRE,* Vol. 1, p. 53).

A recent Yale dissertation (available on microfiche) by J. W. Groves, "Actualization and Interpretation in the Old Testament" (1979), points to a "consensus . . . that cultic actualization . . . does not exist in the Bible"

(p. 123), above all in the sense of a cultic reenactment where time is dissolved and the participant feels he or she is experiencing the original sacred event. Groves prefers to speak of "literary actualization," occurring primarily through written materials and maintaining a difference between the two moments of time involved.

However, an even more recent dissertation by Fritz Chenderlin under J. A. Sanders at Claremont Graduate School, entitled *"Do This as My Memorial"* (1982), reaches slightly different results, admittedly in part against a different philosophical and hermeneutical background. Chenderlin, a Jesuit, concludes that the fullest understanding of the phrases in 1 Cor. 11:24 and 25, to be translated as in his title, allows for both "reminding-man" and "reminding-God," to use his phrases. Chenderlin is concerned primarily with the epistle text as it stands (and not with any meaning to an earlier pre-Pauline form), assuming a Passover and covenantal setting. He treats the reference to *anamnesis* in light of Paul's general teaching on prayer. He concludes that the noun *anamnesis* means "reminder," not "remembering," and the adjective with it *(emēn* in Greek) means "my," not "of me." Hence, "my memorial." Though the tradition Paul presents is heavily Hebraic, it could have been taken by Greek hearers in a sense acceptable to their world, namely, the banquet meal in one of the "hero cults." This would not have been incompatible with views held by some early Christians of Jesus as a heroic figure, now divinized, with power (§295). Chenderlin also notes the *Memorial* of Demetrius to the Great King in the *Letter of Aristeas,* a Jewish document in the Pseudepigrapha. Here (§§28–33) Demetrius, the head of the king's library in Alexandria, was ordered by Ptolemy to draw up a memorial *(eisdosis)* enjoining translation of the Hebrew sacred books. The memorial, when presented to the king, leads to the command to carry the matter out (§§301, 316, 448–49). *A minore ad maius.* Christ serves as a reminder (from and) toward God, the analogy being sensible to Greeks and Jews. With reference to Rom. 8:33–34 Chenderlin makes a great deal of the risen Christ as an "undefeatable advocate" in heaven. From a more general line of argument derived from the way Paul prayed and encouraged prayer, he argues that to pray, or in the case of 1 Corinthians 11 to "do this," including the giving of thanks, provides "factual referent for God's knowing that it is done" (§166, cf. 469).

> The crucified body on the cross and in the role of present advocate would be seen as a blessing-source through God's viewing it as a reminding-God memorial "set forth" by him as his referent of actuality. The communion

part of the cult would serve as a similar memorial and referent, with the difference that it also refers backward in time, like any communion, to the sacrificial event (as well as "upward" to Christ risen). This in the spirit of Divine "new covenant" promise associated with that event and the communion commemoration. (§422)

The treatment is wide-ranging and by no means simple. It leaves us not with a clear, exclusive meaning of Paul but rather with "all the potentialities for memorial significance, by way of denotation and connotation, that the evidence tells us would probably have attached to the term" then (§3). This is perhaps too broad to satisfy.

The meaning of anamnesis thus remains unsettled in biblical studies, in spite of considerable advances beyond notions of mere human recollection. It hovers between the two senses exhibited in Psalm 111: (a) God "has caused his wonderful works to be remembered" *in his congregation* where thanks and praise are given, and (b) *"He* is ever mindful of his covenant" (111:4–5). "Covenant," the last mentioned term, may be part of the solution (see pp. 34–41, below).

One other question about anamnesis can be posed. How much of "the history of salvation" was involved in what the early church "remembered"? Certainly the focal point was the death of Jesus, indeed the exclusive one in 1 Corinthians 11 and in Hippolytus and the church at Rome generally. In time and outside Rome, however, other of the "mighty acts of God" were commemorated—creation, Israel's history, and the promised fulfillment. Jenson, like many modern liturgiologists, regards this limitation to the second article of the Creed as a disastrous "misfortune" where it occurred *(Visible Words,* p. 96).

Can any light be shed on the scope of the history of salvation envisioned in earliest Christianity? The proclamation of the New Testament church in preaching frequently covers the sweep from Exodus to David and then to Jesus (Acts 13:16–40, Paul at Pisidian Antioch), or Abraham to Solomon (and Jesus, cf. Acts 7:2–53, Stephen's speech; for Abraham, cf. also Gal. 3:15–29, 6–9; Romans 4).

But what of materials specifically associated with the Eucharist? The best evidence would seem to be early Christian hymns. The setting in which they were originally used is a matter of guesswork. Baptismal services are usually proposed as the *Sitz im Leben* by form critics, but the next strongest alternative for a "setting in the life of the church" is at celebrations of the Lord's Supper. If one is willing to allow such passages as Phil. 2:6–11 and Col. 1:15–20 as evidence, then these (eucharistic) hymns of praise (which, though ultimately about God, concentrate on the second article of the Creeds, about the Son), especially in the final forms in the epistles, emphasize cross and resurrection but also may bring in creation (Col. 1:15–17) and present exaltation as lord over the cosmos (Phil. 2:9–11; Col. 1:15, 18).

In their presumed pre-Pauline form, these hymns likely emphasized the cosmic claim for Christ's lordship even more. Dahl ("Anamnesis," p. 23) sees a strong "parallelism between creation and salvation through Christ." Explicit references to Israel's history are lacking; perhaps they should just be assumed, at least for Jewish Christianity. The penchant to single out Abraham (as in the *Lutheran Book of Worship's* "Great Thanksgiving) and Sarah (as some pastors in many churches have emended the text, or as in the National Council of Churches' nonsexist lectionary because of sensitivity to the place of women at the Eucharist; cf. Gal. 3:28, in light of recent analysis as summarized in H. D. Betz's Hermeneia commentary, *Galatians* [Philadelphia: Fortress Press, 1979], pp. 184, 189–201) turns out to be sound when viewed in the perspective of the covenant theme (see p. 37, below).

It ought to be added that Nils Dahl's analysis of "remembering" in early Christianity found the motif to be far broader than what happens during the Lord's Supper. To remember leads to shaping one's speech and action ("Anamnesis," p. 13), in fact to "a way of life" (pp. 24–25). One must bear in mind what God has done, the words of Jesus, or what has been known since baptism so as to live in conformity with the gospel. This strong moral or ethical side to anamnesis, so that memory and commemoration do not deal only with faith (doctrine) and worship but also with life (pp. 19, 24–25), has often been overlooked. Yet Paul turned the "Christ-anamnesis" of Phil. 2:6–11 to hortatory purposes (2:1–5) and employed the Words of Institution to deal with disciplinary and, more important, socioeconomic, ethical issues at Corinth (11:17–34). There is even the case in Mark 14:9 and Matt. 26:13 where an unnamed woman anointed Jesus at Bethany for burial, and it is said that the story "will be told" when "the gospel is preached in the whole world," "in memory of her" *(eis mnēmousumēn autēs).*

The Covenant

No one can deny that "covenant" is a prominent theme in connection with the Lord's Supper, or at least the Greek term usually translated "covenant." All four versions of the saying concerning the cup at the Last Supper (see pp. 6–7, above) use the word "covenant," at least in RSV and most standard English translations. Schweizer designates it as the second of his three motifs in the New Testament: "every celebration is a *new confirmation of God's covenant* with his church" *(Lord's Supper,* pp. 2, 16). W. G. Kümmel regards "God's new eschatological covenant with men" as the heart of the saying in the Upper Room and the culmination of Jesus' activity and teaching *(The Theology of the New Testament* [Nashville: Abingdon Press, 1973], pp. 91–95, esp. 94, 129, 132–33).

At the very least, covenant implies fellowship at a meal among those who have covenanted together and with God. That is the sense which some see in what is taken to be the earliest written form of the cup-saying, which interprets the action as a whole: "This cup *is* the new covenant . . ." (1 Cor. 11:24). The adjective "new" suggests Jer. 31:31–34 and conjures up eschatological notions of the kingdom of God, soon to come (1 Cor. 11:26, "until he comes"; cf. Mark 14:25). But Paul's citation goes on to refer to "the new covenant *in my blood,*" and the version in Mark and Matthew equates the cup with Jesus' blood, not with the "new covenant": "This is my blood of the covenant which is being poured out for many" (14:24; 26:28). Here the soteriological sense predominates over that of eschatology and fellowship (Dunn, *Unity and Diversity,* pp. 166–67). Moreover, the background in the Old Testament does not lie in Jeremiah 31 but in Exodus 24 and its description of the covenant-making at Sinai, when Moses took the blood from the sacrificial oxen and "threw it upon the people," saying, "Behold the blood of the covenant which the Lord has made with you in accordance with all these words." Then the leaders and elders of Israel went up into the mountain, "beheld God, and ate and drank" (24:8–11).

There are thus problems with how the cup is connected with the covenant, and with precisely which Old Testament covenant is in mind—for there were covenants (plural) of varying sorts in Israel, and not all of them were associated with "the giving of the law" or with "the promises" (Rom. 9:4). Moreover, "covenant" as a term has had a complicated history in theology. Some, especially among Lutherans, have reacted negatively to the term, preferring "testament" first because that word (more clearly than "covenant") proclaims the monergism of grace and the death of the testator (as Luther argued, *LW,* Vol. 36, pp. 37f., 179ff.); and second because of a feeling that Reformed theology overstressed "the covenant" on an Old Testament basis, making it legalistic and so threatening to obscure the gospel and its nature as promise. At the LCA convention in 1976 there was debate on the floor over whether "covenant" should not be removed from the "Theological Introduction" to the Statement on Communion Practices *(Minutes, Eighth Biennial Convention, Boston* 1976, p. 393). The subject therefore rates further attention.

First of all, there must be a linguistic decision on *how to translate the Greek word diathēkē*. All would agree that in Greek usage the word refers primarily to a "last will and testament," the arrangement whereby someone disposes of his or her goods upon death. It can further denote any legal arrangement between two parties. Since a will involves a one-sided action, where the testator makes the decisions, a *diathēkē* in Greek meant something distinct from a *synthēkē* where two equal parties make an agreement. This flavor to the word *diathēkē,* where a superior designates what is to be done, attracted the translators of the Greek Old Testament to it as a rendering for "covenant," in Hebrew *b͏ᵉrith,* that sort of arrangement into which two individuals might enter (1 Sam. 18:3, Jonathan and David), a king with his subjects (2 Kings 11:4), or, above all, Yahweh with Israel. *Diathēkē (not synthēkē)* is thus the word used two hundred seventy times in the Old Testament for *b͏ᵉrith,* "covenant" such as God made with Noah (Gen. 6:18), Abraham (Genesis 15, 17), Moses and Israel at Mt. Sinai (Exodus 19—24), David (2 Samuel 7), and others.

Our problem is therefore how to render *diathēkē* in the New Testament: in light of its Greek background as "testament" or on the basis of Old Testament usage as "covenant." The rivalry between these two concepts stretches over the centuries. The Latin term *testamentum* won out as our common designation for the two parts of the Bible—"Old" and "New Testaments," though in 1946 the RSV sought to restore on its title page "The New Covenant." "Testament" was used in English translations of the Words of Institution in the Catholic Rheims and Protestant King James versions; the Revised Version of 1881 employed "covenant." The Latin for covenant, *foedus,* had given its name to a particular type of covenantal thinking called "Federal Theology," under Calvinists like Cocceius in the seventeenth century. Both the emphasis on the covenant in modern biblical theologians like Walther Eichrodt and the stress on "dispensationalism" in American Fundamentalism owe something to this latter heritage.

As to the New Testament problem, some exegetes like Ernest De Witt

Burton have argued that *diathēkē* regularly means "covenant" in the New Testament, even in test passages like Gal. 3:15 and 17 (International Critical Commentary series, *A Critical and Exegetical Commentary on the Epistle to the Galatians* [New York: Charles Scribner's Sons, 1920], pp. 496–505). Others have held that even in the latter case "testament" is the right rendering, in part on the grounds that Paul could not employ two different meanings in three verses; so, most recently, H. D. Betz, *Galatians* (Hermeneia [Philadelphia: Fortress Press, 1979], pp. 155–59). The passage is one where Paul says he is going to employ an illustration from everyday life, the case of a man's "last will and testament" (3:15). But by the time we get to v. 17 he has brought in the story of Abraham and—I would render *diathēkē* here—his "covenant" with God.

The evidence would seem to demand—*pace* those attempts to make Paul more consistent than he needs to be—"testament" at Gal. 3:15 (and Heb. 9:16) but elsewhere "covenant." "Testament" as a translation does have, of course, the advantage of keeping before us the emphasis on the death of the testator (Jesus, in this case), but it may suggest too legalistic a notion of what is involved, and above all loses the Old Testament background. In the past few years the translation "covenant," except in a few verses such as those cited, is the usual solution in most discussions—unless one feels from recent studies of Jewish law that, under the influence of Greek *diathēkē* as a loanword in rabbinic Hebrew, the sense of "an arrangement before death between giver and recipients" dominated even in the Words of Institution.

But though we may agree the proper rendering is "covenant," that still does not settle *what model of covenant* the New Testament passages have in mind. The answer is that the old covenant envisioned varies from book to book.

In Hebrews, the old covenant is the covenant under Moses at Sinai seen in *contrast* to the new covenant of Jeremiah 31 (Heb. 10:12–25), mediated by Jesus' death (7:22; 9:11–22). The contrast between Sinai and Calvary is that of shadow and substance (8:5–6; 10:1–10).

For Paul, the covenant of Moses at Sinai is seen in even sharper opposition to the covenant in Christ: the Mosaic arrangement, with its legalistic demands, never functioned to save but only to bring out what sin really is and show its dominance in human life (Gal. 3:17; cf. vv. 16–26; 4:24; cf. vv. 22–31). The new covenant in Christ is what takes away sins (Rom. 11:27). It is characterized by the Spirit, and Christians are ministers of this new covenant (2 Cor. 3:6; cf. 3:7–18; 5:17–21). The major, positive Old Testament category for Paul is *not* the covenant at Sinai but the *promise* of God to Abraham (Galatians 3; Romans 4); if there is salvation history in Paul's thinking, it centers on "the promise to Abraham and his 'offspring,' " that is, the Christ in whom the promise was fulfilled. With regard to past Hebrew history, any anamnesis of Jesus recalls Abraham, not Moses, as prime figure according to Paul.

But what covenant pattern is operative with regard to the words in the Upper Room? Here a great deal of fruitful effort has been spent in recent years in *analysis of the Mosaic and other covenants in the Old Testament* as analogous with the Hittite "suzerainty treaty" form. This approach has become pervasive. The model works well with the Sinai material of Exodus (19:3–8; 20; 24:3–8; cf. Deuteronomy) and with Joshua 24, but those who apply it to the New Testament are puzzled by the absence of certain "covenant-treaty" features. One can list:

Features in Hittite treaties	Exodus 20	Cf. Deuteronomy
(a) Preamble, naming the two parties	"I am the Lord your God" (20:2a)	cf.19:3;1:1—6:3
(b) Historical prologue, on past relationships	" . . . who brought you up out of the land of Egypt" (20:2b; cf.19:4)	cf. 6:4—11:25
and declaration on future relationships	cf. 19:5b–6a	in a sense, the entire book!
(c) Stipulations on the new relationship	19:5a; 21:1—22:25 cf. 20:3–17	12—26
(d) Provision for deposit and public reading	cf. 19:6b–8	31:9–11
(e) List of witnesses (no parallel to use of Hittite gods as witnesses; Yahweh can swear only by himself)		cf. 10:5, the stone tablets
(f) Blessings and curses, possibly followed by an oath	19:5b–6a	11:26–32, chapters 27—28

(see G. E. Mendenhall, "Covenant," in *IDB* 1, pp. 719–21; in *IDBS* there are separate articles on "Covenant, Davidic" [M. Weinfeld] and "Covenant, Mosaic" [P. A. Riemann], pp. 188–97; K. Baltzer, *The Covenant Formulary* [Philadelphia: Fortress Press, 1971]; there is an immense literature on the topic).

The heart of this type of covenant in the Old Testament is part (b), the assertion of what God has done and his promises for the future. But a great deal also depends on the response of the partner Israel: "*if* you will obey my voice and keep my covenant, you will be . . ." blessed (Exod. 19:5). Continuation of the promised covenant blessing depends on living up to the stipulation.

Commentators who try to apply this type of covenant to the Upper Room—and some have done so rigorously and rigidly (cf. Millard, *Apostolic History)*—have come away baffled. One may press hard to find the various items, such as (f) blessings and curses in 1 Cor. 11:27–32, but what remains missing is any note of "stipulations." Therefore it has been suggested that the absence of such obligations is to be explained by the personal relationship which has been created—to list obligations would be superfluous! Or it has been argued that we can discover a stipulation for the Christian's covenant in the "eleventh commandment" found in the Fourth Gospel (13:34), a "new commandment" to love one another; but John lacks any Last Supper references in the Upper Room where he gives that mandate and indeed any "covenant" reference there. It would appear that the Mosaic-Sinai model is the wrong one.

There is an alternative. As Mendenhall puts it, the Old Testament knew not only "covenants in which *Israel* is bound" but also "covenants in which *God* is bound" *(IDB* 1, pp. 717, 718, italics added). The latter type is exemplified by the b^erith or *diathēkē* with Abraham (Gen. 15:7–21) and with David. In this case everything depends, not on obeying conditions or meeting stipulations, but solely upon Yahweh's promise: your house, your throne, will be established for ever (cf. 2 Sam. 7:16). God swears he has made a covenant which he will never violate; it is in light of such a promise that Israel, in darkest despair, could ask God "to remember" (Ps. 89:3–4, 28–37; cf. 89:39, 47, 50). Such a promise to Abraham is what Paul saw as analogous to the new covenant in Christ.

What, then, of the *Upper Room?* It seems obvious that New Testament usage generally has in mind, in contrast to the Mosaic covenant at Sinai, a parallel to the Abrahamic covenant of promise when it speaks of a *diathēkē—bᵉrith* which God has effected in Christ. This suggests that the covenant set forth with the eucharistic cup is one dependent on God's word, not upon human obedience to stipulations. But there are several things to give us pause. While the "new covenant" of Jeremiah 31 is not to be like the one with Moses at Sinai (31:32) but is to be based upon Yahweh's doing (31:33–34), so that 1 Cor. 11:25 (= Jer. 31:31) is not Mosaic in its orientation, Jeremiah's "new covenant" does assume that God will write the law within human hearts (cf. the "heart" and "new spirit" of Ezek. 11:19) and torah will then be obeyed. Moreover, Mark 14:24 *is* reflective of Exod. 24:8 ("the blood of the covenant"), unless the enigmatic Zech. 9:11 is involved. Was it simply the link to the *death* of Jesus as blood sacrificed "for many" which the phrase had in view, or were there also overtones in the Markan-Matthean wording of some hint of a Sinai-covenant pattern with its stipulations? A final answer for today will depend on matters more broad than the historical exegesis of the phrases, including the degree to which we conceive of "gospel" and "promise" as including imperatives (cf. Gen. 18:1b) and ethical admonition (cf. for example, the Sermon on the Mount) or parenesis (Romans 12—14).

In any case, it will not do to call the one type of covenant—that of promise— a "covenant of pure grace" and the other (Sinai) type something less. For grace is always grace. The Sinai pattern, of initial declaration in the indicative mood about what God has done in the past, followed by imperatives graciously given to guide Israel's daily response, is just as much a product of God's loving kindness or grace as the call to Abraham and David and the promises to them. The Lord's Supper as covenant is a matter of grace whether it is based on the Abraham model or reflects something of Sinai. And like the Exodus experience or David's divine prerogatives, it could be abused (cf. Exod. 32:4, 6; Num. 25:1–18; 21:5–6; 16:41–49; in light of 1 Cor. 10:1–11). The covenant aspect of the Christian Sacrament is a topic not yet exhausted in modern analysis.

One of the services of Klaus Baltzer's study of the ancient Near Eastern and Israelite *covenant formularies* is the fact that he carried his research on to seek *reflections* in later Jewish and *early Christian writings*. In particular, he made a case for the way the historical prologue or prior history on past relationships with God was recited at the synagogue service, whence it came into Christian preaching and liturgy. Narrative-recital or confession of what God has done, beginning with Abraham or the Exodus, or with creation, would thus be a part of worship, amounting to kerygmatic proclamation or profession of the community's faith. Against a covenant background, ethical teaching and didache would likewise have had a natural role in Christian literature and life. Baltzer even suggested that the very structure of the New Testament letter form owes something to the covenant-sequence of a *Vorgeschichte* followed by stipulations; Romans 1—11 is a recital of God's deeds and promises; 12—14 provides "stipulations" for how believers live. Obviously in an eschatological community blessings and curses would be very much alive too.

All early Christian parallelization of the Last or Lord's Supper to the Passover, we may add, carries with it implications for a covenant motif: just as Yahweh's bringing Israel up out of Egypt resulted in a covenant relationship, so God's delivery of Jesus from death led to a new covenant. If there is anything to the notion of an annual Christian Passover service or of a celebration of the resurrection each year at the empty tomb, as has been proposed, one may ask whether these services were at all similar to what Israel celebrated as a "covenant-renewal" ceremony?

Further, Christian prayers of thanksgiving at the Eucharist for what God has done in salvation history may owe something to the covenant: they share in the practice of reciting and remembering God's saving deeds. The New Testament references plainly commit the church to remember Jesus at the Lord's Supper within a covenant context (1 Cor. 11:24). How much more of salvation history was then recalled may owe something, in the differing instances, to the whole covenant background and practices (cf. J. Reumann, "Heilsgeschichte in Luke," *Studia Evangelica IV* [Texte und Untersuchungen 102; Berlin: Akademie-Verlag, 1968], pp. 110-15).

Participation/Fellowship

These two words have been used to express what is involved in the Greek term *koinōnia,* a word not found in the sayings from the Upper Room but prominent in Paul, a word closely related to "covenant" and to "fellowship meals" (see pp. 4-5, above).

To derive benefit from what God has done in Christ one must "participate" or "have a share" in that death, and since this is done with coparticipants, there is a "fellowship" or "participation" together in the Son, in the gospel, and in the Spirit, for example (cf. 1 Cor. 1:9; 9:23; 2 Cor. 13:14; Phil. 1:5). If the view is correct that the central theme in Paul's whole "pattern" or system of thought is "participationalist eschatology" (E. P. Sanders, *Paul and Palestinian Judaism* [Philadelphia: Fortress Press, 1977], pp. 502–8, 511–15, 543, 549, though materially this means the same thing as justification by faith), *not* "covenant nomism" as in Judaism, then we are here at the core of Paul's Christianity.

Roth makes participation a major term for grasping the meaning of the Lord's Supper *(Meaning,* pp. 23–25). Within the last thirty years koinonia has become a piece of "pop-Greek" in English garb, meaning "fellowship." The word is also the basis for terming the Lord's Supper a "communion" (1 Cor. 10:16, RSV note).

Actually the goal of a koinonia between gods and men, or of people with each other, was a widespread one in the Greek world. Pythagoreans and Stoics sought it. Others dreamed of a past golden age when such things had been. Ancient Israel regarded itself very much as a nation, people, and community under its God and looked forward, at least in later apocalyptic literature, to a messianic age to come (though the *koinōnia* family of words is rare in the Greek Old Testament). Later, various Pharisaic groups and Qumran formed what were called *haburim*, societies for fellowship to share the Passover or a common life.

Luke's reference to the early Christian community at Jerusalem, which speaks of the baptized as devoting themselves to "the apostles' teaching and fellowship [*koinōnia*], to the breaking of bread [see pp. 16–17, above], and the prayers" (Acts 2:42), probably means to convey the notion that this ideal society has been realized in the church. While koinonia here has been taken as "communion" or "liturgical fellowship in worship," it more likely refers to the Jerusalem community's practice then of having "all things in common" *(koina,* 2:44–45) and to its financial collection system and distribution of relief (4:32–37, 6:1–6). That was "sharing" too.

The really pertinent passage is in *1 Cor. 10:16.* Here Paul quotes what most take to be a pre-Pauline eucharistic formula, doubtless familiar to the Corinthians, for he goes on in v. 17 to make a further point on the basis of it. The original formula, with its exact parallelism, minus Paul's recasting of it, we have already noted above (see pp. 14–15, for a translation). The bread we break and the cup for which we bless God and give him thanks are each "a participation in the body/blood of Christ," that is, in Christ himself, more specifically in the benefits of his atoning death. We have here a Lord's Supper formulation which, like 1 Cor. 11:23–25, is older than the letter to Corinth. For this reason its theme of koinonia deserves prominence in any list of key New Testament themes.

Paul, it may be noted, applies this christological statement to make an *ecclesiological* point. He comments,

> Because there is "one bread" [the term is the same as was used in the formula in v. 16], we, the many, are one body, for we all partake [the verb is different, not from the *koinōnia* root] of the one bread. (10:17, au. trans.)

Paul has moved here from the one loaf, broken in the sacramental meal, to an emphasis on the oneness of the community. He has done this via the phrase "body of Christ." Paul's usual application of the phrase is to the church (cf. 1 Cor. 12:12–27). So it is here. He does not mean that the church is Christ's body *only* when it eats Christ's body or even that it is at *most* the body of Christ at the Eucharist, for it is that at all times. Rather Paul strikes a blow against individualist notions of the sacrament and insists, in the face of Corinth's troubles (cf. 11:17–22), that above all at the meal-celebrations there can be no place for divisiveness. The congregation

> is the place where the love of the Lord given in death is to be experienced, and therefore "edification" in responsibility for the brethren is the only criterion . . .

for life together (Günther Bornkamm, "Lord's Supper and Church in Paul," *Early Christian Experience*, p. 152). But that means discerning the brothers and sisters in Christ as well as the Lord's love at the Supper.

Paul goes on to argue (1 Cor. 10:18–30) that all peoples participate and share in "the divine" in one way or another:

> Old Testament Israelites were participants (partners) in *the altar* (i.e. *God,* through sacrifices, v. 18);
>
> Pagans are participants/partners in the table of *demons* (vv. 19–20);
>
> Christians participate in the body of *Christ* (crucified and risen) at the Lord's Supper.

Precisely because of these realities, sacramental participation carries with it real dangers and calls for discerning judgments. Be careful when you pronounce a *berakah* or prayer of thanksgiving (10:30)—in giving glory to God (10:31) one is also affecting the neighbor (10:24).

That brings us to the matter of *discernment.* The chapters about the

Lord's Supper in 1 Corinthians are full of terms from the root *krinein* meaning to "judge" (10:15, 29, RSV "determined"; 11:31–32), "discern" *(diakrinein,* 11:29, 31), and related words (10:25, 27, to "raise a question" of judgment; 11:29, 32, 34, judgment, chasten, condemn).

Some Christians—and I take Lutherans as the chief example—have perhaps been overscrupulous on the theme of judgment, and that in a particular way. They begin with the warning in 11:27 about eating the bread and drinking the cup of the Lord *unworthily,* so as to be "guilty of profaning the body and blood of the Lord." Their approach is abetted by a textual tradition in some Greek manuscripts (reflected in English by the KJV) which underscored the point in v. 29 by adding the words italicized below (these words should now be dropped as the insertions of later manuscripts), "he that eateth and drinketh *unworthily,* eateth and drinketh damnation to himself, not discerning the body *of the Lord"* (KJV adapted). In these ways the sin of unworthy participation was doubly driven home. Lutherans then took all these references to be warnings against the error of not perceiving the true presence of the whole Christ as "body and blood" "in, with, and under" the bread and wine. Articles in periodicals some twenty-five years ago discussed, however, whether interpretation might also allow a reference here to the body of Christ in the sense of the church, as Paul takes it in 10:17 (cf. *Lutheran Quarterly* 8 [1956]: 67, 271; and 9 [1957]: 61).

Since then the pendulum has definitely swung, and common opinion is on the side of the argument which sees an ecclesiological reference in these verses. William F. Orr and James Arthur Walther, in *I Corinthians* (Anchor Bible [Garden City, N.Y.; Doubleday & Co., 1976], p. 273) are typical: v. 27 refers "to the mistreatment of persons present and not to misinterpretation in liturgical procedures." But this goes too far. Conzelmann describes v. 27 as "a principle of sacral law: the man who offends against the elements, offends against the Lord himself," though he adds, "we must bear in mind that the idea of the church as the body of the Lord has a part to play" *(1 Corinthians,* p. 202). The transition is probably made between v. 27 and v. 29. The former refers to "elements" (both body *and blood):*

> whoever, therefore, eats the bread or drinks the cup of the Lord in an unworthy manner will be guilty of profaning the body and blood of the Lord. (11:27)

The further statement, after a reference to self-examination (v. 28), refers to participation in the meal-sacrament at Corinth but takes "the body" (blood is unmentioned) in the ecclesiastical sense of 10:17:

> Any one who eats and drinks without discerning the body eats and drinks judgment upon himself. (11:29)

In any case, a double discernment is called for, before and in participating: discernment of the elements, that Christ is present, and discernment of the communing community, that Christ's people are present. Direct consequences follow where one fails in either discernment (vv. 30–32).

We must remember Paul was writing these words when confronted by problems from two extremes. There was the Scylla of those who regarded the sacraments as a quasi-magical medicine, insulating them from sinning and providing assured immortality here and now (cf. Schweizer, *Lord's Supper,* pp. 5–6; Dunn, *Unity and Diversity,* pp. 164–65). The Charybdis was an attitude inherited from the Corinthian environment that such fellowship gatherings were a matter of one's own feasting and drinking tastes, in quality, quantity, and company. The two tendencies had a common fault: they failed to discern that it is the *Lord's* body (the church) participating in the *Lord's* Supper (body and blood). It had overlooked that Christ is always judge and not a talisman at our disposal, or simply a congenial companion.

It is not easy to state the discernment theme as part of participation today so as to keep a balance between *koinōnia* as participation in the death-benefits of the risen Lord (10:16) and as a horizontal dimension involving relationships with each other. Jenson *(Visible Words,* p. 87) captures the priority of the "presence of Christ as bread and cup" but also brings out the importance of the community of fellow believers, "the church-body of Christ," toward whom a wrong understanding (in thinking of them as "mere individuals rather than as one entity") may be directly exhibited. "If I fail in my discernment of [the presence of Christ], it is not it but I who am destroyed."

The dilemma, in an age where interpersonal relations and social structures readily fall apart, is how much to emphasize our inclinations to highlight the person-oriented, social-ethical aspect of the sacrament, while still keeping the "presence-of-Christ, participation-in-him" motif. Apartheid, for example, is rightly said to become a confessional issue when it occurs at the communion table. Economic, social divisions dare not separate believers "before the Lord." But can the vertical aspects of our relationship with God be kept if too much stress is put upon the horizontal ties? Can "fellowship" serve as the right bridge to cover both directions? No contemporary view of the Eucharist dare overlook these issues brought to light by the participation-discernment motif.

Some Other Emphases

A few other themes arise in the New Testament, sometimes noted above in passing, that ought to be singled out.

1. *The Spirit,* while not mentioned in the Words of Institution—of course not, because the Spirit is not prominent in the Synoptic Gospels, and one may say it is a sign of fidelity to the tradition that Paul has not added a reference—appears prominently, though briefly, in the discussion in John 6 (6:63, see p. 20, above).

In Paul's argument, however, in 1 Cor. 10:1–13, that ancient Israel possessed "sacraments" akin to baptism and the Lord's Supper, yet nonetheless fell when tempted and suffered punishment, he describes the people in Moses' day as eating a "supernatural" or "spiritual" food and drinking a "supernatural" or "spiritual" drink from the "supernatural" or "spiritual" Rock which followed them, that is, Christ. The Greek word *pneumatikos*, here translated in the two different ways indicated in the RSV text and noted each time it occurs, need mean nothing more than "allegorical" or "typological," or could derive from the mystery cults (suggesting the sense, they ate and drank "Christ"). But others think Paul reflects Christian views of their own sacraments and so describes Israel's sacraments as *"imparting* the Spirit" (Ernst Käsemann, *Essays on New Testament Themes,* trans. W. J. Montague [London: SCM Press, 1964; Philadelphia: Fortress Press, 1982]) or even *"containing* the Spirit" (cf. Conzelmann, *1 Corinthians,* p. 166). In this way, the Holy Spirit would be involved with Holy Communion, long prior to the later development of an invocation or *epiclesis* of the Spirit, an invocation to be present. (Cf. J. E. L. Oulton, *Holy Communion and Holy Spirit* [London: SPCK, 1951], for a maximalizing of relationships.)

2. *Faith.* Though this concept no more occurs in the Synoptic Upper Room scenes (or in 1 Corinthians 11) than "the Spirit" does, it remains implicit because a group of "believers" is assumed at the meal.

Again it is the Fourth Gospel that makes the theme explicit in connection with the Eucharist. In Chapter 6, note the verses where the verb, never the noun, is dynamically used: the whole chapter contrasts those who believe Jesus and never thirst but have eternal life (6:29, 35, 40, 47,

69) and those who do not (6:30, 36, 64). Perhaps any "original" discourse here made even more decisive the factor of believing that God gives the bread of life in Jesus and his words. The presence of vv. 51c–58 applies the need for faith to the eating and drinking of the Son of man's flesh and blood. Dunn (Unity and Diversity, p. 170) regards "the language of 'eating,' 'munching,' 'drinking' as metaphors for believing in Jesus: the need to believe in Jesus is the central emphasis of the whole passage."

Paul's general understanding of "faith" as the response of confession, trust, obedience, and hope, with confidence yet not without an element of fear (cf. R. Bultmann, Theology of the New Testament [New York: Charles Scribner's Sons, 1951–55], Vol. 1, pp. 314–24) corresponds well with key elements we have seen in the Lord's Supper, such as proclamation, presence of the crucified, risen Lord, renewal of covenant relationship, and an eschatological horizon.

An Achilles' heel in sacramentology, especially for some Christians, has often been the difficulty of fashioning a view of the Lord's Supper that neither makes everything depend upon "subjective" faith nor, in its search for an "objective" sacrament, on magical notions. Though there are exceptions to all generalizations, the tendencies in recent years have probably been more in the direction of eucharistic objectivization than in a stress upon faith.

3. *Frequency and centrality* for the Eucharist in early Christianity is widely presumed. A celebration "every Sunday" or even daily of what is taken to be "the central act of worship" for the primitive church is widely asserted. The fact of the matter is that we have little evidence and do not know how often or when communions were held in the New Testament period, or when, let alone how frequently, believers received the Lord's Supper.

For the second century, even the latter part of it, and the "Pre-Nicaean" period, things were too varied and there is enough of a "caesura," that one can scarcely take that period as a norm for all later Christianity (G. Kretschmar, TRE, Vol. 1, pp. 59–60). By then shifts from the agape to just a bread-and-wine sacrament, from (Saturday) evening to Sunday morning service, from one Christian community in a place to several congregations, from eschatological imminence to structured stability, from blessing God to what became more and more a thank offering (eucharistia) to God—were well under way. Even so, our records are sparse. The tendency has often been to read later views back into the second and first centuries (for example, Alan Richardson, *An Introduction to the Theology of the New Testament* [London: SCM Press, 1958], pp. 13, 364–87, esp. 380–81).

For the first century our general view is probably clouded by the romantic reconstruction Luke gives of Christianity in Jerusalem (see p. 16, above). His "breaking of the bread" may or may not have been eucharistic. If daily, the celebration points in the direction of regarding *every* family meal as a vehicle for Jesus' presence. But that is not the same as making every meal a Lord's Supper. What if, at the other end of the spectrum, there was an annual Christian Passover service, known to Luke? (Jewish Christians once a year, using bread and water, were thus said to imitate the church Eucharist.) Would we then have a range of daily meals, "real" Lord's Supper celebrations (how often?), and a "super" annual "special service"? In the Pauline congregations we cannot tell how often Corinth had its sacrament-cum-meal. The assumption is too easy, however, and to be resisted that every Sunday gathering was a Eucharist or that every worship service was sacramental (as Cullmann proposed). Likely there was considerable variety.

4. There is little in the New Testament directly applicable to the controversy in recent years over *"child" or "infant Communion."* New Testament studies did see a debate in the 1950s and 1960s between Joachim Jeremias, who sought to demonstrate *Kindertaufe* or the baptism of *children* already in the first century, and Kurt Aland, who argued that the records show that *Säuglingstaufe* or *infant* baptism can be demonstrated with direct evidence only back to the third century. Aland seems to have had the better of the arguments, though he added that the later practice of baptizing infants is to be justified on the basis of our understanding of the gospel message, even if it was not New Testament praxis (cf. Dunn, *Unity and Diversity,* pp. 160–61).

If there was no practice of infant baptism in the first century, there could have been no infant Communion—unless one wants to conjecture a practice of communing the unbaptized.

5. Though it surfaced at times in our discussions above (cf. p. 44), the *"judgment theme in the sacraments"*—as C. F. D. Moule termed it (in *The Background of the New Testament and Its Eschatology,* Dodd Festschrift [Cambridge: Cambridge University Press, 1954], pp. 464–81)—has been a neglected note in recent years, with all the emphasis on joy and

triumph and life. Yet John 6 (belief or unbelief as the result of encounter with Jesus and his flesh and blood), Acts (with its graphic picture of retribution on those in the community not living up to its standard, like Ananias and Sapphira, a contrast in 5:1-11 to the koinonia portrayed in 4:32-37), and Paul (1 Cor. 11:26-32) show clearly that the presence of the Lord can result in woe as well as weal.

CONCERNING THE BIBLICAL FINDINGS

Origins

Scholarship in recent years has loosened our hold on the Upper Room as *the* origin for the Lord's Supper in Christianity, at least as a single direct-line cause. All the records agree that something occurred there, but historians cannot agree on which version is primary at certain points or on what Jesus said. Although doubts are cast on a New Testament verbatim of what his words were "on the night in which he was betrayed," firmer links are established to other portions of Jesus' ministry. The church's Supper expresses what was genuinely characteristic of Jesus in eschatology, Old Testament backgrounds, and assertion of God's good news. But it does so after Good Friday and Easter.

Developmental Lines, Variety, and Unity

Recent scholarship has more clearly traced out the probable lines of development for the meal-sacrament in New Testament Christianity. One is struck here by the changes that occur and the variety that must have existed in the fifth and sixth decades of the first century and afterward. However, the view that there were two clear, antithetical types of meals competing—in the manner of Tübingen-School reconstructions, for example,

Lietzmann:	Jerusalem	and Pauline types
Lohmeyer:	Galilean	and Jerusalem (!) types

let alone R. D. Richardson's two types (cf. Marxsen, *Lord's Supper,* pp. xvii-xx for details), which eventually combined (so that one can debate whether "Easter joy" as in Acts *or* the death of Christ as in 1 Corinthians 11 is *the* original leitmotif)—is less prominent than it used to be. The same is probably true of Dom Gregory Dix's widely influential analysis (in *The Shape of the Liturgy* [Chicago: Alec R. Allenson, 1950; London: Dacre Press, 1945]) of four essential actions (took, blessed, broke, gave), for these seem characteristic of *all* ancient religious meals.

Though some views have faded in influence, the general impression today which any observer must have from reading the recent literature on early Christian eucharistic practice and piety is one of variety. But that does not mean that everything was allowed in the early church, for there were surely perimeters and limits and central themes which occur again and again.

The next steps in New Testament research will likely involve more precise reconstructions of developments in separate Christian communities of the first century, such as the Johannine community (for example, Raymond E. Brown, see pp. 20–21, above; further, Brown, *The Churches the Apostles Left Behind* [New York: Paulist Press, 1984], pp. 87–90, 100), the Pauline School, or Luke-Acts. For the patristic centuries Arthur Vööbus (in *Meaning,* pp. 39–74) pointed in 1961 to considerable evidence for varying views and practices, especially in Eastern Christianity—more evidence than has yet been assimilated. Georg Kretschmar *(TRE,* Vol. 1, p. 86) speaks of the difficulty in deriving the whole course of eucharistic development for the first four centuries from any one impact. The problem of the origin and rise of the anamnesis he regards as the central liturgical-historical and theological theme. (Is it to be connected with covenant recital-theology?) But the unity of the Lord's Supper he finds not in any " 'perennial theology' or liturgy *[theologia oder liturgia perennis]* but in the anamnesis of Christ which refers back to Jesus' cross and resurrection, exalts the Lord who is present, awaits the Coming One, and so imparts the gifts of the eucharist in the Communion."

Emphases for Us

The several themes which do emerge prominently in the New Testament analysis of the Lord's Supper include the eschatological aspects of future hope and fulfillment, touching "the now" proleptically; the proclaiming and remembering of God's deeds of grace, Jesus' death and resurrection being the sine qua non; the covenant, with its aspects of promise, fulfillment, and the corporate implications of community; and participation as personal appropriation of what God is offering, yet fellowship not only with Christ but also with brothers and sisters in the faith as well. Discernment, anamnesis, Spirit, faith, salvation, and judgment inevitably loom large. No Eucharist today can be faithful to its biblical roots and norms without reflection of all of, or at least many of, these aspects.

As seen in current scholarship, the New Testament thus provides us with a general picture of eucharistic origins, something of the course of early development, and emphases and aspects for the sacrament today, within the context of the gospel as a message of justification, reconciliation, and forgiveness, and of a community of believers. Later developments, of which there were many over the centuries, must be measured within this biblical framework, above all with regard to whether the sacrament conveys the gospel and person of Jesus the Lord.

FOR FURTHER READING AND REFERENCE

Allmen, Jean-Jacques von. *The Lord's Supper.* Ecumenical Studies in Worship 19. Richmond: John Knox Press, 1969. Seminal essay for the work of the Faith and Order Commission; see chap. 3, pp. 137ff., below.

Bernas, C. "Eucharist (Biblical Data)." *New Catholic Encyclopedia,* Vol. 5. New York: McGraw-Hill, 1967. Pp. 594–99.

Chenderlin, Fritz. *"Do This as My Memorial." The Semantic and Conceptual Background and Value of* Anamnēsis *in 1 Corinthians 11:24–25.* Analecta Biblica 99. Rome: Biblical Institute Press, 1982.

Delling, Gerhard. *Worship in the New Testament.* Trans. Percy Scott (German, 1952). Philadelphia: Westminster Press, 1962. Older, broader account by author of the *TRE* article.

Dunn, James D. G. *Unity and Diversity in the New Testament. An Inquiry into the Character of Earliest Christianity.* Philadelphia: Westminster Press, 1977. Pp. 161–73.

Hahn, Ferdinand. *The Worship of the Early Church.* Trans. David E. Green (German, 1967). Philadelphia: Fortress Press, 1973. Tradition-historical approach by German scholar whose subsequent, untranslated articles are cited especially by Jenson for their concise summaries.

Heron, Alasdair I. C. *Table and Tradition.* Philadelphia: Westminster Press, 1984.

Jeremias, Joachim. *The Eucharistic Words of Jesus.* Trans. Norman Perrin, 3d German ed. of 1960 with author's revision. New York: Charles Scribner's Sons, 1966. Philadelphia: Fortress Press, 1978.

Kilmartin, Edward J. *The Eucharist in the Primitive Church.* Englewood Cliffs,

N.J.: Prentice-Hall, 1965. Reflective of emerging Roman Catholic scholarship.

Marxsen, Willi. *The Lord's Supper as a Christological Problem*. Trans. Lorenz Nieting, from the German of 1963. Facet Books Biblical Series 25. Philadelphia: Fortress Press, 1970. Reprinted in Marxsen, *The Beginnings of Christology* (Philadelphia: Fortress Press, 1979).

Moule, C. F. D. *Worship in the New Testament*. Ecumenical Studies in Worship 9. Richmond: John Knox Press, 1961. Pp. 9–46.

RGG, Vol. 1 (1956). "Abendmahl I. Im NT," has been translated; see Schweizer, Eduard, below. Cf. also G. Kretschmar, "IV. Liturgiegeschichtlich," cols. 40–44.

Schweizer, Eduard. *The Lord's Supper According to the New Testament*. Trans. James M. Davis, from *RGG* article of 1956, as rev. by the author. Facet Books Biblical Series 18. Philadelphia: Fortress Press, 1967.

Thurian, Max. *The Eucharistic Memorial*. Trans. J. G. Davies (French, 1959). Eucumenical Studies in Worship 7 and 8. 2 vols. Richmond: John Knox Press, 1960, 1961. An outgrowth of the Faith and Order meeting at Lund, Sweden, in 1952, this liturgical-theological monograph on the Eucharist as sacrifice is the work of the Taizé (Protestant) monk who later helped draft *Baptism, Eucharist and Ministry*.

TRE, Vol. 1. Berlin and New York: Walter de Gruyter, 1977; articles in Lieferungen 1 and 2, 1976:

Ström, Å. V. "Abendmahl I. Das sakrale Mahl in der Religionen der Welt." Pp. 43–47.

Delling, Gerhard. "Abendmahl II. Urchristliches Mahl-Verständnis." Pp. 47–58.

Kretschmar, Georg. "Abendmahl III. Das Abendmahl in der Geschichte der christlichen Kirche. III/1. Alte Kirche." Pp. 59–89.

————· "Abendmahlsfeier I. Alte Kirche." Pp. 229–78.

Hauschild, Wolf-Dieter. "Agapen I. In der alten Kirche." Pp. 748–53.

2

Some Developments in the History of Holy Communion Through the Centuries

IT WOULD BE attractive to move directly from biblical motifs about the Lord's Supper to the convergences in ecumenical discussions today about the Eucharist, for those seem the areas of greatest breakthrough for Christians seeking to come to a closer fellowship at Holy Communion. The intervening centuries and their developments seem to many specifically what divide us.

Yet some find their stance on this sacrament to have been shaped precisely during these centuries, in councils of the church or confessional statements, for example, in the sixteenth century. Others find the solution to eucharistic problems in early but post–New Testament centuries, such as the third or fourth. In no case will we understand the recent ecumenical discussions without attention to the developments and understandings and barriers of past centuries, which bilaterals or the Faith and Order Commission must face. And so just as one cannot do theology with simply a Bible in one hand and today's *New York Times* in the other (for there must be attention to the intervening centuries)—and just as in liberation theology one pays attention not only to Jesus and Scripture, on the one hand, and praxis and reflection in the local situation today, on the other, but also to intervening events and thought (a good example in Jon Sobrino's *Christology at the Crossroads: A Latin American Approach* [Maryknoll, N.Y.: Orbis Books, 1978] is the attention to the Chalcedonian Formula)—so we must consider some highlights in the history of the Eucharist since New Testament times.

It should be plainly stated that no comprehensive outline of that enormous topic will be attempted here. A variety of treatments exist, some of which are described under "For Further Reading and Reference" at the end of this chapter. Our emphasis will be on developments, for better or

53

for worse, that especially find echo in the ecumenical discussions reported in chapter 3. The following pages link, as it were, these two areas of Scripture and ecumenism today.

The arrangement of such a history of highlights is a matter of some dispute. Strictly speaking, one should write historically of a time of "origins," coupling biblical and other early sources together (as was done somewhat in chapter 1). But most Christian groups regard the scriptural materials as standing in a privileged position, indeed as normative, however much these groups also stress the church fathers (so, for example, the Anglican Communion in its Lambeth Quadrilateral of 1888). How then should postbiblical developments be labelled? The "age of the fathers" and "patristic period" after the New Testament are terms frequently employed (though now criticized as "noninclusionist terminology" by feminists). Yngve Brilioth's use of "the Early church" followed by the "Middle Ages" is not precise enough. Darwell Stone in 1909 and Bernard Cooke in 1967 distinguish, for good reasons, the Ante-Nicene Period and the period of "the Great Councils." Stone was particularly careful to separate Eastern and Western development in theology from the sixth century on. Aware of these concerns, we shall with some ecumenists speak of what follows the primary documents of the New Testament as a period in which the church—before and after Constantine—was building up its life and thought, here with regard to the Lord's Supper.

THE BUILDING PERIOD

J. J. von Allmen once wrote, ". . . during the first millennium the Church experienced no violent controversies or notable heresies concerning the Eucharist" (The Lord's Supper, Ecumenical Studies in Worship 19 [Richmond: John Knox Press, 1969], p. 16). There is some truth in this if one counts the first controversies to be those in the ninth and eleventh centuries involving Paschasius Radbertus and Berengarius (see below). The contention could also gain support in some quarters if one put the Eucharist under "church order," rather than under "faith," as Arthur Darby Nock once did even for the New Testament (St. Paul [New York: Harper & Brothers, 1938], p. 186). A dissertation on Eucharist and Excommunication: A Study in Early Christian Doctrine and Discipline by Kenneth Hein (European University Papers, Series 23, Vol. 19 [Bern: H. Lang; Frankfurt: P. Lang, 1973]) suggests that "eucharistic excommunication" was used in discipline and disputes, even if the differences were not over the Eucharist itself. (Hein, incidentally, hoped personally that in modern ecumenism the Lord's Supper might be used not just as a *goal* of fellowship but a *means* to it.) For evidence from antiquity, however, one ought not to overlook Werner Elert's study, *Eucharist and Church Fellowship in the First Four Centuries* (trans. N. E. Nagel; St. Louis: Concordia Publishing House, 1966), with its conclusion (pp. vii, 80–81) that "confessional divisions" are by no means "a phenomenon reserved for modern times" and its evidence for "closed communion" in this period (chap. 7)—"Holy things for holy ones"; "first be reconciled" before offering your gift at the altar, as Matt. 5:23–24 said, and that came to be applied to the Eucharist.

We argued in chapter 1 that the variety of views in the New Testament period about the meal was far greater than supposed, and if our discussion of the Johannine community is at all correct (let alone the "Church of the Beloved Disciple" in contrast to other positions held by New Testament communities), there were apparent controversies. The statement of von Allmen seems an extension over the subsequent centuries of a rather romantic picture of Christian origins. We can say perhaps more accurately that, since "church fellowship is eucharistic fellowship," many problems that confronted the church in the early centuries, such as Docetism in Christology, Gnosticism, or the Donatist controversy, had ramifications for the Eucharist. F. C. Conybeare is at the other end of the spectrum from von Allmen. In remarks about the transubstantiation debate (for which he cites opinions beginning with Serapion in the fourth century) Conybeare describes how people began to ask what the Eucharist meant:

> Rival schools of thought sprung up, and controversy raged over it, as it had aforetime about the *homoousiŏn,* or the two natures. Thus the sacrament which was intended to be a bond of peace, became a chief cause of dissension and bloodshed, and was often discussed as if it were a vulgar talisman. *(Encyclopaedia Britannica* [1910]: 9, 872)

The picture in the church's building period lies somewhere between von Allmen's idyllic description and a notion of bloody doctrinal and disciplinary battles.

For the second and following centuries, we may ask, What significant developments were taking place with regard to the New Testament motifs noted in chapter 1? We have already stressed that there were lines of development there. Some of these continued, others withered. There is no single "trajectory."

Obviously, the New Testament's often intense perspective of imminent eschatology could not be sustained: "the hope" chiefly became a distantly future one, sometimes expressed in actual sacramental celebration there and then. Geoffrey Wainwright has concluded that "the eschatological dimension of the eucharist retained a fair degree of prominence at least as long as the church was exposed to persecution and martyrdom" (Eucharist and Eschatology [New York: Oxford University Press, 1981], p. 124). At the Eucharist the theme of Jesus' death was in the post–New Testament centuries related not only to his resurrection but also to other events in his life, including, in a salvation-historical view, the incarnation. Emphases in the Words of Institution like "(new) covenant" continued but were subject often to a less Semitic–Old Testament understanding and more and more to a Greco-Roman one, as in this case "testament."

In what Bernard Cooke speaks of as "a startling shift" in the second century from the "a-cultic" mentality of the New Testament to one that moves "in the direction of cult categories reminiscent of Old Testament thought" and "is accelerated in the third century" (Ministry to Word and Sacraments: History and Theology [Philadelphia: Fortress Press, 1976], p. 537, cf. 525), we may pick out the following aspects.

The agape or meal, often in the evening and already subject to strictures in 1 Corinthians 11, increasingly disappeared from the scene. While Ignatius (Smyrnaeans 8) and the letter by Pliny to Trajan early in the second century refer to it, Justin Martyr does not. By the time of Cyprian the Eucharist was separate. The agape survived at points as a "charity supper." From time to time, biblically inclined pietist groups have restored the "love feast," and in some ecumenical circles in the 1960s it was discussed as a possibility even for a World Council of Churches' Assembly (see New Directions in Faith and Order: Bristol 1967, Faith and Order Paper No. 50 [Geneva: WCC, 1968], pp. 64–66).

With the bread and wine in the Eucharist separated from a meal-setting and increasingly paralleled with each other, as we suggested was already happening in the New Testament period, attention was given more and more to "the elements." Prayers of thanksgiving were addressed to God; the Lord or the Spirit was invoked—Mar anatha, "Our Lord, come"; and without much speculation as to how, the crucified and risen Lord was regarded as present. This presence was sometimes talked of in seemingly figurative terms, with words like "antitype," "likeness," the bread as "figure of the body," "representing" the body (Tertullian). Sometimes the imagery was more realistic, as with Irenaeus *(Against Heresies,* V.2.3): the bread "receives the Word *(logos)* of God and it becomes the eucharist, the body of Christ, from which the substance of our flesh grows and is formed." A blessing of the elements led to views of their change, though this was not yet spelled out in ontological categories: "we invoke the Holy Spirit to constitute this offering, both the bread body of Christ and the cup the blood of Christ" (Irenaeus, frag. 36, Harvey ed. 2, p. 500). To "give thanks" *(eucharistein)* was more and more coming to mean "consecrate" and was eventually to mean "offer sacrifice" (Kretschmar, *TRE,* Vol. 1, pp. 61f., 69–73). The link was "saying a prayer of thanks" over "offerings" (Greek *anaphora,* Latin *oblationes,* both then technical terms of "offertory"), so that elements were "consecrated."

Along with this development went a growing stress on sacrifice. The New Testament had spoken of a "sacrifice of praise," meaning human prayer and confession, using Old Testament language metaphorically (Heb. 13:15). Such language was given a more literal meaning because of what was happening with the understanding of ministry.

By the end of the second century, "priest" (Greek *hiereus,* Latin *sacerdos)* was being applied not only to Christ (cf. Hebrews, the "Great High Priest") and to the whole people of God (1 Peter 2:9 and 5 = Exod. 19:6) but also to "overseers" and "elders" or, as they increasingly came to be regarded in a threefold (ordained) ministry, the bishops and presbyters who stood over the deacons. What priests did in Israel and in contemporary pagan temples had to find parallel in the church: the Eucharist became the sacrifice they offered. The "understanding of priesthood that evolves in this [ante-Nicene] period is inevitably linked with the evolution of thought about the nature of the Eucharistic action," and "by the time of Nicaea, whatever reluctance there had been in Christian circles to utilize the term *'hiereus/sacerdos'* has disappeared" (Cooke, *Ministry,* pp. 541, 554, cf. 543–47). We need not trace out here resulting cleavage between clergy and laity, or hierarchical understandings of ministry, or the view that this pattern was *jure divino,* by God's plan and will; Cooke supplies details and bibliography.

As ministry thus developed, the Eucharist became more and more that sacrifice offered by the presiding clergyman (male), functioning in Christ's stead, imitating what Christ did. Paul's words, "Do this in memory of me" could "to pagan ears mean 'this do ye sacrifice' " (Conybeare, *Encyclopaedia Britannica,* p. 872). The human priest takes Christ's place and imitates his action by offering in church a true and full sacrifice to God the Father (Cyprian, *Ep.* 63). The liturgical "president [*proestos*] of the brethren," whatever was meant in Justin's *First Apology* 65, is now clearly "clergy." The cult mystery *(mystērion,* no longer as in the New Testament sense with a Semitic background of meaning; in Latin, *sacramentum)* takes on an increasing note of awe, even remoteness. A later contributing influence (sixth century on) was the growth of "private masses," encouraging the notion that the priest "does mass" and people if present simply "attend" (Cooke, *Ministry,* p. 560).

As previously mentioned in chapter 1, G. Kretschmar in *TRE* (Vol. 1, pp. 78–79) has emphasized Christ-*anamnesis* in this period of development: "remembrance" becomes an imitation of the drama of salvation, with the ordained priest (Christ's image) presenting bread and wine (Christ laid on the table to be sacrificed): through the Holy Spirit they become Christ's body and blood—"the awesome sacrifice, the ineffable mysteries" (citing the Antiochene theologians Theodore of Mopsuestia, *Catechetical Homilies* 15–16, and, for the phrase directly quoted above, John Chrysostom, *Homilies on Acts* 21, 4). The other developments Kretschmar selects are "the presence of the Incarnation in the eucharist" and the truth-reality of symbols, so that eternal, heavenly realities are what confront one in the Eucharist (these themes especially in Eastern theologians); and in Ambrose and Augustine, in the West, he emphasizes the power of the Word of God and the role of faith. Hearing the word, rather than seeing the mystery, was to be a theme in Western Christianity.

We need not dwell on examples of such points, either typical, vivid, or bizarre (Conybeare, *Encyclopaedia Britannica,* p. 872, cites the Greek custom of the priest "stabbing with 'the holy spear' in its right side the human figure planned out of the bread, by way of rehearsing in pantomime the narrative of John xix. 34"). But we need to remind ourselves that the diversity in Christian thought and practice was probably much greater than some handbooks about "the catholic tradition" suggest, particularly if one looks at Syrian evidence and what we increasingly know of "gnostic" Christianity. Such influences on sacramental developments have yet to be fully assessed.

If the development of ministry as priesthood is a post–New Testament factor affecting understanding of the Lord's Supper, so also is what took place with regard to baptism. As is well known, the baptism of infants was a later development. Adult baptism of converts was the initial New Testament norm. Possibly, children of Christian households might have received baptism in the first century; for by the second or third generation the question of baptizing newborn infants could have led to such a practice. But in the debate between Joachim Jeremias (seeking to prove baptism of children in the New Testament) and Kurt Aland (arguing that baptism of babies was not at that time likely), the historian's verdict seems to go to Aland: infant baptism is not clearly verifiable as the practice till the end of the second century. (Cf. Jeremias, *Infant Baptism in the First Four Centuries* [Philadelphia: Westminster Press, 1960]; Aland, *Did the Early Church Baptize Infants?* [Philadelphia: Westminster Press, 1963]; Jeremias, *The Origins of Infant Baptism: A further study in reply to Kurt Aland* [Studies in Historical Theology, 1; Naperville, Ill.: Alec R. Allenson, 1963].)

Once infant baptism became common a new question arose involving baptism, "chrismation" or "confirmation," and Eucharist. New Testament texts speak of "making disciples," "baptizing," and "teaching them," as in the Great Commission at Matt. 28:19–20. Passages in Acts refer to the Jerusalem apostles "laying hands" upon those baptized so that they might receive the Spirit and the gifts or signs of the Spirit; this gift of the Spirit (usually by laying on of hands) might come *after* baptism (Acts 8:16–17; 19:5–6) or *before* it (10:44–48), or during baptism. In addition, there are references to "chrismation," that is, receiving the *chrisma* or "anointing" from God, as in the case of Jesus (Acts 4:27; 10:38; Luke 4:18—a reference to his baptism) and of all Christians (2 Cor. 1:21–22, God has "established" [=confirmed] and "commissioned [=anointed] us . . . and given us his Spirit"). All these passages and terms were to play a part in centuries of debate and development, and we go beyond the early centuries in outlining the options.

How could infant baptism, the element of teaching (catechetical instruction), anointing (with the Spirit) (by laying on of hands), and the Lord's Supper be put together for the individual? One could, of course, combine baptism, chrismatism, and admission to the Eucharist in one single, sacramental occasion, a "Super Sunday" or Easter Eve. This worked well enough with adult converts, and catechetical instruction could be beforehand or afterward or both. With infant baptism, the instruction would have to come later. But at what point, then, should an individual participate in Communion?

1. One model—found in the Eastern Orthodox churches to this day and developed from early, though not earliest, centuries and reflected in the West until the Middle Ages—involved giving a child baptism, chrismatism, and Eucharist at one and the same service. Variations (besides the question of bread only for infants, no wine, or similar changes for the sake of the baby) included: (a) such communion only at the initial service, the child begins to receive the Eucharist regularly at a later age; (b) periodic eucharistic reception by the child, though parents and child would not necessarily commune at every service they attend.

2. Another model, developed especially in the West, stressed infant baptism, a later sacrament or rite of "confirmation" (after instruction, usually, with prayer for the renewal of the gifts of the Spirit given in baptism), and then Holy Communion. Variations included: (a) Holy Communion could first be administered at the same service as confirmation or at least the very next Sunday; (b) first Communion could be administered at an earlier age, say six or seven, with confirmation at a later time. We need not discuss here the history of confirmation, nor the disputed use of Acts texts on the issue. It probably remains true that the first model stresses "mystery" more, and the second instruction and understanding.

3. There is a third possibility, classically developed by Baptist groups in the Reformation period: revert to the New Testament practice of adult baptism upon profession of faith. Believing parents could, of course, have a child "dedicated" to the Lord, but only upon personal commitment is that child baptized, receiving the gifts of the Spirit. In this system the rite or ordinance of the Lord's Supper may not play the same role as in the other models.

We cite this problem area to indicate how, in the interrelatedness of baptism and Eucharist, the connections with Christian initiation and ongoing Christian life pose various possibilities for the practice of the Lord's Supper. The matter of the Communion of babies and children is put before the churches today by *BEM*. The issue and attempts at solution began in the early centuries. (On "chrismation"—I have deliberately used the Eastern Orthodox term—cf. Cyrille Argenti's essay in Faith and Order Paper No. 116, *Ecumenical Perspective on Baptism, Eucharist, and Ministry* [Geneva: WCC, 1984], pp. 46–67.)

A fuller history of the Eucharist ought to pay attention at some point to subsequent developments in the East, an area all too often overlooked in Western theology. For although the East claims "continuance and unanimity of its teaching that the consecrated elements are the body and blood of Christ, that the consecration is effected by the work of the Holy Ghost elicited by the invocation of Him in the Liturgy, and that the Eucharist is a sacrificial presentation of Christ to God," there is development, for example, in the distinction that "before the consecration the elements are the *image* of the body of Christ, and that, on becoming His *actual body* at the consecration, they cease to be the image" (Darwell Stone, *A History of the Doctrine of the Holy Eucharist* [London: Longman, Green, 1909], Vol. 1, p. 192, cf. pp. 148–50, italics added). This last statement about "image" reflects the controversy in the East in the eighth century over icons. The position adopted led to veneration of the sacrament *before* consecration as "antitypes" of the body and blood which they become upon the descent of the Spirit at consecration.

Thus the East developed in one way, the West in another. Curiously, two Eastern emphases that will crop up in modern discussion both deal with the Holy Spirit: that there *must* be an invocation of the Spirit in the Eucharist, but the Spirit, according to the Creed, proceeds from the Father, *not* the Son. This latter issue, of the *Filioque* or "double procession of the Holy Ghost," contributed to the split between East and West, along with political and other factors. In 1054 the papal legates delivered a sentence of excommunication upon the Orthodox patriarch in Constantinople, a move to which he responded with similar denunciation of the pope. The problems were not solved by the Council of Florence (1438–45), by which time the use of unleavened bread in the West versus leavened bread in the East had also become an issue. These questions continue into modern discussions.

Such discussions today have also involved contacts with the ancient Oriental Orthodox churches that never accepted the Definition at Chalcedon (451) of Christ as "One Person in Two Natures," which are united "unconfusedly, unchangeably, indivisibly, inseparably." This "first major split in Christendom," as it had been called (cf. Vatican II's Decree on Ecumenism, #13), concerned Christology, but led to separation in eucharistic fellowship. Present Eastern Orthodox–Oriental Orthodox discussions on such matters began in 1964 as part of ecumenical dialogue (see Nils Ehrenström and Günther Gassmann, *Confessions in Dialogue: A Survey of Bilateral Conversations Among World Confessional Families,*

1959–1974, Faith and Order Paper No. 74 [Geneva: WCC, 1975], pp. 46–47).

THE MIDDLE AGES, REFORMATION, AND ROMAN CATHOLIC RESPONSE

It may seem strange to group the Protestant Reformation with the medieval church, rather than as a new start, as is often done in the history of doctrine, but recent work on Luther in particular has indicated how much his heritage lay in medieval predecessors and schools of theology. This suggests the Schoolmen, the Reformers, and the Counter-Reformation are to be looked at in a certain continuity of Western church faith and life. It does not necessarily mean, however, that the Reformation impulses (or the Roman Catholic reply or even medieval Scholasticism) were simply a storm in a Western teacup, for the appeal in all three cases was back to councils of an undivided church, early fathers in the East and West, and especially the reformers to Scripture. In assessing Protestantism on the Eucharist, therefore, one needs to keep in mind not only its biblical concerns but also its basically Western heritage. The Schoolmen and Council of Trent would not want to be regarded as bereft of scriptural foundations in their heritage. That is why the biblical motifs emerge as so important, as an ecumenical meeting ground today.

In the Middle Ages there developed what clearly must be termed "doctrinal controversies" over how Christ is present in the Eucharist. In whatever way one may wish to assess the view that Ambrose had stressed a change of the bread and wine into "actual body and blood of Christ" but that Augustine had stressed "presence in the eucharist in spirit and in power," in the ensuing centuries "two conflicting tendencies" appeared, one tending to crude "realism," the other to vague "symbolism" (J. McCue, in *The Eucharist as Sacrifice,* Lutherans and Catholics in Dialogue III [New York: U.S.A. National Committee of the LWF and the Bishops' Committee for Ecumenical and Interreligious Affairs, 1967], pp. 89-90). Paschasius Radbertus (c. 785–c. 860), a Benedictine from Corbie, for example, wrote that when the priest says the Words of Institution nothing remains save body and blood under the outward form of bread and wine: present is the flesh that was born of Mary, suffered on the cross, and was raised, miraculously now multiplied at each consecration. But Ratramnus, another monk at the same monastery of Corbie at about the same time, took the position that the change is spiritual and figurative, not corporeal. A similar view was articulated in the eleventh century by Berengar of Tours (c. 999–1088), who denied material change in the elements or that Christ would come down to every altar from God's right hand in heaven prior to the last judgment; therefore the presence is that of a sacramental counterpart to Christ's body in heaven, the bread and wine sensible symbols of that Christ. Berengar's great opponent, Archbishop of Canterbury Lanfranc (c. 1005–89), insisted against such a "rationalist" view that the sacred species contain the invisible body of Christ, identical with that born of Mary but now hidden under signs of bread and wine. Such a position was to win out.

New conceptual tools for expressing how Christ is present in the Eucharist came with the use of Aristotelian philosophy and its distinction between "accidents" and "substance." Thomas Aquinas (c. 1225–74) especially applied these tools in the doctrine of transubstantiation. This view stood in its day in contrast to "consubstantiation" and "annihilation." The "new" philosophical view held that bread and wine in their substance are "transubstantiated" or converted into the body and blood of Christ, only the "accidents" of bread and wine remaining. In consubstantiation it was believed that the substances of both Christ's body and blood *and* of bread and wine coexist after consecration, while in annihilation it was believed that the elements of bread and wine are destroyed in the change. For Aquinas an objective validity is achieved *ex opere operato*, "by the performance of the act," automatically, or as he says in the *Summa Theologiae*, "by the work of Christ." Representation of the passion is "effected in the consecration itself, in that the body and blood as the inner sacrament *(res et sacramentum* [that is, both signified reality and sign]) are effective signs of the sacrificial act of Christ" *(TRE,* Vol. 1, p. 95). So the Eucharist is both sacrament and sacrifice.

The Fourth Lateran Council in 1215 decreed, "The body and blood of Jesus Christ are truly contained in the sacrament of the altar under the species of bread and wine, the bread and wine respectively being transubstantiated into the body and blood by divine power" (DS #802). As liturgical and calendrical expression of "the body of Christ" in the Eucharist, the feast of Corpus Christi was instituted (A.D. 1264; DS #846), with hymns written by Aquinas, to be celebrated on the Thursday after Trinity Sunday.

The medieval period also saw growing emphasis on the Mass as *propi-*

tiatory sacrifice (from the Latin of Rom. 3:25); Christ the victim is "immolated." Development of the doctrine of "concomitance"—that Christ's body and blood are each present in both the bread and the wine, so that to receive either element is to receive the whole Christ— undergirded the practice of withholding the cup from laity. Communion in only one kind became the practice.

Most of these doctrinal and practical developments were to be the object of Reformation attacks. Transubstantiation, the sacrifice of the Mass as propitiatory, Communion in one kind, as well as the growth of votive Masses, are issues that continued into modern ecumenical debate. They were objected to by Protestants, and on occasion, as with a Western doctrine like transubstantiation, by the Orthodox as well. Paradoxically, the medieval period was marked by a high esteem for the sacrament, but relatively little communion. Thirteenth-century practice has been estimated at once a year for laity and only three or four times a year in convents (T. G. Tappert, in Lehmann, *Meaning*, pp. 82–83; Iserloh, *TRE*, Vol. 1, pp. 98–99). The reform movement would challenge sacramental practices as well as doctrines, even if it did not begin with such things.

Luther's protests did not begin with the Eucharist, but by 1520 he was attacking transubstantiation, the withholding of the cup from the laity, propitiatory sacrifice, the notion of the Mass as a good work, and in all these things the use of ecclesiastical power to impose such views without or against scriptural teaching. Luther never did relate the Eucharist to his all-central doctrine of justification pervasively, but again and again he saw the Supper as "pure gospel," a gift to us from God. He never followed through on whatever liturgical instincts were his to revamp the Mass into the service of Holy Communion, where God serves us and brings us into intimate fellowship, for after the experiments with the *Formula missae et communionis* (1523) at Wittenberg and the *Deutsche Messe* (1526) his attention with regard to the Eucharist was more and more given to defending the presence of Christ in the Supper and to opposing the more radical views of other reformers. (On Luther's exegesis, cf. David C. Steinmetz, "Scripture and the Lord's Supper in Luther's Theology," *Interpretation* 37 [1983]: 253–65.)

Where then lies Luther's contribution? Perhaps in shaping an evangelical view of the sacrament that claimed consonance with the catholic heritage, while appealing above all to the New Testament foundations. As a conservative reformer, he retained much that had developed through the centuries, though appealing to the Words of Institution as a criterion. His approach was that of Augustine—Word and faith. Luther's struggles in a two-front battle with Rome on the right and other reformers on the left were informed by his view of the gift-character of this gospel-sacrament, his trust in Christ's promise to be present in the bread and wine, a refusal to try to explain how Christ was present, and an emphasis on the benefits of receiving the elements as earthly means through which God comes to human beings. Cooke *(Ministry,* pp. 594–96) has further sought to clarify Luther's eucharistic views by stressing how Luther, in the face of then-current cleavage between the clergy (as priests) and the laity, inclined to the pastoral role of "administering the sacrament" in contrast to the cultic role of "offering sacrifice." In addition, Luther sensed the priestly role of all the Christian baptized, while granting a special function to pastors to preach the gospel, with its always assumed linkage to public administration of the sacraments.

It must be remembered, however, that Luther is not all there is to Lutheranism. So both in the sixteenth-century debate and in modern ecumenical dialogue somewhat varying positions of his colleagues do exist and are to be noted. Moreover, confessional documents like the Augsburg Confession (1530) have an official standing among Lutherans that Luther's own voluminous writings do not.

What Melanchthon wrote in the *Confessio Augustana* for the Lutheran representatives at Augsburg was variously received by the Roman theologians in their response, the *Confutation.* Article 10 of the Augsburg Confession, "that the true body and blood of Christ are really present in the Supper of our Lord under the form of bread and wine," was affirmed. Those "matters in dispute" in 1530 which the Augsburg Confession mentioned in Articles 22 (Communion in both kinds) and 24 (use of the vernacular in the Mass, abolition of private Masses, and the position that "the holy sacrament was not instituted to make provision for a sacrifice for sin—for the sacrifice has already taken place—but to awaken faith and comfort our consciences") were condemned by the *Confutation's* writers as instances of disobedience contrary to "the custom of the Holy Church." Likewise rejected were the criticisms in Article 28 on how bishops institute such customs and obligatory ceremonies "contrary to the Gospel." Lutheran-Roman Catholic dialogue in the 1960's had to reckon precisely with such views, drawing both on the Confessions and Luther, in addition to other voices of the day.

An example of the need and difficulty to interpret a phrase in its historical situation is the oft-cited opening sentence of Article 24 in the *Confessio Augustana:* "We are unjustly accused of having abolished the Mass."
Obviously that does not mean Lutheran retention of what they termed its
abuses. Nor does it mean any and all types of Masses, as the rest of the
article makes clear. (Masses said for "special intention" were discontin-
ued "in our churches.") Especially stressed in Article 24 is not mere
celebration but reception. Nor need Mass be "held on every day that the
people assembled," for (in the passage being discussed from the sixth-
century monk Cassiodorus) "services were held without Mass" (that is,
without "remembrance of the sacrifice").

But what does this passage from Article 24 tell us about the question of
whether one should have Eucharist every Sunday as the normative service? It is the historian's job to ask whether the Augsburg Confession was
trying here to describe a fact in 1530, namely, that most "Lutheran"
parishes had the Lord's Supper at each Sunday service or at least a service; or was the Confession trying apologetically to impress the Roman
representatives with Lutheran catholicity; or were the authors explaining
in what ways and when they retain the sacrament? There is a further
question of the Augsburg Confession's place as authority in a Lutheran
"hierarchy of authorities" in relation to its place as one document in a
historical process of evolution of belief and practice.

We cite this example because of the assertions that will appear in *BEM*
and the Lutheran–Roman Catholic and Lutheran-Anglican dialogues
about the "oughtness" of the Eucharist as service every Sunday. (Cf. the
Faith and Order statement "Eucharist," ##30–31, discussed below ["celebrated frequently," "at least every Sunday," "frequently (received)"];
and the more nuanced statements in *Anglican-Lutheran International
Conversations* [1973, #94], "in both Churches, the Holy Communion is
coming back into the centre of the picture as the principal service of each
Sunday," and *The Eucharist* of the Lutheran/Roman Catholic Joint Commission [Geneva: LWF, 1980, #76]. "Catholics are convinced that
Lutherans should seek . . . more frequent celebrations of Holy Communion.")

As an example of using a Luther quote not in the Lutheran Confessions,
the U.S. Lutheran–Roman Catholic dialogue at a crucial point in its treatment of *Eucharist as Sacrifice* (pp. 189–90, n. 6) invokes a much-
debated citation from a 1520 tract by Luther. The dialogue employs it to
support the point that "the Catholic affirmation that the Church 'offers

Christ' in the mass has . . . been increasingly explained in terms that answer Lutheran fears that this detracts from the full sufficiency of Christ's sacrifice"; hence we can say, through the "union between Christ and Christians, the eucharistic assembly 'offers Christ' by consenting in the power of the Holy Spirit to be offered by him to the Father." Then the Luther quote: "not that we offer Christ as a sacrifice, but that Christ offers us"; through faith we—and Luther means "all Christian men . . . all women"—"we offer ourselves . . . in Christ [and through Christ], and thereby we offer Christ [to God, that is, we move Christ and give him occasion to offer himself for us and us with himself]" ("A Treatise on the New Testament," *LW*, Vol. 35, pp. 98–101; bracketed material above is in Luther but is not quoted in dialogue statement; but cf. also *Eucharist as Sacrifice*, pp. 54-61, esp. 58 and 61). Here the historian must elucidate Luther's meaning at that point in his career and to what extent it is consonant with his later, developed views, and those in dialogue must decide when rightly to cite Luther, when the Confessions, and when to give attention to actual parish praxis. What has been noted here by way of example from Luther and Confessions in the Lutheran tradition holds also for use of statements, for example, from John Chrysostom and the Ecumenical Councils for the Orthodox faith, or from Thomas Aquinas and the Councils of Trent, Vatican I and II for Roman Catholic teaching, or the Thirty-Nine Articles and Richard Hooker for the Anglican tradition.

For a contrast to Luther's views within the general Reformation movement we could turn to Andreas Karlstadt who, on Christmas Day 1521, is said to have celebrated "the first Protestant Communion service"—no vestments, no canon of the Mass, no elevation of the host, laity receiving both bread and wine. Or we could turn to Johannes Oecolampadius, the reformer in Basel, who took any presence in the Lord's Supper to be "pure spirit," not in the bread and wine, and attacked Luther as that "Saxon idol" whose followers drink blood and worship a "baked God." Luther wrote vigorously against each man's position. But a better example is Ulrich Zwingli (1481–1531), the Swiss reformer in Zurich. By 1524 he was preaching against the sacrifice of the Mass, and in 1525 Zurich did abolish the Mass. Zwingli's position stressed preaching, not cult. The division with Luther is most dramatically seen in their Marburg Colloquy of 1529 and Luther's contention that Zwingli was of "another spirit."

The Zwinglian position, perhaps best expressed in the statement *Ratio*

Fidei that Zwingli submitted to the 1530 Diet at Augsburg, maintained that since Christ has ascended into heaven his body cannot be present in ten thousand churches at each Mass. (To this Luther responded that, in Christ's "ubiquity," God's right hand is everywhere.) Further, Zwingli went on, the flesh of Christ—even if it were present—"profits nothing," only the Spirit matters (John 6:63). Celebration of the Lord's Supper is therefore basically a "Eucharist," that is, a supper where Christians offer thanks to God for all that has been done for us by Christ. It is a public expression by the community of its faith, but there is no eating ("masticating with our mouth or teeth") of Christ's body. "This *is* my body" means "This signifies. . . ." Christ is "present" as faith contemplates him at the Eucharist, which becomes almost an "aid to devotion." It has been argued that while Zwingli thus rejected transubstantiation of the elements or any change in them, he did teach that the congregation is changed, in effect that the citizens of Zurich were "transubstantiated" at their Eucharists. This is an overreading of the statements from Zwingli himself. But what needs to be emphasized is that, unlike the individualism suggested in the views of other Reformed theologians, Zwingli strongly emphasized the corporate, the community at worship in the Eucharist, and in this he especially gave the Holy Spirit a role. In Brilioth's words *(Eucharistic Faith and Practice, Evangelical and Catholic* [London: SPCK, 1930], p. 157), "the sense of Communion-fellowship recovers with Zwingli something of its primitive intensity."

The French reformer John Calvin (1509–64) had views somewhat between those of Luther and those of the Swiss Reformed like Zwingli. They are probably closer to Luther's, though the Formula of Concord (Solid Declaration VII: 8, 119–23) rejects what was taken as the Calvinist position, to wit, that one receives "only bread and wine" at the Holy Supper and is to "look away from the bread . . . to that place in heaven where Christ is present with his body and there to partake of him."

Calvin, a lawyer with great systematic powers of mind and an able exegete, was the reformer of Geneva, but his influence spread far beyond. In a sense "second generation" in the Reformation, he did not have to contend against the Mass as sacrifice or against transubstantiation so much as he was compelled to seek ways to close the gap in existing ideas and practices among Lutherans and Reformed. He allowed a sense of "mystery" to the sacrament (Brilioth, *Eucharistic Faith,* p. 167, calls it "the religious center of Calvin's view"). He brought in the note of thanksgiving—but preferably as praise expressed in the world as a *response* to the blessings from the Lord. He thus made room for "sacrifice" language, referring to Christ's death on Calvary and our oblation of "praising and exalting God." And while rejecting extremes of sacramental realism, he did allow a "real presence" (literature in Cooke, *Ministry,* p. 630, n. 68). Compare Calvin's letter to Bullinger in 1562, "Though the flesh of Christ is in heaven, we are nourished by it truly on earth, because Christ, by the unfathomable and ubiquitous power of his Spirit, so makes himself ours that he dwells in us without changing place" (cited in F. Wendel, *Calvin* [London: Fontana Books, 1965], p. 269). Note "the Spirit" as the means of presence.

If the Reformed (Presbyterian) positions on the Lord's Supper are marked by a certain diversity, those in Anglicanism are even harder to pin down. Cook *(Ministry,* p. 600) points to "pluralism of theological opinion and the oscillation of official policy within the Church of England," as well as to "political pragmatism," as factors in the origins of the Reformation there. Henry VIII was named "Defender of the Faith" by Pope Leo X in 1521 because he wrote a treatise against Luther on the seven sacraments. The king then defended (and continued to defend) transubstantiation. On the other hand, his archbishop of Canterbury, Thomas Cranmer, was Reformed in his outlook on the Lord's Supper, whether closer to Zwingli or Calvin continues to be debated (literature in Cooke, *Ministry,* p. 600, nn. 98–100). Article 28 of the Thirty-Nine Articles of Religion (1563) is Reformation thinking in its rejection of transubstantiation and emphasis on faith, but distinctly Reformed in asserting that the body of Christ is eaten in the Supper "only after a heavenly and spiritual manner." This Zwinglian or perhaps Calvinist position is borne out in the (in)famous statement printed at the end of the Holy Communion service in the *Book of Common Prayer.* (It appeared without Parliamentary authority in the 1552 Prayer Book and it was deleted in 1559 and restored in 1662 with a slight but important change noted below. The rule is referred to, in a nineteenth-century coinage, as "the Black Rubric," from the color of the ink employed before red began to be used for rubrics.) With regard to kneeling to receive the sacrament, it is declared:

> No adoration is intended, or ought to be done, either unto the Sacramental Bread and Wine, there bodily received, or unto any real and essential Presence of Christ's natural Flesh and Blood. For the Sacramental Bread and Wine remain still in their very natural substances, and therefore may not be adored (for that were idolatry . . .); and the natural Body and Blood of our Saviour Christ are in Heaven, and not here; it being against the truth of

Christ's natural Body to be at one time in more places than one. (Text, in *Encyclopaedia Britannica,* Vol. 9, p. 874; cf. Brilioth, *Eucharistic Faith,* p. 205.)

In 1662 the words "real and essential" were replaced with "corporeal," thus allowing some sense of "(real) presence."

If these Anglican views were thus of a Reformed type, when did a view more closely resembling Luther's sacramental realism or of traditionally Catholic doctrine develop? The U.S. Lutheran-Episcopal dialogue suggests, "It was Richard Hooker (1554?-1600) who gave Anglicanism its normative approach to eucharistic doctrine by teaching that the elements of bread and wine are the instruments of participation in the body and blood of Christ" *(The Report of the Lutheran-Episcopal Dialogue Second Series 1976-1980* [Cincinnati: Forward Movement Publications, 1981], p. 26). Hooker, while rejecting notions of the celebrant offering sacrifice, did put more emphasis on the sacrament as a source of grace and (against the Puritans) on the power of the ordained minister "over both the mystical and natural body of Christ" (Cooke, *Ministry,* pp. 600–601). On the other hand, he has been described as teaching that bread and wine remained unchanged as the communicant receives them along with the true body and blood of Christ ("receptionism"). Others, like Cooke (p. 601), would see the balanced Anglican position, as both Reformed and Catholic, arising in the work of the Caroline divines; Lancelot Andrewes (1555–1626), Jeremy Taylor (1613–67), William Laud (1573–1645), the archbishop of Canterbury who implemented many of these emphases which developed during the reigns of Charles I and II. Sacramental and sacrifice aspects came into further prominence. As Taylor wrote in 1660 in *The Worthy Communicant* 4.3, "The Lord's Supper is an appointed enunciation and declaration of Christ's death . . . a sacramental participation of it," with Christ continuing his priestly activity in heaven and through the ordained priest who is Christ's minister on earth. (Cf. Stone, *History of Doctrine,* Vol. 2, pp. 328–37.)

This ebb and flow of views among Anglicans of course makes modern dialogue difficult not only for the partners in the discussion but also for Anglicans themselves. (Cf. discussion of the Anglican and Episcopal dialogues in chapter 3 below.)

Against these varying positions on the Eucharist and related topics like the ministry held by Protestants of several sorts, the Roman Catholic Church responded, especially in the decrees of the Council of Trent (1545–63). At session XIII in 1551, statements were made on the Holy

Eucharist. At sessions XXI–XXIII in 1562–63, after all hopes of reconciliation were long past and the Counter-Reformation under way, the
Council spoke on eucharistic Communion, the sacrifice of the Mass, and
Orders, that is, priesthood. Each decree is accompanied by canons that
anathematize those who take differing positions. While these anathemas
were sometimes aimed at Lutheran, Zwinglian, Calvinist, Anglican,
Anabaptist, and other positions, one cannot always be sure which the
canon meant; opponents then—partners in dialogue today—can also
question whether the position condemned was actually the one they held
or hold today. So the historian must sort through the story of how each
statement at Trent developed and what it says or does not say (see the two
essays by Harry J. McSorley in Lutherans and Catholics in Dialogue IV,
Eucharist and Ministry [New York: U.S.A. National Committee of the
LWF and the Bishops' Committee for Ecumenical and Interreligious
Affairs, 1970], pp. 120–37, 283–300, for examples).

Trent reasserted transubstantiation: "by the consecration of the bread
and wine a conversion takes place of the whole substance of the bread into
the substance of the body of Christ our Lord . . ."; anyone who says
"there remains the substance of bread . . . together with the body . . . of
our Lord Jesus Christ . . . , let him be anathema" (session XIII, "Decree
on the Most Holy Eucharist," chap. 4 and canon 2; trans. of DS, by R. J.
Deferrari, *The Sources of Catholic Dogma* [St. Louis: Herder, 1957], pp.
267–68, 270; DS ##1642, 1652). Christ's body and blood are present not
only in use, that is, while people partake of the sacrament, but also afterward in the hosts or consecrated particles that remain after Communion
(canon 4, p. 270; DS #1654). Therefore the faithful offer "to this most
Holy Sacrament" the worship *(latria)* "due to the true God" (chap. 5;
DS #1643).

The 1562 pronouncement "on the Most Holy Sacrifice of the Mass"
linked the Christ who " 'once offered himself' in a bloody manner [Heb.
9:27]" on the altar of the cross with the same Victim now offering himself
by the ministry of priests, Christ now "immolated in an unbloody manner," in a propitiatory oblation (session XXII, chap. 2). The sacred canon
of the Mass (or consecratory prayer)—consisting both of "words of God"
and "traditions of the apostles" and "instructions of the holy pontiffs,"
all "free of all error"—is to be recited with loud voice at only a few
points. Most of it, including the *verba,* is spoken in low tone or silently;
but lights, incense, and vestments are to help raise the minds of the faithful to meditation on divine things. Masses are not to be in a vernacular

language. If there are no communicants and the priest is receiving alone, such Masses are approved (session XXII, chaps. 2, 4–6, 8; Deferrari translation, pp. 289–91; DS ##1743, 1745–47, 1749).

Another statement insisted that lay people and even priests not officiating receive bread only, not both species. Further, the holy synod taught "that little children without the use of reason are not bound by any necessity to the sacramental communion of the Eucharist" ("On Communion," chaps. 1, 3, 4; Deferrari translation, pp. 286f.; DS ##1726, 1729–30).

Finally, speaking in 1563 on the Sacrament of Orders, Trent intertwined priesthood and sacrifice so that ministry became primarily "the power of consecrating, of offering and administering" Christ's body and blood "and also of forgiving and retaining sins." Anathema be everyone who denies in the New Testament "a visible and external priesthood." (The argument is that, in saying "*Do* this in memory of me," Christ made the apostles priests.) ("On Orders," chapter 1 and canon 1, plus canon 2 of "The Most Holy Sacrifice of the Mass"; Deferrari translation, pp. 293–94, 292; DS ##1764, 1771, 1752.)

The bull "Iniunctum nobis" of Pius IV, in 1565, set forth the Roman Catholic position in credal terms:

> I profess that in the Mass there is offered to God a true, proper sacrifice of propitiation for the living and the dead, and that in . . . the Eucharist there is truly, really, and substantially present the body and blood together with the soul and divinity of our Lord Jesus Christ, and that there takes place a conversion of the whole substance of bread into the body, and of . . . wine into the blood; and this conversion the Catholic Church calls transubstantiation. I also acknowledge that under one species alone the whole and entire Christ and the true sacrament are taken. (DS #1866; Deferrari, *Sources,* p. 303)

By the 1560s the lines of division were thus basically set with which today's ecumenical movement has had to contend regarding the Lord's Supper.

INTERNAL DENOMINATIONAL DEVELOPMENTS FROM THE SEVENTEENTH TO TWENTIETH CENTURIES

It would not be accurate to claim there was no development in eucharistic theology and communion liturgies from the late 1500s till the ecumenical discussions in the twentieth century and especially since about 1965.

But most of these developments, save very recent ones, took shape within the framework of basic confessional positions already hammered out in previous periods. For example, the lines are set for Roman Catholics by Trent, for Lutherans by the *Book of Concord,* for the Reformed churches by various Confessions of the late sixteenth century.

The relative unimportance of these last three to four centuries is evidenced in the fact that the bilateral and multilateral statements on the Eucharist seldom pay much attention to this period. Dialogue statements rarely mention them, and published essays as from the U.S. Lutheran–Roman Catholic dialogue do not deal much with the Eucharist in this period.

A related fact to be observed is that, especially in Europe, certain trends affected all groups in these centuries. In broad terms, there was a period of "orthodoxy," then a rise of Pietism; the rationalist movement known as the Enlightenment left its influence in many areas; and beginning in the nineteenth century we have the rise of critical historical and theological scholarship, often revamping the views earlier generations had held about the past. One may wish to say these currents affected the Lutherans and Reformed (and Anglicans) more than other groups, or that the effects came later in Roman Catholic circles. But to one degree or another there were similar influences in many camps, such as Liberalism or Modernism in the late-nineteenth and early-twentieth centuries.

For Lutheran doctrine and praxis—typical also for other groups—a good account is provided by T. G. Tappert (Lehmann, *Meaning,* pp. 113–28). Lutheran Orthodoxy sharpened its teaching against both Rome and the Reformed. Oddly enough, use of Artistotelian terminology and speculation over when, for instance, the presence of Christ (the *unio sacramentalis)* began and when it ended brought such Lutheranism closer to Roman Catholic modes of expression. Pietism meant little change in doctrine but put a premium on the warmth of experience, sometimes within conventicles of like-minded persons within a larger congregation. Rationalism meant an emphasis on the sacrament as a memorial to truth and virtue in Christ's life and our lives. If most people had communed four times a year under Orthodoxy and Pietism, the average now declined, and what we term "secularism" was increasingly to become a factor (cf. *Anglican-Lutheran Dialogue: The Report of the Anglican-Lutheran European Regional Commission, Helsinki, August–September 1982* [London: SPCK, 1983], pp. 23–28, where these inroads today are discussed). But if liberalism had eroded eucharistic emphasis even more, the so-called Old Lutheranism movement stressed the Lord's Supper. For Wilhelm Loehe, "all of Lutheranism" was "embraced in the sacrament of the altar" (Tappert, in Lehmann, *Meaning,* p. 124). On the other hand, Neo-orthodoxy, whether that of Karl Barth or Emil Brunner, seems not to have left a special imprint on the understanding of the Lord's Supper.

For Anglicanism we have already noted the formative influence of the Caroline theologians. A further push toward the catholic, rather than the evangelical, side came from the Tractarian, or Oxford, movement in the nineteenth century.

The pietist movement in the Church of England led to the creation of a separate Methodist church. While the background of Wesleyan thought on the Lord's Supper is contained in the Thirty-Nine Articles and the *Book of Common Prayer,* it has been argued that a particular contribution from John Wesley was the theme of "covenant renewal," which could be combined with a service of Holy Communion (Cooke, *Ministry,* p. 626). Usually, only the hymns of John and Charles Wesley are given attention in regard to the Sacrament (as in Stone, *History of Doctrine,* Vol. 2, pp. 510–14).

Roman Catholic thought on the Eucharist was expressed abundantly during these centuries. In general, it rests within the Tridentine framework until Vatican II. But all sorts of almost speculative theories came into existence. For example, the Jesuit John de Lugo (1583–1660) argued for a "destruction" at the consecration of the elements: Christ's human nature is destroyed at this change into a lower state where the object is to be consumed as food. Similarly the Vatican I theologian Johann Cardinal Franzelin stated that immolation in the sacrifice consists in the humiliation of Christ's human nature when it is clothed in the species of bread and wine to be consumed by human beings.

In French Catholic spirituality the views of Pierre Cardinal de Bérulle (1575–1629) had great influence. He stressed Jesus' redeeming sacrifice, the self-immolation of Jesus that continues in the Eucharist, the priest's offering of Christ's sacrifice to God, and the ideal of sacrifice for all Christians (Cooke, *Ministry,* pp. 610–11). In considering many thinkers who dealt with Christ's oblation, we note the position of Maurice de la Taille (1872–1933). Against those who insisted on an immolation in the Mass, de la Taille claimed the one real immolation was on the cross, to

which Jesus' self-offering *(oblatio)* in the Upper Room pointed forward
and to which the Mass looks back. In the Mass the church offers God the
sacrifice that had been prepared on the cross. This was a change from
Trent's talk about "unbloody immolation" in the eucharistic sacrifice.
Another emphasis of de la Taille was on the meal-aspect of the Eucharist.

Finally in Roman Catholic thought and beyond, mention must be made
of the Benedictine Odo Casel, whose 1932 book on the Christian "cult-
mystery" brought to the fore the "mystery" dimension of the Eucharist
(trans., *The Mystery of Christian Worship* [Westminster, Md.: Newman
Press, 1962]). Often against the backdrop of history-of-religions
research, he stressed mystery as the *representatio* of the history of salvation through cult. Some hail this as the sort of breakthrough Darwell
Stone had a generation before hoped for with the "scientific study of
history" and of religions *(History of Doctrine,* Vol. 2, p. 649). Others
dispute Casel's derivation of the concept, attribution of it to the first century, and wholesale application of it in the Eucharist.

As interesting as such ideas may be, many of the persons in the centuries of eucharistic discussion since the Reformation and Trent are today
just names, figures of little influence in ecumenical discussion. However,
Vatican II cannot be underestimated for Roman Catholics as a further
stage and perhaps a new beginning in many areas of theology and church
life. Trent mattered and "post-Tridentine" developments had less significance; Vatican II overshadowed both. But in his encyclical *Mysterium
Fidei* (1965), Pope Paul VI reemphasized that Trent's words still stand by
calling for transubstantiation as the way of expounding the real
presence—words like "transignification" or "transfinalization" will not
do; and Christ's presence continues after Mass, so that adoration by
Christians is correct.

With regard to the Eucharist specifically, we mention finally two movements of great impact. One is the so-called liturgical movement. The fact
that scholars from many confessions met and worked together for some
years in liturgical research and developed great commonality of method
and outlook provided a vast reservoir of thinking on the Lord's Supper
that cut across denominational lines. Hence the agreement in a statement
like that on Eucharist in *BEM,* #27, about the outline of what a Communion service should be.

The matter is similar with critical biblical studies, a movement important for Protestants since the nineteenth century and for Roman Catholics

since the papal encyclical *Divino Afflante Spiritu* of 1943 and the "Bible study movement"; and for both, in the 1950s, "biblical theology." A most significant example has to do with the emphasis on eschatology. In 1901, Albert Schweitzer, following in the wake of Johannes Weiss, "recovered" eschatology as an ("the," Schweitzer said) important element in Jesus' thought, above all at the Last Supper (Mark 14:25). Indeed, Schweitzer's desire to establish what happened in the Upper Room led to his enormously influential "quest of the historical Jesus." (Cf. Schweitzer's *The Lord's Supper in Relationship to the Life of Jesus and the History of the Early Church*, Vol. 1: *The Problem of the Lord's Supper According to the Scholarly Research of the Nineteenth Century and the Historical Accounts*, trans. A. J. Mattill, Jr., with an introduction by J. Reumann [Macon, Ga.: Mercer University Press, 1982]). New Testament studies have kept this theme prominent ever since, and it has more recently emerged as a constitutive component of ecumenical statements on the Lord's Supper. (Cf. Wainwright, *Eucharist and Eschatology*; and *BEM*, Eucharist, ##22, 26.)

These trends in liturgics and biblical studies were to make their contributions as ecumenical discussion progressed.

FOR FURTHER READING AND REFERENCE

Betz, Johannes, J. A. Jungmann, and L. Scheffczyk. "Eucharist," in *Sacramentum Mundi: An Encyclopedia of Theology*. New York: Herder & Herder, 1968. Vol. 2, pp. 257–76. A recent standard Roman Catholic treatment.

Brilioth, Yngve. *Eucharistic Faith & Practice: Evangelical and Catholic*. London: SPCK, 1930. By a Swedish Lutheran professor and later archbishop.

Conybeare, F. C. "Eucharist." *The Encyclopaedia Britannica*, 11th ed., 1910–11. New York: Encyclopaedia Britannica. Vol. 9 (1910), pp. 868–76. This old edition is still worth consulting for its voluminous articles on religion, and this one by an Oxford fellow in New Testament and patristics is no exception.

Cooke, Bernard. *Ministry to Word and Sacraments: History and Theology*. Philadelphia: Fortress Press, 1976. Pp. 525–657. Ecumenically reflective, strong on Roman Catholic views, especially in light of Vatican II.

DS. *Enchiridion Symbolorum*. Edited by H. Denzinger and A. Schönmetzer. Freiburg: Herder, 34th ed., 1967. Standard collection of Roman Catholic source statements, cited by DS number, even though quoting the Deferrari translation, which is convenient but not always as accurate as might be wished.

Stone, Darwell. *A History of the Doctrine of the Holy Eucharist.* 2 vols. London: Longman, Green, 1909. Long a basic work.

Tappert, Theodore G. "Meaning and Practice in the Middle Ages," pp. 75–86; "Meaning and Practice in the Reformation," pp. 87–112; and "Meaning and Practice in Europe since the Reformation," pp. 113–34. In *Meaning and Practice of the Lord's Supper,* edited by Helmut T. Lehmann. Philadelphia: Muhlenberg Press, 1961.

TRE, Vol. 1:

Kretschmar, G. "Abendmahl III. Das Abendmahl in der Geschichte, der christlichen Kirche. III/1. Alte Kirche." Pp. 59–89.

Iserloh, Erwin. "2. Mittelalter." Pp. 89–106.

Staedtke, J., and E. Iserloh. "3. Reformationszeit." Pp. 106–31.

Peters, Albrecht. "4. Von 1577 bis zum Beginn des 20. Jh." Pp. 131–45.

Kuhn, Ulrich. "Das Abendmahlsgespäch in der ökumenischen Theologie der Gegenwart." Pp. 145–212.

New Catholic Encyclopedia. New York: McGraw-Hill, 1967.

Dewan, W. F. "Eucharist (as Sacrament)." Vol. 5, pp. 599–609.

Kilmartin, E. J. "Eucharist (as Sacrifice)." Vol. 5, pp. 609–15.

Kosnicki, T. A. "Eucharist (Worship and Custody)." Vol. 16 (*Supplement 1967–1974*), pp. 170–71. Summarizes 1967 *Instruction on Eucharistic Worship,* especially on reservation of the host.

Powers, J. "Eucharist (theology)." Vol. 16 (*Supplement 1967–1974*). Pp. 169–70. Reflective of Vatican II on real presence and transubstantiation.

3
Ecumenical Motifs:
Dialogue and Convergence in
Recent Decades

BECAUSE OF THE variety of emphases already found in the New Testament and because these have been exacerbated by centuries of varying practices and doctrinal judgments in a growing number of denominational traditions, the Lord's Supper has become in modern times the storm center of intra-Christian differences. Instead of serving as the sacrament of oneness for the one body of the church (1 Cor. 10:17), its celebration often became precisely the moment of greatest divisiveness. For Reformed and Lutheran Christians the chief issue between them was the doctrine of Lord's Supper as exemplified by the Marburg Colloquy between Zwingli and Luther in 1529. It was the same with Protestants and Roman Catholics. "The Mass in the papacy," declared Luther in the Smalcald Articles of 1537, is "the greatest and most horrible abomination because it runs into direct and violent conflict" with what the Reformers confessed about Christ and faith (SA, Part II, Article II).

In the face of such separated, armed denominational camps, the ecumenical movement took shape in the twentieth century to break old impasses and transcend inherited barriers, especially at the Lord's Table. In the last fifteen or twenty years the impact of ecumenism has been felt at all levels, ranging from church leaders with their necessary rules for discipline and often-heady theological statements to parishes and concerned everyday people at the grass roots. It is a major force for change—and hope—regarding the sacraments.

A Note on Terms and Degrees of
Eucharistic Sharing

The terminology for eucharistic sharing varies, as we might expect. Lutherans have traditionally spoken of "altar and pulpit fellowship" (in

German, simply *Abendmahlgemeinschaft)*. "Intercommunion" is a
word that is increasingly more widely used. But intercommunion allows
many degrees between "closed communion" (limited to a church's own
members) and "full communion" (open to others, with ministers fully
recognized). The Faith and Order Conference in 1952 at Lund, Sweden,
posited seven gradations; a decade later at its Montreal Conference the
Faith and Order Commission distinguished more between "admission"
to the Sacrament by communicants and "celebration" of the Sacrament
by mutually recognized clergy who officiate.

Most people think of intercommunion as their being allowed to partake
of Holy Communion in a church of another denomination. But intercommunion involves a further desideratum, namely, the acknowledgment
that the ministers of each church rightly carry on a sacramental ministry
and then the recognition of the other's clergy. Current statements, for
example, such as that of the ALC/LCA, suggest when and how their
members are to decide to accept hospitality offered at another church's
altar. Eventually the further step of public acknowledgment of the other
churches' ministers and finally some sort of interchange of clergypersons
must follow, if "full communion" is to be achieved. But in this area of the
(mutual) recognition of ministries the ordination of women has already
become a barrier to intercommunion for some.

The degrees of eucharistic fellowship therefore vary considerably at
this stage in the ecumenical scene. Indeed, the picture is somewhat
ironic.

1. Lutherans, for example, usually do not question the validity of ministers in other Lutheran churches, but they have not always declared "fellowship" at the altar with them and in some cases discourage it. Thus the
Lutheran Church—Missouri Synod has had no such fellowship officially
with the LCA. In 1977 and again in 1979 the LCMS declared its earlier
recognition of altar and pulpit fellowship with the ALC, voted in 1969, to
be now "fellowship *in protest,*" partly over the ordination of women by
the ALC, and at its 1981 convention voted that it was no longer in such
fellowship with the ALC.

2. Lutherans and Roman Catholics do not yet by official declaration
recognize each other's clergy to be "engaged in a valid Ministry of the
gospel" (though their theologians have recommended precisely that).
However, *de facto* in some parishes and on certain occasions members of
one church commune at the altar of the other, rules notwithstanding.

3. Protestant, Anglican, and Lutheran bodies vary, often geographically, in the degree to which they have some sort of open, of undeclared, communion among themselves, at least when members of another church present themselves to receive the elements. U.S. Episcopalians and Lutherans have had an official if interim arrangement since 1982.

4. The situation with the Orthodox churches seldom encourages eucharistic fellowship, for even the concept of "intercommunion" is alien to them. The negative attitude in canon law may, Orthodox theologians stress, be at times ameliorated by concerns for pastoral needs. But dialogue has very far to go in Orthodox relations.

The ecumenical spirit has for some decades attacked these problems in common concert and more recently bilaterally. The Faith and Order movement in particular has brought dozens of churches together to discuss the Sacrament of the Lord's Supper. Important work accomplished here has influenced all other discussions. But with the increasing number of churches and variety of viewpoints involved in recent years—including Pentecostal voices, the Third World, and above all Roman Catholic participation since the late 1960s—it became imperative to proceed in a more manageable way, by just two or three groups talking together at once. These "bilateral" dialogues have emerged as the vehicle for current progress. But after noting examples of Lutherans and Anglicans speaking in both directions with Reformation "opponents," we must ask, as many have, about the consistency of results in two-party discussions. Do these dialogues agree with each other?

FAITH AND ORDER: THE MANY AND THE ONE

The great nineteenth-century missionary wave and Christian experiences of both denominational cooperation and division on far-flung foreign fields gave impulse to the World Missionary Conference at Edinburgh in 1910, and that event in turn gave impetus to desire for a forum where together many Christians of divergent beliefs and practices could air their differences concerning theology, church, and ministry and seek oneness. The Faith and Order movement provided this forum by holding world conferences, commission meetings, and study programs. Along with the Life and Work movement, it helped create in 1948 the World Council of Churches, of which it is now a part. See Figure 1 for an outline of these developments and of the sequence of meetings which detail the genesis of what the multilateral discussions have had to say on the Eucharist and which in turn lead to the *Baptism, Eucharist and Ministry* statement at the 1982 Lima meeting of the Faith and Order Commission.

Already at the Lausanne Conference in 1927, Faith and Order included a section on the sacraments, and at Lund in 1952 one on "intercommunion." The meeting in Montreal 1963 found agreement in one of its sections on the Holy Communion as "a sacrament of the presence of the crucified and glorified Christ until he come, and a means whereby the sacrifice of the cross, which we proclaim, is operative within the Church," and stressed in another group the process of "growing together" in each locality where Christians are. Commission meetings during the next few years took up "the Eucharist, a Sacrament of Unity." The emerging report, combined with statements on baptism and the ordained ministry, was approved at the Commission meeting in Accra, Ghana, in 1974, for circulation among member churches. *One Baptism, One Eucharist and a Mutually Recognized Ministry: Three agreed statements* (Paper No. 73) was thus a major contribution of Faith and Order on matters sacramental and a step on the way to *BEM.*

This sort of ecumenical work has moved in the course of the years from the bookkeeping of "comparative symbolics"—where each tradition laid out on the table what it believes and practices, so that apples and apples (rather than apples and oranges) could be usefully compared—to more creative pooling of insights and beyond (though the suspicion lingers, from reading the minutes, that compromise often leads to statements which the group as a whole "will buy"). There have been attempts to get around old stalemates by moving in provocative new directions, "on the way to communion in the Eucharist," as a 1969 document put it.

Faith and Order was the workshop where many Protestants learned to speak of God's work in sacraments without ingrained fears of "magic" (notably at the North American Conference on Faith and Order, Oberlin, Ohio, in 1957) and to become acquainted with strange Greek terms like *anamnēsis* and *epiklēsis*. The first means "reminder" or "remembrance" or "memorial" and has been used for "the act of 'calling to mind' what is now present before God" *(Ecumenical Terminology* [Geneva: WCC, 1975], p. 193). The second, often spelled "epiclesis" as a loanword in English, means "invocation," specifically in the Eucharist the invocation of the Holy Spirit to act and manifest Christ in the Lord's

FIGURE 1

"Faith and Order" Within the World Ecumenical Context*

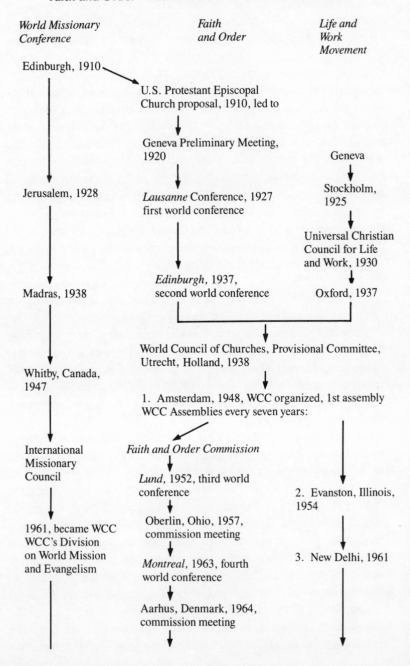

World Missionary Conference	Faith and Order	Life and Work Movement
Edinburgh, 1910		
	U.S. Protestant Episcopal Church proposal, 1910, led to	
	Geneva Preliminary Meeting, 1920	Geneva
Jerusalem, 1928	Lausanne Conference, 1927 first world conference	Stockholm, 1925
		Universal Christian Council for Life and Work, 1930
Madras, 1938	Edinburgh, 1937, second world conference	Oxford, 1937
	World Council of Churches, Provisional Committee, Utrecht, Holland, 1938	
Whitby, Canada, 1947	1. Amsterdam, 1948, WCC organized, 1st assembly WCC Assemblies every seven years:	
International Missionary Council	Faith and Order Commission	
	Lund, 1952, third world conference	2. Evanston, Illinois, 1954
1961, became WCC WCC's Division on World Mission and Evangelism	Oberlin, Ohio, 1957, commission meeting	
	Montreal, 1963, fourth world conference	3. New Delhi, 1961
	Aarhus, Denmark, 1964, commission meeting	

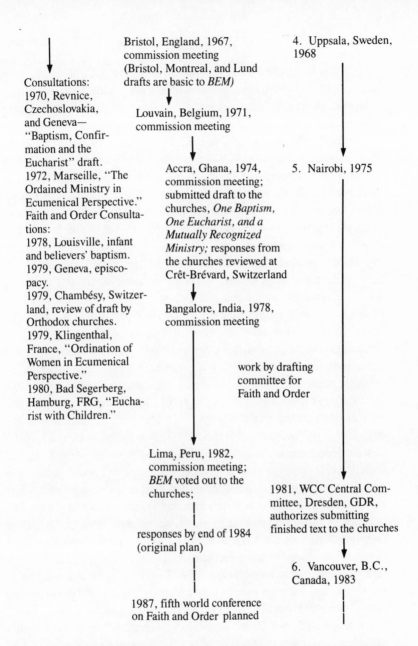

Consultations:
1970, Revnice, Czechoslovakia, and Geneva—"Baptism, Confirmation and the Eucharist" draft.
1972, Marseille, "The Ordained Ministry in Ecumenical Perspective."
Faith and Order Consultations:
1978, Louisville, infant and believers' baptism.
1979, Geneva, episcopacy.
1979, Chambésy, Switzerland, review of draft by Orthodox churches.
1979, Klingenthal, France, "Ordination of Women in Ecumenical Perspective."
1980, Bad Segerberg, Hamburg, FRG, "Eucharist with Children."

Bristol, England, 1967, commission meeting (Bristol, Montreal, and Lund drafts are basic to *BEM)*

Louvain, Belgium, 1971, commission meeting

Accra, Ghana, 1974, commission meeting; submitted draft to the churches, *One Baptism, One Eucharist, and a Mutually Recognized Ministry;* responses from the churches reviewed at Crêt-Brévard, Switzerland

Bangalore, India, 1978, commission meeting

work by drafting committee for Faith and Order

Lima, Peru, 1982, commission meeting; *BEM* voted out to the churches;

responses by end of 1984 (original plan)

1987, fifth world conference on Faith and Order planned

4. Uppsala, Sweden, 1968

5. Nairobi, 1975

1981, WCC Central Committee, Dresden, GDR, authorizes submitting finished text to the churches

6. Vancouver, B.C., Canada, 1983

*For background and historical details, see T. Tatlow, "The World Conference on Faith and Order," in *A History of the Ecumenical Movement 1517–1948*, ed. R. Rouse and S. C. Neill (Philadelphia: Westminster Press, 2d ed. 1967), pp. 405–41, and M. B. Handspicker, "Faith and Order 1948–68," in Vol. 2 of the same History, *The Ecumenical Advance, 1948–1968*, ed. H. E. Fey (1970), pp. 143–70. There is a list of church negotiations leading to full or limited intercommunion in Vol. 1, p. 499. All Faith and Order consultations are listed, with information on publications, in *Six Hundred Ecumenical Consultations 1948–1972*, ed. A. J. van der Bent (Geneva: WCC, 1983), pp. 17–34.

Supper. It was also for Faith and Order in 1937 that F. C. N. Hicks, then Anglican bishop of Lincoln, brought his earlier findings on "sacrifice" in biblical thought influentially into the ecumenical picture. (On Hicks's subsequent influence, cf. p. 105, below.)

The three agreed statements of Faith and Order at Accra in 1974 treat "the Eucharist"—alongside baptism (the "once performed and never repeated" sacrament)—as "constantly repeated and always including both word [preached Word] and sacrament" (#1; cf. #13), the sacrament where "we proclaim and celebrate a memorial of the saving acts of God. . . . Christ himself, with all He has accomplished for us and for all creation, is present in the eucharist" (#1). Among the rich variety of meanings in this "meal of bread and wine" with its "promise of the presence of the crucified and risen Christ" (##4–5) are thanksgiving to the Father, *anamnēsis* (representation and anticipation of Christ), invocation and gift of the Spirit, and communication *within* the body of Christ (##6–22). Some of the statement's strongest words are directed against our "estrangement, separation and fragmentation. . . . A mockery is made of the eucharist when the walls of separation destroyed by Christ on his cross are allowed to reappear in Church life: those between races, nationalities, tongues, and classes" (p. 22, #20). There is also a firm emphasis on "mission to the world" and upon Christians, "reconciled in the eucharist," as "servants of reconciliation" in the world (p. 23, #25). Since celebrations are also "always concerned with the whole Church," there is a catholicity to local celebrations, it is argued, which is obscured when "the right of baptized believers and their ministers to participate in and preside over eucharistic celebrations in one church is called into question by those who preside over and are members of other eucharistic congregations" (p. 26, #27). The Faith and Order statement also lists a dozen liturgical items to be included in a celebration (pp. 26–27, #28) and makes recommendations (pp. 27–28, ##34–35) even about how to treat bread and wine left over from a service (if "reserved," it is to be used for the sick and those absent, or respectfully consumed).

To this Faith and Order Agreed Statement over ninety member churches of the World Council, plus fifty other groups, sent replies as requested (in itself a new step toward achieving consensus). These responses were of great variety and ranged from one to sixty pages in length. Perhaps typical was the response of the Lutheran Church in America in 1977 with appreciation but with reference, in light of the

Lutheran Confessions and LCA convention statements, to Lutheran difficulties with the concept of "sacrifice" and with "eucharist," as *the* term for the Sacrament of the Altar, not to mention questions over use of the elements after Communion (Ninth Biennial Convention, 1978, *Bulletin of Reports*, pp. 361–63, 366–67; *Minutes*, pp. 754–62).

The Faith and Order Standing Commission (in its Paper No. 84, *Towards an Ecumenical Consensus*) then issued "A Response to the Churches." Here it asked the average person's question (p. 2) "Why can't Christians worship God together around the Common Table?" and pointed to consensus and "common language" emerging on many points. But at issue, admittedly, remain such questions as how in faith "the divine gift for which we give thanks" is expressed, how far the community using the sacrament may extend, and how to handle the "disposal of the bread which is not consumed in the communion."

At its Bangalore meeting in 1978 the Commission pledged itself to move on with *BEM*, seeking to revise the text and converge toward consensus, so as to present it at the next World Council Assembly in 1983. But it recognized a thicket of problems—"child communion," the relation between baptism and confirmation, "eucharistic presence," and "the ministry," including ordination of women. Indeed, by 1979, Anglican division on the latter issue, Orthodox intransigence, and Pope John Paul II's firm stand against women in ministry had again brought the question of women clergy to the fore. It became a "burning issue" no longer "on the periphery" (cf. Faith and Order Paper No. 105, *Ordination of Women in Ecumenical Perspective* [Geneva: WCC, 1980]). For there can be no sacramental fellowship, according to many traditions and churches, without agreement on the ministry. (See pp. 137ff., below, for the further work of Faith and Order.)

BILATERAL DIALOGUES: PROGRESS TWO BY TWO

Discussing differences with one denomination or confessional group at a time made increasing sense as the number of churches and therefore of viewpoints grew and grew in recent years. There are earlier examples of bilateral discussions in church history: for instance, Luther and Zwingli at Marburg in 1529 agreed to disagree about the Lord's Supper. Modern examples seem to begin with the 1959 session on "Justification" between representatives of the Evangelical Church in the Federal Republic of Germany (EKD) and the Russian Orthodox Moscow Patriarchate. By the late 1960s such bilaterals were becoming commonplace, both on the national and international levels. They proliferated even more in the 1970s.

Figure 2 lists with some, but not absolute, completeness the bilateral dialogues, consultations, and conversations dealing with the Lord's Supper/Eucharist. The list is chronological from 1964 on, with place for each meeting indicated since agreements are sometimes referred to by the place name where the statement was approved. Thus one can see when and where in the world the topic was under discussion. An attempt is also made in the figure to indicate the relative place of the dialogue partners in each discussion by noting with an asterisk in a series of columns for church group where each fits within a spectrum of Christian confessions. These range from those especially stressing the Eucharist within a hierarchical ministry (the Orthodox, Roman Catholics, and others) in the left-hand columns through the Reformation churches, to those in the Free Church tradition on the right in the series of columns. Fuller data on each conversation through 1974 are provided in Nils Ehrenström and Günther Gassmann, *Confessions in Dialogue: A Survey of Bilateral Conversations among World Confessional Families, 1959–1974*. Faith and Order Paper No. 74. (Geneva: WCC, 3d ed. 1975); hereafter cited as Ehrenström-Gassmann. The abbreviations (explained at the first occurrence of each) generally follow those employed there, with the pages cited for the discussion in the third edition of Ehrenström-Gassmann, where further bibliography is also supplied. For references since 1974, see Harding Meyer and Lukas Vischer, *Growth in Agreement: Reports and Agreed Statement of Ecumenical Conversations on a World Level*. Faith and Order Paper No. 108 (New York: Paulist Press, 1984); hereafter cited as Meyer-Vischer; and J. Puglisi, *A Workbook of Bibliographies of Interchurch Dialogues* (Rome: Centro pro Unione, 1978), supplemented by "A Continuing Bibliography for the Study of Interchurch Dialogues," in the *Centro Pro Unione bi-annual Bulletin*, No. 15, Spring 1979 (cited as "*Bulletin* 1979"); No. 17, *Bulletin* 1980; No. 19, *Bulletin* 1981; No. 21, *Bulletin* 1982; No. 23, *Bulletin* 1983; and No. 25, *Bulletin* 1984.

From such a chart it can be readily seen how bilaterals about the Eucharist multiplied, especially from 1966 on into the 1970s. One sees, as is to be expected, the impetus for and concentration on the topic in churches that stress this sacrament. There is a paucity of conversation on the

FIGURE 2
Bilateral Conversations on the Eucharist
(Old Catholics noted in Roman Catholic column)

	Orthodox	Roman Catholics	Anglicans	Lutherans	Reformed and Free Churches
1964					
L-R/usa (Lutheran-Reformed), New York, 27–29 Feb., "Christology, the Lord's Supper and its Observance in the Church" (pp. 93–96). Puglisi, *Workbook,* pp. 45, (46).				*	*
A-O/usa (Anglican-Orthodox), New York, 15–16 April, "The Eucharist" (pp. 57–60). Puglisi, *Workbook,* pp. 25, (29).	*		*		
L-R-U/eur (Lutheran-Reformed-Union churches in Europe), April 1964 through 1973, Leuenberg Agreement (pp. 98–101). Puglisi, *Workbook,* pp. 46, (47).				*	*
1965					
A-RC/usa (Episcopal-Roman Catholic) began; and continued into		*	*		
1966					
Kansas City, Mo., 2 Feb., "The Eucharist, Sign and Cause of Unity"; Providence, R.I., 10–12 Oct., "The Ministry of the Eucharist." (pp. 69–72). Puglisi, *Workbook,* pp. 33–34, (36).		*	*		
A-EKD (Church of England-Evangelical Church in Germany), Bethel, Federal Republic of Germany, March, "Word and Eucharist" (p. 53). Puglisi, *Workbook,* pp. 22, (27).			*	*	*
L-RC/usa (Lutheran-Roman Catholic), Washington, D.C., 23–25 Sept., "Eucharist as Sacrifice" (pp. 103–8). Puglisi, *Workbook,* pp. 48–(50).		*		*	
1967					
A-RC/usa, Milwaukee, Wisc., 24–26 May, "The Eucharist" (pp. 69–72).		*	*		
L-RC/usa, New York, 7–9 April, and St. Louis, Mo., 29 Sept.–1 Oct., *Eucharist as Sacrifice* (pp. 103–8).		*		*	
O-RC/usa (Orthodox-Roman Catholic), Worcester, Mass., 5 May, intercommunion; and	*	*			

	Orthodox	Roman Catholics	Anglicans	Lutherans	Reformed and Free Churches

1968

Maryknoll, N.Y., 7 Dec., the Eucharist, leading to an agreed statement, Worcester, Mass., 12 Dec. 1969 (pp. 117–20). Puglisi, *Workbook,* pp. 56, (56).
    Orthodox * Roman Catholics *

CC-RC/usa (Christian Church, Disciples of Christ–Roman Catholic), St. Louis, Mo., 29 April–1 May, "A Responsible Theology for Eucharistic Intercommunion in a Divided Church," *Midstream* 7 (1967–68): 90–91 (pp. 74–76).
    Roman Catholics * Lutherans *

M-RC/usa, (Methodist–Roman Catholic), London, 31 Aug.–4 Sept., "Eucharist," *Book of Proceedings of the Twelfth World Methodist Conference* (Nashville: Methodist Pub. House, 1972) (pp. 40–43). Puglisi, *Workbook,* pp. 36, (38).
    Roman Catholics * Lutherans *

L-RC/usa, 5 meetings through 1970, resulting in *Eucharist and Ministry* (completed at Bermuda meeting, Feb. 1970).
    Roman Catholics * Anglicans *

1969

A-O (Anglican–Orthodox), Jerusalem, 15–19 Sept., (pp. 19–22).
    Orthodox * Anglicans *

1970

L-O/f-r (Finnish Lutheran–Russian Orthodox churches), Turku, Finland, March 1970, "The Eucharist as Manifestation of the Unity of Believers" (pp. 86–88). Puglisi, *Workbook,* pp. 41, (43).
    Orthodox * Lutherans *

OC-RC/eur (Old Catholic–Roman Catholic), Netherlands, Switzerland, Germany, Austria, discussions recommending limited eucharistic communion took up "transubstantiation among other topics" (pp. 112–13).
    Roman Catholics * *

A-RC (Anglican–Roman Catholic), Windsor, England, 9–15 Jan., "Intercommunion and Ministry; Eucharist," and Venice, 21–28 Sept.
    Roman Catholics * Anglicans *

A-RC/eng (Anglican–Roman Catholic), London, 22 Oct., "The Eucharist"; continued 1971 on A-RC papers (pp. 62–64).
    Roman Catholics * Anglicans *

L-RC/phil (Lutheran-Roman Catholic, Philippines), 1970–72, "Progress Report . . . on the Holy Eucharist," reflecting L-RC/usa. Puglisi, *Workbook,* pp. 47, (48).
    Roman Catholics * Lutherans *

	Orthodox	Roman Catholics	Anglicans	Lutherans	Reformed and Free Churches
A-L/usa (Episcopal-Lutheran), Milwaukee, Wisc., 7–9 April, "The Relation of the Church's Worship and Sacramental Life to the Unity of the Church" and			*	*	
1971 New York, 10–12 Nov., "What Would Be Needed for Full *Communio in Sacris* between Our Two Churches?" (pp. 55–57).			*	*	
OC-O (Old Catholic–Eastern Orthodox), three meetings since 1967 conclude with declaration of agreement, also listing areas needing further study, such as Eucharist as propitiation and inter-communion.	*	*			
L-RC (Lutheran–Roman Catholic), Malta Report, 21–25 Feb., based on annual sessions since 1967 (pp. 36–40).		*		*	
A-RC/lam (Anglican–Roman Catholic, Latin America), Bogota, Columbia, 9–14 Feb., "Ministry and Eucharist" pp. 65–66. Puglisi, *Workbook,* pp. 30, (33).		*	*		
M-RC (Methodist–Roman Catholic), Denver Report, includes "V. Eucharist" (Rome: Secretariat for Promoting Christian Unity, Information Service, No. 21, 1973 III, 22–38; *Proceedings of the Twelfth World Methodist Conference.* Denver, 1971 [Nashville: Abingdon]). Stresses Charles Wesley's hymns, sacrifice as "re-enactment of Christ's triumphant sacrifice," and for Methodists "presence" as "not fundamentally different from" that in preaching; indeed, "for some Methodists" preaching "provides a more effective means of grace than the Eucharist." Meyer-Vischer, pp. 325–28. See also 1967.		*			*
A-RC, Windsor, 1–8 Sept., "The Eucharist—Joint Statement" (pp. 22–28). Meyer-Vischer, pp. 68-72. Puglisi, *Workbook,* pp. 4–11.		*	*		
L-O/f-r (Finnish Lutheran–Russian Orthodox), Zagorsk, USSR, 12–16 Dec., "The Eucharist, especially its Sacrificial Nature" (pp. 86–88). Puglisi, *Workbook,* pp. 41, (43).	*			*	

	Orthodox	Roman Catholics	Anglicans	Lutherans	Reformed and Free Churches
1972					
A-RC/eng, London, 10 March. "Agreed Statement on the Eucharist" (pp. 62–64). Puglisi, Workbook, pp. 28, (31).		*	*		
A-RC/usa, Cincinnati, Ohio, 12–15 June.		*	*		
A-RC/can (Anglican–Roman Catholic, Canada), 18 March, on Windsor Statement. Puglisi, Workbook, pp. 27, (30).		*	*		
A-L/aus (Anglican-Lutheran, Australia), 22 March, Puglisi, Workbook, p. 23.			*	*	
A-RC/usa, Cincinnati, Ohio, 12–15 June, "Eucharistic Presence" and Windsor Statement (pp. 69–72).		*	*		
A-RC/jap, Tokyo, Japan, 14 Oct., translation of Windsor Statement (pp. 64f.). Puglisi, Workbook, pp. 29, (32).		*	*		
A-L (Anglican-Lutheran), Pullach, nr. Munich, Federal Republic of Germany, 4–8 April, "Word and Sacrament" and "Pullach Report" (pp. 14–18). Meyer-Vischer, pp. 22–23.			*	*	
RC-PR/usa (Roman Catholic–Presbyterian Reformed), cf. Journal of Ecumenical Studies 9 (1972): 589–612, on ministry.		*			*
1973					
L-R-U/eur, Leuenberg Agreement, 12–16 March (see above, 1964) (pp. 98–101). Puglisi, Workbook, pp. 46, (47).				*	*
A-RC/jap, Tokyo, 19 May, discussion of the Windsor Statement. Puglisi, Workbook, pp. 29, (32).		*	*		
A-OC (Anglican–Old Catholic), Oxford, 25–29 June, "The Meaning of Full Communion" (pp. 18–19).		*	*		
L-R/usa (Lutheran–Reformed), Grand Rapids, Mich., 25–27 Oct., "The Role of the Eucharist in the Life of the Church" (pp. 96–98). Puglisi, Workbook, pp. 45, (46).				*	*
EKD-O (Evangelical Church in Germany–Russian Orthodox), Zagorsk, USSR, 26–29 Nov., "The Eucharist" pp. 78–84). Puglisi, Workbook, pp. 37, (39).	*			*	*

ECUMENICAL MOTIFS: DIALOGUE AND CONVERGENCE 91

	Orthodox	Roman Catholics	Anglicans	Lutherans	Reformed and Free Churches
1974					
A-RC/scot (Anglican–Roman Catholic, Scotland), publication of *The Ecclesial Nature of the Eucharist* (Glasgow: J. S. Burns). Puglisi, *Workbook*, pp. 32, (35).		*	*		
A-RC/usa, Vicksburg, Miss., 6–10 Jan., "The Church as a Eucharistic Community" (pp. 69–72).		*	*		
R-RC (Reformed–Roman Catholic), Woudschoten/ Zeist, the Netherlands, 18–23 Feb., the Eucharist (pp. 49–52).		*			*
L-O/f-r, 23–28 May, Järvenpää, Finland, "The Doctrine of the Eucharist and Priesthood" (pp. 86–88). Puglisi, *Workbook*, pp. 41, (43).	*			*	
1975					
EKD-0 (Evangelical Church in Germany–Ecumenical Patriarch of Constantinople), October, "Eucharist." Puglisi, *Workbook*, pp. 39, (41). *Bulletin* 1979, p. 20; 1980, p. 24.	*			*	*
1976					
EKD-O (Evangelical Church in Germany—Russian Orthodox), Arnoldshain, Federal Republic of Germany, 6–10 June, "The Sacrifice of Christ and the Sacrifice of Christians" (German *Das Opfer Christi und das Opfer der Christen*, Beihefte zur Ökumenischen Rundschau 34 [Frankfurt: Lembeck, 1979]).	*			*	*
A-O (Anglican-Orthodox), "Moscow Statement," 26 July–2 Aug., includes "The Church as the Eucharistic Community" and "The Invocation of the Holy Spirit in the Eucharist." Meyer-Vischer, pp. 45–46; bibliography in Puglisi, *Workbook*, pp. 2–(3).	*		*		
M-RC (Methodist–Roman Catholic), "Dublin Report," includes "VI. The Eucharist"; based on 1971 Denver Report, influenced by A-RC "Windsor Statement," as discussed by the English Roman Catholic/Methodist Commission, 1973–74. Some "differences of approach" emerge more fully than in 1971. Rome: Secretariat for Promoting Christian Unity, Information Service, No. 34, 1977/II, 11–20; *Proceedings of the Thirteenth World Methodist Conference*, Dublin 1976 (Nashville: Abingdon). Meyer-Vischer, pp. 351–56.		*			*

	Orthodox	Roman Catholics	Anglicans	Lutherans	Reformed and Free Churches
1977					
R-RC (Reformed–Roman Catholic), "The Presence of Christ in Church and World," includes "The Eucharist" (##67–92). Rome: Secretariat for Promoting Christian Unity, Information Service, No. 35, 1977/III–IV, 18–34. Meyer-Vischer, pp. 449–56; Puglisi, *Workbook,* pp. 21, (26).		*			*
B-R (Baptist-Reformed), includes brief reference in ##30–32 of the Report of the Theological Conversations sponsored by the World Alliance of Reformed Churches and the Baptist World Alliance, 1973–77 (Geneva: WARC; Washington: BWA, 1977). Meyer-Vischer, pp. 147–49.					* *
1978					
L-RC (Lutheran–Roman Catholic), *Das Herrenmahl* (Paderborn: Bonifacius-Druckerei; Frankfurt: Lembeck); Eng. trans., *The Eucharist* (Geneva: LWF, 1980). Meyer-Vischer, pp. 190–214; Puglisi, *Workbook,* pp. 13–14, (18–19); considerable literature cited in *Bulletin* 1979–83.		*		*	
1979					
A-RC (Anglican–Roman Catholic), Salisbury, England, 12–20 Jan., "Eucharistic Doctrine: Elucidation" (reprinted in ARCIC, *The Final Report* [London: SPCK, 1982], pp. 17–27). Meyer-Vischer, pp. 72–77; *Bulletin* 1980–1983.		*	*		
A-RC/scot (Anglican–Roman Catholic, Scotland) *Priesthood and the Eucharist: A Common Statement* (Glasgow: J. S. Burns). *Bulletin* 1982, p. 13.		*	*		
A-L/usa (Episcopal-Lutheran), Sewanee, Tenn., August, "The Eucharistic Presence," incorporated at final session in November 1980, in *The Report of the Lutheran-Episcopal Dialogue Second Series 1976–1980,* pp. 25–29. *Bulletin* 1980–83.			*	*	
1980					
A-L/erc (Anglican-Lutheran, European Regional Commission), Edinburgh, "Worship and Eucharistic Theology," included in its report, *Anglican-Lutheran Dialogue* (London: SPCK, 1982), pp. 11–14.			*	*	

	Orthodox	Roman Catholics	Anglicans	Lutherans	Reformed and Free Churches
EKD-O (Evangelical Church in Germany–Roumanian Orthodox Church), Jassy meeting, "The Sacraments of the Church of the Augsburg Confession and in the Orthodox Confessions of the 16-17 Centuries." *Bulletin* 1983, p. 17.	*			*	*
L-RC/aus (Lutheran–Roman Catholic, Australia), *Bulletin* 1981, p. 15.		*		*	
O-RC (Orthodox–Roman Catholic), Rhodes Conference. *Bulletin* 1981, p. 18.	*	*			

1981

	Orthodox	Roman Catholics	Anglicans	Lutherans	Reformed and Free Churches
L-R/f (Lutheran-Reformed, France), "The Supper of the Lord." *Bulletin* 1982, p. 17; 1984, p. 25.				*	*
M-RC (Methodist–Roman Catholic), "Eucharist, Ministry, Authority: Statements agreed by Roman Catholics and Methodists" (Abbots Langley: Catholic Information Services, 1981). *Bulletin* 1982, p. 25; 1983, p. 19.		*			*

1982

	Orthodox	Roman Catholics	Anglicans	Lutherans	Reformed and Free Churches
L-RC/nor (Lutheran–Roman Catholic, Norway). Resulted in "considerable agreement." *Bulletin* 1982, p. 24; 1983, p. 19.		*		*	
L-O-R/f (Lutheran and Reformed [Protestant]-Orthodox, France), Paris. *Bulletin* 1983, p. 17.	*			*	*
O-RC (Orthodox–Roman Catholic), Munich, 30 June–6 July, "The Church, the Eucharist, and the Trinity." *Origins* 12 (1982): 10, 157–60. *Bulletin* 1983, pp. 21–22; 1984, pp. 29–30.	*	*			

1983

	Orthodox	Roman Catholics	Anglicans	Lutherans	Reformed and Free Churches
O-RC/usa (Orthodox–Roman Catholic), New York, 23–25 May, discussion of 1982 Munich statement. *JES* 20 (1983): 745.	*	*			
L-R/usa (Lutheran-Reformed), Techny, Ill., 30 Sept.–2 Oct., third round completed with recommendation for "eucharistic fellowship." *An Invitation to Action: The Lutheran-Reformed Dialogue, Series III, 1981–1983* (Philadelphia: Fortress Press, 1984).				*	*

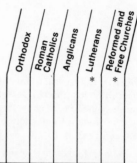

1984

L-M (Lutheran World Federation–World Methodist Council), Bossey, Switzerland, 3–8 March. The final report, after five years of dialogue, recommended that "our churches take steps to declare and establish full fellowship of word and sacrament," with "visible expression in full sacramental communion."

Lord's Supper among those in the Free Church tradition. That Baptists, Quakers, and even Methodists would take up the Lord's Supper among themselves as a prime issue calling for doctrinal agreement is unlikely. That they discuss it as part of a common agenda with Roman Catholics, for example, is to be expected. One may also note how certain agreed statements such as the Anglican–Roman Catholic (1971) "Windsor Statement" or the U.S. Lutheran–Roman Catholic statements of 1967 and 1971 on the Eucharist have had a ripple effect, being taken up in other dialogues worldwide, for instruction, testing, and local adaptation.

Since it is impossible here to survey all these conversations (and the Ehrenström-Gassmann and Meyer-Vischer volumes provide coverage), we shall turn to four examples that are of considerable depth and significance. Two involve Lutherans and sixteenth-century "opponents," the Reformed-Presbyterian denominational family and the Roman Catholic Church. Another takes up Anglican–Roman Catholic discussions. The final one, concerning Anglicans and Lutherans, provides us with the one case study where practical, if limited, results have occurred in a U.S. agreement in 1982 among the churches involved that may prove a model for other dialogues as well.

Lutheran-Reformed Agreements

Arnoldshain

As background, we must look at spadework done before the dialogues of the 1960s, particularly by New Testament exegetes, work which seemed at the time to lead to no direct results. Experiences during the "emergency fellowship" of the Hitler period led German churches—

Reformed, Lutheran, and Union—to band together in 1947 into a federation, the Evangelical Church in Germany (Evangelische Kirche in Deutschland or EKD). This EKD convened a series of conferences to discuss inherited differences over "the Lord's Supper problem." Some Lutherans, particularly Professor Peter Brunner, strongly stressed their confessional heritage in the face of such efforts, and the VELKD (United Evangelical Lutheran Church in Germany), in its own study, a volume entitled *Koinonia* (1957), insisted "the *mode* [italics added] of the self-impartation of the Lord in the Lord's Supper is essential," that is, as "body" and "blood," not just as "person" but as objective things *(Dinghaftigkeit*, so Ernst Sommerlath). But it soon became apparent that developments in New Testament studies had brought about a changed situation.

From 1951 to 1957 a commission including some of the best-known New Testament scholars of the day labored to produce a set of eight theses on "what we, as members of the One, Apostolic Church, hear as decisive content of the biblical witness about the Lord's Supper." Julius Schniewind led the group initially, with fire and openness, until his disappearance during the Russian occupation of East Germany in 1948. To Sommerlath he had insisted, "The gift is Christ in person" (John 1:14). Against the background of the Dead Sea Scrolls, Karl G. Kuhn of Heidelberg emphasized Mark 14:22 ("This is my body") as a *logion* (saying) of Jesus pointing to his death, interpreted by Paul as the institution of a cultic act ("Do this . . ."). Ernst Käsemann took Mark form-critically not as a glimpse into Maundy Thursday night during Jesus' lifetime but as testimony of the church, with "not the action, but the elements" as midpoint, real presence, and power. Eduard Schweizer's famous judgment was made in these discussions: that if asked to explain "the elements," a Jewish Christian would have answered as a Reformed pastor does now, a Hellenistic Christian as a Lutheran does!

The resulting *Arnoldshain Theses* (published in 1958 and named for an Evangelical Academy site near Frankfurt where work was done) stated, among other things:

1. "The Lord's Supper which we celebrate is based on the institution and command of Jesus Christ, who has given himself for us in death and who is our risen Lord. . . ."

2. "Present in the Holy Spirit through the Word," he acts in that which the church does, bestowing forgiveness of sins.

3. The Lord's Supper is an act of worship, the meal joined with proclamation of Jesus' saving death.

4. Our Lord Jesus Christ gives us, as his words promise to those who believe in his promise, the victory of his lordship, forgiveness, life, and blessedness.

5. Notions of "supernatural substance," "repetition" of the salvation event, and separation of "physical and spiritual eating" are inadequate.

6. Christ, himself "the beginning and crown of a new creation," incorporates us into his body, the "community of brethren" and "beginning of a new humanity."

7. "The Lord's Supper places us on the way of the cross of Christ," free in our tasks "to share all that we are and have with those in need."

8. "Faith receives what is promised to it and builds on this promise. . . ." Misuse calls down God's judgment. "All members of [the Lord's] church are invited to his meal, and the forgiveness of sins is promised to all who desire God's righteousness."

Signed by Günther Bornkamm, Jeremias, Käsemann, Schweizer, systematic theologians like Peter Brunner, Gollwitzer, Kreck, and Schlink, among others, the *Arnoldshain Theses* were meant to push the churches toward further discussion on a biblical basis. The VELKD and other groups were generally positive, but questions were raised about whether the theses were specific enough in relating the Lord's Supper to the Last Supper or about the unique presence of Christ in the elements.

Lutheran-Reformed Dialogue in North America

The initial bilateral experience in America for most of the churches involved was an attempt, begun in 1962, to heal a breach dating from at least 1529 between two mainline Reformation groups. It involved representatives of the North American Area of the World Alliance of Reformed Churches Holding the Presbyterian Order and those designated by the U.S.A. National Committee of the Lutheran World Federation. The first series of these dialogues (which included three Canadian Presbyterians) concluded in 1966 with a report to sponsoring organizations that

> As a result of our studies and discussions we see no insuperable obstacles to pulpit and altar fellowship and, therefore, we recommend to our parent bodies that they encourage their constituent churches to enter into discussions looking forward to intercommunion and the fuller recognition of one another's ministries. (*Marburg Revisited*, ed. Paul C. Empie and James I. McCord [Minneapolis: Augsburg Publishing House, 1966], p. 191)

Of course, other topics had been taken up, including Scripture, justification and sanctification, law and gospel, and ethics, even the meaning of subscription (by ministers and members) to church confessions. But the healing of old divisions was particularly apparent with regard to the Lord's Supper, examined in the light of Christology. Key arrangements in a summary statement of 1964 (printed in the final volume, *Marburg Revisited*, pp. 103–4, the title a nod to Luther and Zwingli's colloquium in 1529) included these:

1. As "windows are opening between Protestants and Roman Catholics" (an allusion to Pope John XXIII's Council), we find we share a common Reformation heritage. Our differing terms and concepts, in the past misrepresented by each other, are "often complementary rather than contradictory."

2. "The same gift is offered in the preached word and in the administered sacrament." The presence of Christ in the sacrament is "effected by the Holy Spirit through the word." It is "not effected by faith but acknowledged by faith," faith which acknowledges "the Lordship of Christ, his presence in the sacrament, and the fellowship of the brethren in the common Lord."

3. "Sacrifice" applies to the atoning, "perfect self-offering of the Son of God . . . whereby our self-offering to God in worship and in loving gift to the neighbor is made possible and acceptable."

4. Christology assures us that the total Christ "is present in the sacrament, but it does not explain how he is present."

Additional agreements in 1966 observed that in an age of population mobility "intercommunion . . . is not only permissible but demanded *wherever there is agreement in the gospel" (Marburg Revisited*, p. 183, italics added in light of the next statement concerning "a false witness" where the gospel is denied).

This "breakthrough" statement reflects a period of ecumenical optimism. We must remember that five Reformed and three Lutheran churches were involved which, on closer inspection, varied among themselves and therefore toward the spectrum of churches on the other side. When the second series of dialogues took place from 1972 through 1974, the mood had changed to one of greater ecumenical caution. In particular, new leadership in the Missouri Synod was directing that church away from fellowship not only with other Christians but even with fellow Lutherans.

The second series of meetings (1972–74) was set up specifically "to assess the consensus" of the 1960s and the "remaining differences in the theology and life of the participating churches" (p. 54 of *An Invitation to Action: Lutheran-Reformed Dialogue, Series III, 1981–1983,* ed. James E. Andrews and Joseph A. Burgess [Philadelphia: Fortress Press, 1984]). But only two of the nine or ten participants on each side had been in the first series, and the climate was now changed among Lutherans. No volume of essays and findings resulted from the second series, just a six-page report (which the Missouri Synod delegation refused to sign, issuing a Minority Report of its own). The "Lutheran-Reformed Dialogue II: Report and Recommendations" was subsequently printed in *An Invitation to Action* (pp. 54–60). Its summary makes clear that the Lord's Supper received particular attention, not only in terms of *Marburg Revisited* but also the Leuenberg Agreement (a Reformed-Lutheran effort in Europe; see pp. 99–100, below) and further discussion on requirements for fellowship and on the Eucharist in the life of the church. The final report disappointedly tells of the failure: "We attempted to express our unity in terms other than Leuenberg but were unsuccessful" (p. 56). However, it was agreed that, except for the Missouri Synod, there exists

a consensus of Lutheran and Reformed churches concerning the following *doctrinal* points: the Lord's Supper is (1) a sacrament; (2) a means of grace, in which (3) the true (proper) body and blood of Jesus Christ are present and are eaten and drunk. Disagreement remains between Lutheran and Reformed churches, and among Reformed churches, concerning the *mode* of Christ's presence. (p. 57)

Furthermore, while the Reformed churches practice "Communion open to all Christians" and recognize the ordinations of other churches, Lutherans refrain here "for doctrinal reasons" (Missouri Synod), or practice "selective fellowship" (ALC and LCA). Among the limited recommendations was one that individual church bodies (not whole church families) approach one another in dealing with altar fellowship.

Lutheran-Reformed talks in Canada (1972–74) and discussions on a worldwide level under the Lutheran World Federation (LWF) and the World Alliance of Reformed Churches (WARC) seem not to have touched especially on the Lord's Supper. Progress in the United States was to wait nine more years until a third series of meetings was completed (see pp. 100–102 below). Meanwhile, in the Old World, European churches made a striking advance.

Leuenberg

Although the *Arnoldshain Theses* and other meetings between Reformed and Lutheran theologians in Europe between 1955 and 1960 came to naught because of lack of institutional backing, a new state of endeavor was reached in a series of meetings between 1964 and 1967 at Bad Schauenburg in Switzerland, aided by the Faith and Order Commission, the LWF, and the WARC. The findings of these meetings launched in turn a series of sessions (1969–73) which pounded out at Leuenberg, a retreat center near Basel, an agreement for Reformation and pre-Reformation churches (like the Waldensians and Czech Brethren). The forty-nine paragraphs of the Leuenberg Agreement are not a new confession of faith (indeed, the "binding force" of old statements is left "intact") but a "consensus" about "central matters," which allowed the fifty-six churches signing it by 30 September 1974 to enter into full altar and pulpit fellowship.

Starting from the common Reformation heritage, but aware of changes over four hundred years (including "advances in biblical research" and "the ecumenical horizon"), the Leuenberg Agreement moves from the gospel (articulated, with the richness of modern scriptural interpretation, in terms of justification as the message of God's free grace) to preaching, baptism, and the Lord's Supper. After stating new agreements with respect to old areas of anathemas, the Leuenberg Agreement declares church fellowship for those accepting the consensus about the gospel and sacraments and then points to ways for realizing such fellowship. Just two paragraphs are devoted to the Lord's Supper as a way to spread the gospel of justification:

(15) In the Lord's Supper the risen Christ imparts himself in his body and blood, given up for all, through his word of promise with bread and wine. He thereby grants us forgiveness of sins, and sets us free for a new life of faith. He enables us to experience anew that we are members of his body. He strengthens us for service to all men.

(16) When we celebrate the Lord's Supper we proclaim the death of Christ through which God has reconciled the world with himself. We proclaim the presence of the risen Lord in our midst. Rejoicing that the Lord has come to us, we await his future coming in glory.

With these few lines—plus paragraphs 18–20 which assert that "faith receives the Lord's Supper for salvation, unfaith for judgment" and that communion with Christ cannot be separated from "the act of eating and drinking"—it became possible to overcome the animosities of four and one-half centuries. No one festively celebrated the four hundred fiftieth anniversary of the Marburg Colloquy in 1979.

U.S. Recommendations from Series III

A third series of dialogues involving churches in the United States took place between 1981 and 1983. It resulted in agreements and proposals far beyond the ecumenical fruits from similar conversations up to that date. Spurred on by Leuenberg and their own discussions and in light of Lutheran-Reformed consensus in series I and II, the theologians involved called on their churches "to encourage the practice of eucharistic fellowship with one another," to recognize each other as churches "in which the gospel is preached and taught," and also to recognize the "validity of one another's ministries." Their proposals thus went further than "interim sharing of the eucharist" to which U.S. Lutherans and Episcopalians had agreed in 1982 (see pp. 117ff., below), for this dialogue asserted a "validity" to the other group's ordained ministry that the Lutheran-Episcopal agreement had addressed more circumspectly.

The four U.S. Lutheran churches represented in series III differed from the bodies involved in 1972–74 because both the Lutheran Church—Missouri Synod and the group that had left Missouri to constitute itself as the Association of Evangelical Lutheran Churches (AELC) participated. The four Reformed bodies included the Presbyterian Church (U.S.A.), formed in 1983 by a merger of the United Presbyterian Church in the U.S.A. and the Presbyterian Church in the U.S. during the course of the dialogue; the Reformed Church in America; the small Cumberland Presbyterian Church; and the United Church of Christ. As in 1972, the Missouri Synod representatives wrote a Minority Report stating that their synod establishes fellowship "only after substantial agreement has been reached in all the doctrines of scripture" (*An Invitation to Action,* p. 8). The other Lutherans stated, "We believe that the burden of proof rests with those who would deny reconciliation in the supper with churches that preach and teach the gospel and administer the sacraments according to the ordinance of Christ" (news release, Lutheran Council in the U.S.A. 83–86, and LWF Information 39/83; cf. *An Invitation to Action,* p. 117, where it is phrased differently). While the majority Lutheran statement accompanying the common statement thus affirmed unity "in eucharist and pulpit hospitality," it added that "organic union" was not being proposed (pp. 108-9).

What the 1983 statement did propose included joint celebrations of the Lord's Supper between congregations of the two traditions, with the ordained pastors of each tradition invited to preach in the congregation of the other tradition and to preside at the communion, for "there are no substantive matters concerning the Lord's Supper which should divide us" (p. 17). This wording picks up *Marburg Revisited* and its phrases about "no insuperable obstacles to pulpit and altar fellowship" and "intercommunion and fuller recognition of one another's ministries." But it goes beyond the historic Lutheran practice of "selective fellowship" at pulpit and altar with other Lutherans only and opts for that degree of eucharistic sharing where the clergy of the two churches become interchangeably acceptable at each other's celebrations.

In achieving this new level of agreement the seventeen Reformed and Lutheran theologians involved drew upon not only previous series of dialogue between their two traditions in the United States and Europe but also upon other bilaterals and multilateral work. The phraseology in the recommendations about churches "in which the gospel is preached and taught" and especially that about the "validity" of one another's ministries (pp. 4, 5) derives from U.S. Lutheran–Roman Catholic recommendations (especially *Eucharist and Ministry,* Lutherans and Catholics in Dialogue IV, 1970). At other key points language is drawn in from the Faith and Order statement *Baptism, Eucharist and Ministry,* which had been published midway in the course of Lutheran-Reformed series III.

For all the significant agreement thus reached by the final session at Techny, near Chicago, in October 1983, it must be added that the results are stultified without appropriate action in the respective churches. And here the two groups vary. Most of the Reformed churches, as one participant put it, have "never felt it was necessary to negotiate such agreements formally. Lutherans in America have." Thus on the Lutheran side, something like the convention action would be needed that was taken jointly with Episcopalians in 1982 (see pp. 127ff., below). In 1984 the LCA convention voted to engage with the AELC, ALC, and "churches of the Reformed tradition in careful study of the Dialogue report," looking to recommendations to its 1986 convention. Similarly the other Lutheran bodies.

In the Reformed-Presbyterian family of churches, most people probably already assume the "validity" of the ministry of other Christian clergy, Lutherans included, though the term "validity" would probably not naturally come to mind, let alone call for convention action. The situation is somewhat different in the United Church of Christ, a merger of German Reformed and Evangelicals and of English Congregational-Christians. Here the tradition of local polity and a nonconfessional approach to theology led to both a great variety of outlooks about the Lord's Supper and a certain freedom about who ministers. The process of "reception" here, even where there is a series of theological agreements on paper, is less fixed than in a hierarchical church. On the other hand, the disposition is present, and in many local congregations has for some time often been put into practice, simply to go ahead sharing in each group's meal, recognizing each other's ministry.

Evaluation

The task force report by U.S. Lutherans in 1977, assessing the consistency of the several dialogues then existing, described the first series (1963–66) as "successful for the most part in carrying out" its mandate, though its summary and supplementary statements were deemed often too general. But this series was a pioneer undertaking. The second series (1972–74) failed, of course, to fulfill its mandate, but "its failure . . . was only partial," given the situation. It stated conclusions but did not give explanations (*Lutherans in Ecumenical Dialogue: An Interpretive Guide* [New York: Lutheran Council in the U.S.A., Division of Theological Studies, 1977], pp. 10–12). An LWF study, *Ecumenical Relations of the LWF: Report of the Working Group on Interrelations between the Various Bilateral Dialogues* (Geneva, 1977), dealt only with European conversations leading up to the Leuenberg Agreement and emphasized the treatment of justification by faith along with considerations of old divisions about the Lord's Supper. If history makes the decisive evaluations, then the results—that European churches have for several years lived within the framework of the Leuenberg Agreement and that U.S. Presbyterian, Reformed, and Lutheran churches have on the basis of dialogue called for official eucharistic and ministerial recognition—are significant.

In Europe, as a follow-up to Leuenberg, there have been a series of regional conferences on other theological topics (cf. for example, for the period 1976-81, *Konkordie und Kirchengemeinschaft reformatorischen*

Kirchen im Europa der Gegenwart, ed. A. Birmelé [Ökumenische Perspektiven 10; Frankfurt: O. Lembeck, J. Knecht, 1982]). The ecumenical institutes in Bern, Bensheim, and Strasbourg have explored even broader Protestant involvement than just that of Lutheran and Reformed churches together in ecumenical dialogues. In Holland, there has been consideration of the small Lutheran church there entering into a proposed merger of Reformed bodies.

Lutheran–Roman Catholic Proposals

Traditionally the barriers here were so great, above all regarding the Lord's Supper, that little change could have been predicted by anyone in the late 1950s. Yet even before the Second Vatican Council had begun, U.S. Lutherans, sparked by Paul C. Empie, had made overtures to begin discussions. Of course, there had previously been voices theologically fresh and hopeful within Catholicism (such as that of Karl Rahner). The impact of the biblical studies movement—set loose by a 1943 encyclical of Pope Pius XII, *Divino afflante Spiritu*—was increasingly becoming an influence in the late 1960s. But Vatican II, with its new questions and unaccustomed ways of thought and its broadening and counterbalancing of old dogmas, was the biggest factor making change possible. Indeed, no other church has had anything comparable to the council which John XXIII began.

The U.S. Lutheran–Roman Catholic dialogue began with single sessions in 1965–66 on "the Nicene Creed as dogma" and on baptism. Then came over a year's work to produce what may be the single most important bilateral volume for our subject, *Eucharist as Sacrifice* (1967). Based on the success achieved here, the dialogue then sought to move directly into "intercommunion" as a theme—only to discover that neither group really had a developed theology on the topic. It also came face to face with the stubbornly held position that for Catholics in particular no Eucharist could be "valid" unless performed by a clergyman properly ordained—that is, by a bishop in succession to other bishops and in proper communion with the bishop of Rome, the pope. As a reflection of its concern for ultimate eucharistic fellowship, the dialogue turned to the ministry which performs the Eucharist (1968–70) and then papal ministry in two phases—papal primacy (1971–73) and infallibility (1973–78). "Justification" was treated next in 1979–83, and discussion on Mary and the saints began in 1983.

The Eucharist as Sacrifice (1967)

The volume *The Eucharist as Sacrifice,* Lutherans and Catholics in Dialogue III, sought to overcome a basic problem on each side. For Catholics it was "the presence of Christ" in the Lord's Supper: did Lutherans really believe Christ is "in, with, and under" the elements of bread and wine? Is Christ "substantially" present? This problem, unexpected by the Lutheran theologians, was met by five agreements about Christ's presence: (1) He is present in *manifold* ways, in his people, in baptism, in the reading of Scripture, and in preaching. (2) He is present "wholly and entirely, in his body and blood, under the signs of bread and wine" in the Lord's Supper. (3) We *affirm* rather than *explain* this presence. (4) "By the power of the Spirit through the word," rather than by our own faith, his presence comes about. (5) This presence runs "throughout the eucharistic action" and does not occur merely "at the moment of reception."

On the other hand, Catholics had to deal with Lutheran objections, prominent since the Reformation, about terming the Eucharist a "sacrifice." For Lutherans, "sacrifice" had never been the only or even necessarily primary category for the Supper. By making Eucharist so central, they had in Lutheran eyes tended to obscure other forms of divine presence (hence agreement that [1] above was important). By stressing the role of the minister as "sacrificing priest," offering up "the victim to God" as propitiation, traditional Catholic theology and practice seemed to add—blasphemously, for Lutherans—something to the work of Christ at Calvary. On many of these points more recent Catholic thought helped correct misunderstandings and reassure Lutherans of a more gospel-oriented intent. After three meetings it was agreed that (1) the Christ who is present is the *Crucified* One and that (2), following Faith and Order phraseology, our offering of "praise, thanksgiving, and intercession" at the Eucharist is the church's sacrifice. Further agreements came with decreasing unanimity:

(1) agreed, Christ's sacrifice on the cross is "unrepeatable";
(2) fears over "offering Christ" in the Mass were answered by insisting that Christians united to Christ consent to be offered by him to the Father (K. Rahner: our yes to God is not what moves God to forgive; reconciliation exists only through the cross; in the Mass God takes hold of us to work effects by prayers and actions in the world);

(3) "propitiatory" can be used as a term to affirm that Christ's sacrifice on the cross is "efficacious" for forgiveness and life, but to apply it to the dead needs further discussion;

(4) there exist other divisive problems, like celebrating a Mass without a congregation, which need attention.

Here—but not only here, and far more prominently than in Reformed dialogue—"sacrifice" entered into Lutheran eucharistic vocabulary. The very title of the volume probably helped convince Catholic readers that Lutherans believed in a genuine "presence." For Lutherans the way to this language had been prepared by biblical studies like that of Bishop Hicks (see p. 84, above), with his insistence that the meaning of ritual sacrifice is to identify oneself with the offering upon the altar. Faith and Order had mediated the concepts.

Eucharist and Ministry (1970)

Eucharist and Ministry, Lutherans and Catholics in Dialogue IV, concentrates more on the latter than the former topic, but it does conclude (pp. 22, 32), in light of findings about the proposed validity of each other's ministries, that

Lutheran churches be urged to declare formally their judgment that . . . the body and blood of our Lord Jesus Christ are truly present in [Roman Catholic] celebrations of the sacrament of the altar,

and that

the Roman Catholic church recognize . . . the presence of the body and blood of Christ in the eucharistic celebrations of the Lutheran churches.

The *Malta Report* (1971) and *Das Herrenmahl* (1978)

With full awareness of this progress in the United States, the international Joint Lutheran/Roman Catholic Study Commission was meeting on "The Gospel and the Church" from 1967 to 1971. Its final document, covering the gospel and tradition, the world, ministry and church unity, was formulated at a session on the island of Malta. This report does not go into the Eucharist but does close with sections (68–74; cf. 64) on intercommunion. "Altar fellowship" is termed "an essential sign of church unity." It is known that "in some places members of our churches have met together at the Lord's table." "Unthinking . . . irresponsible actions are a hindrance to a final solution," but all the experimenting going on in

common celebrations ought to spur authorities on to responsible steps.
Baptism provides a starting point. Any Eucharist "suffers from imper-
fection" when all baptized believers present are not in principle invited to
the table. Lutherans felt that common celebrations could occasionally be
recommended, even pending full mutual recognition of ministries.

Since 1973 Lutheran–Roman Catholic working groups from this dialogue have tackled, among other topics, the Lord's Supper. A 1978
report, *Das Herrenmahl/The Eucharist,* lists agreements and unresolved
questions, with representative liturgical texts to illustrate contemporary
understandings and practices. On sacrifice it is helpful: Christ's once-
for-all sacrifice "can be neither continued, nor repeated, nor replaced,
nor complemented; but rather it can and should become effective ever
anew in the midst of the congregation." But it must be added, "There are
different interpretations among us regarding the nature and extent of this
effectiveness" (p. 20).

At least three things strike the reader in this statement. One is the extent
to which it rests upon and quotes other ecumenical statements—U.S.
Lutheran–Roman Catholic, Anglican-Lutheran, Anglican–Roman Catholic, Faith and Order (Accra Statement), and the report of the Group of
Les Dombes, from French-speaking theologians (see p. 134, below).
Some are even double quotes, U.S. Lutheran–Roman Catholic citing
Faith and Order at Montreal (p. 13). On occasion (pp. 7, 14) one-half to
two-thirds of a page consists of direct quotes. This can give an impression
of a pastiche. But then why reinvent the wheel?

It is, however, precisely this deliberate, catholic alertness to the broad
ecumenical advance in the totality of discussion that gives the book a
certain comprehensiveness. Its "Joint Witness" concerns not simply
what has been traditionally divisive or points of convergence but, in the
very outline (in boldface) and the subtopics, a rather comprehensive
spectrum of topics:

    I. **The Legacy** (Vermächtnis) of Christ According to the Scripture
        (the *verba* of Jesus);

    II. **Mystery of faith** (salvation, salvation history, and the triune God
        as mystery, "only accessible to us through the divine gift of
        faith"; thus a doxological setting is provided for the entire state-
        ment);

    III. **Through, With, and In Christ** (each preposition is taken up in
        this christocentric section, so emphatic on Christ Jesus as the

origin of, presence in, and gift of the eucharistic meal);

IV. **In the Unity of the Holy Spirit** (through whom Christ works, in the Eucharist, for "ecclesial community"); all this is to the

V. **Glorification of the Father** (to whom union with Christ through the power of the Spirit leads; hence Eucharist as proclamation of, thanksgiving and intercession and praise to, God, and self-giving by Christ and us);

VI. **For the Life of the World** (that is, for all, through prayer for humankind and the call to service, seeking "bread, justice, and peace");

VII. **With a View to the Future Glory** (at the Lord's coming; the glory of which one receives as "initial revelation" in the "fraternal meal," a here-and-now mediation of eternal life).

The statement concludes with reference to how "controverted positions" on presence, sacrifice, communion (reception), ministry, and fellowship (with the saints and possibilities with each other) are being overcome but may still need further attention. A "basic pattern" for the liturgical form of eucharistic celebration is presented, which draws heavily on the Faith and Order statement then being developed (Accra version, 1974) and is best discussed in connection with *BEM,* Eucharist, section 27 (see pp. 168–69, below).

Third, to the Lutheran/Roman Catholic Joint Commission statement are appended six supplementary statements, by individual dialogue members on "the degree to which historical research and ecclesial developments can now overcome" past divisive issues. Received by the Commission, these statements—on such matters as presence, word and proclamation, *sola fide* and *ex opere operato*—may be of less authority in the dialogue, but they are helpful examples of thinking for the future. Is, however, the Reformation condemnation that the bread not be "locked up in the tabernacle" or "carried about as a spectacle and for adoration" (Formula of Concord, Solid Declaration VII: 108; Tappert ed., p. 588, cf. 585)—"because the Lord's Supper and the presence of Christ are wholly oriented towards reception" (H. Meyer, in *The Eucharist,* p. 65)— met by noting that the Council of Trent "described the reservation of the host as 'custom' " (not a doctrine, therefore?) and that a Vatican II directive calls communion of the sick the "first and original purpose" of the usage (V. Pfnür, p. 65)?

Eucharistic Hospitality (1973)

Mention should also be made of the statement from the Institute for Ecumenical Research (LWF), Strasbourg, France, on *Eucharistic Hospitality*. It argues, in light of the many Lutheran-Catholic dialogue documents and convergences in doctrine and practice, that "occasional acts of intercommunion" are meaningful and "Lutheran churches should officially agree" to them, for example, in mixed marriages or at ecumenical events. Among factors it urges Lutherans to further stress in practice are eucharistic prayers, the note of joy, sacrifice, and the "community-creating character" of the Lord's Supper.

Evaluation

The Lutheran–Roman Catholic dialogues have been acclaimed widely for their progress and depth. With regard to the series in the United States, the Lutheran task force evaluating bilaterals in 1977 commended it for not only its detailed findings but also for the valuable methodological stimuli to other interconfessional dialogues. Criticisms were raised, including the observation that while "the article of justification may have guided the Lutheran participants in this dialogue implicitly, the explicit discussion" of the topic is needed (a step completed in 1983). But the dialogues were "commended for their style of operation, contribution to theological scholarship, and pursuit of ecumenical understanding" *(Lutherans in Ecumenical Dialogue*, pp. 16–18). The review and critique by a study committee of the Catholic Theological Society of America in 1979, as in 1972, stressed "the admirably high scholarly standards" in biblical, historical, and theological presentations *(Proceedings*, 1979, pp. 264–71). Long-established and well-supported by its participants and their churches, the Lutheran-Catholic efforts—nationally and internationally—have been perhaps the most productive theologically, if not as yet in practical results, of the bilaterals.

Anglican–Roman Catholic Reports

Few dialogues have begun with such prospects of auspicious conclusions. Both the Anglican and Roman communions are liturgical churches, have the threefold ministry of bishop, priest, and deacon, and stress the Eucharist or Holy Communion. They stand in the same Western, Latin tradition, yet in modern times each has also sought closer relations with the Orthodox churches of the East. Current bilateral discussion was initiated upon contacts at the highest level, between the pope and the archbishop of Canterbury. Periodic contact between these leaders has furthered Anglican–Roman Catholic relationships. The theological dialogue has been unusual in the care taken in preparing for it, and in a network-effect whereby national discussions have contributed to the international undertaking and vice versa.

Nonetheless, Anglican–Roman Catholic dialogue has not been without its difficulties. While the Church of England remained traditionally catholic in much of its life and faith, its Thirty-Nine Articles of Religion, as tenets of belief accepted in 1563, are for the most part Calvinistic in outlook. Article 28, "Of the Lord's Supper," rejects transubstantiation as "repugnant to the plain words of Scripture," but likewise rejects Zwinglian views; however, it has been interpreted either in terms of "real presence" or of "receptionism" (to use a nineteenth-century coinage), the view that bread and wine remain unchanged after consecration but that at reception the faithful receive Christ's body and blood with the bread and wine. The fact that for over the past hundred years confessional subscription by the clergy to these Articles has been merely an affirmation that the tenets are "agreeable" to the Word of God and more recently the stance that the Articles are of historical, rather than juridical, value leave Anglican doctrinal positions rather flexible. Thus positions have ranged from those of Evangelicals to "Broad Church" to Anglo-Catholics, from "low" to "high" not merely in liturgical practice but also in eucharistic understandings.

The apparent agreement on the structure of ministry was, moreover, set back in 1896 by the encyclical of Pope Leo XIII, *Apostolicae Curae,* which declared Anglican orders "absolutely null and utterly void." The pronouncement came in the face of efforts by Viscount Halifax, head of the English Church Union, a High Church group, to promote reunion with Rome. Later efforts, likewise promoted by Viscount Halifax through the "Malines Conversations" in Belgium (1921–25), involving Cardinal D. J. Mercier, the archbishop there, had the effect of keeping alive such desires for rapprochement but left certain scars because the secrecy of the first meeting suggested a clandestine operation.

The Second Vatican Council brought a change, however. Its Decree on Ecumenism (1964), in referring to the Reformation, singled out the Anglican Communion as occupying "a special place" "among those in which some Catholic traditions and institutions continue to exist" (section 13; W. M. Abbott, ed., *The Documents of Vatican II* [New York: Guild, America, and Association Presses, 1966], p. 356). In 1966 the archbishop of Canterbury at that time, Michael Ramsey, made an official visit to Pope Paul VI in Rome. Their Common Declaration announced that "a serious dialogue" would be inaugurated, to "lead to that unity in truth, for which Christ prayed," a phrase subsequently echoed in several national Anglican–Roman Catholic dialogues.

National and International Efforts
Toward "Full Communion"

In England theological talks soon began between Evangelical Anglicans and Roman Catholics (under the Church of England Evangelical Council and Cardinal Heenan), thus seeking to avoid the mistake at Malines where only Anglo-Catholics were involved. In Canada, "personal 'bilateral' conversations" began as early as 1965 among ecumenists (Ehrenström-Gassmann, p. 61).

Official, international dialogue developed through the work of a Joint Preparatory Commission, meeting in 1967 and 1968. Its Malta Report, unfortunately leaked to the press while still confidential in 1968, called for a "quest for the full, organic unity of our two Communions." This impressive final goal was to be the aim of the step of dialogue carried out through the Anglican–Roman Catholic International Commission (ARCIC). The first topic of three which ARCIC took up—Eucharist, Ministry, Authority—was dealt with in meetings at Windsor Castle, England, in 1970 and 1971, and one meeting in Venice, Italy, between the British sessions.

How the Windsor Statement on the Eucharist (1971) was produced ought to be noted. At the very first ARCIC meeting three subcommittees were formed, to take up the three topics. At the second meeting in Venice 1970, enough progress had been made to allow publication of "working papers" that, through "an administrative mishap," appeared in print without planned critical notes (in *Theology* 74 [Feb. 1971]: 49–67; *The Clergy Review* 57 [1972]: 62–67). They were, as one participant put it, "not warmly received," but an English postal strike diverted full attention from them (Charley, *The Anglican–Roman Catholic Agreement*, p. 7). An extensive rewriting was done by the subcommission, and when presented at the Windsor meeting in September 1971, the draft became a "breakthrough." Consensus was reached on "real presence" and "sacrifice."

It should be added that behind the draft lay the fruits of what might be called "Evangelical Anglican—Anglo-Catholic dialogue" within the Church of England, for the volume *Growing into Union: Proposals for forming a united Church in England,* by C. O. Buchanan, E. L. Mascall, J. I. Packer and the bishop of Willesden (London: SPCK, 1970) has been said by participants to have been helpful in providing an "interim agreement" between Anglican parties that then could be taken up in discussion with Roman Catholics (Charley, *Anglican–Roman Catholic Agreement,* p. 18, n. 3).

The Windsor Statement was, as already noted, then analyzed in the national dialogues between Roman Catholics and Anglicans. These examinations of it and their comments led in turn to the later "Elucidations" on the 1971 statement by ARCIC in 1979. Perhaps no other dialogue has achieved this type of coordination and pattern of testing work, revising it, and then publicly commenting on it in the face of responses.

The Windsor Statement (1971) and Its *Elucidation* (1979)

The twelve numbered paragraphs of the initial relatively short document completed at Windsor seek to provide "a consensus at the level of faith, so that all of us might be able to say, within the limits of the Statement: this is the Christian faith of the Eucharist" (Co-Chairmen's Preface 1971, *The Final Report,* p. 11). From the "substantial agreement" reached, it was claimed that "if there are any remaining points of disagreement they can be resolved on the principles here established" (section 12). Ultimately, *The Final Report* by ARCIC (1981) would put the discussion of Eucharist, Ministry and Ordination, and Authority, within the setting of *koinonia* ("communion") as an overarching theme *(Final Report,* pp. 5–8, 30, 50, 53–56, 68, 78, 86, 89, 93, and 98), but that Greek term appears neither in the Windsor Statement of 1971 nor in its 1979 *Elucidation.*

The terminological question is noted first: "Lord's supper, liturgy, holy mysteries, synaxis [Greek for "assembly," a term used for any public worship but especially in the East for the "liturgical synaxis" or Eucharist], mass, holy communion," all can be used. "The eucharist has become the most universally accepted term" (section 1). After a paragraph about how God through Christ "has reconciled man to himself" and "calls us into a new relationship . . . inaugurated by baptism into Christ through the Holy Spirit, nurtured and deepened through the eucharist, and expressed in a confession of one faith and a common life of loving service" (section 2), three themes are taken up.

Under the heading of "The Mystery of the Eucharist," what happens when people gather to commemorate God's saving acts is described: "Christ makes effective among us the eternal benefits of his victory and elicits and renews our response of faith, thanksgiving and self-surrender. Christ . . . builds up the life of the Church, strengthens its fellowship and furthers its mission." We, on our part, "proclaim the Lord's death," receive "a foretaste of the kingdom to come, we look back with thanksgiving to what Christ has done for us, we greet him present among us, we look forward to his final appearing." When we partake, it is in "commitment not only to Christ and to one another but also to the mission of the Church in the world" (sections 3–4).

The two crucial "breakthrough" areas dealt with sacrifice and presence. As to the former (section 5), it is strongly asserted that "there can be no repetition of or addition to what was then [on the cross, the culmination of a whole life of obedience] accomplished once for all by Christ." The Eucharist is the means of making Christ's atoning work effective in the church. The "notion of *memorial" (anamnēsis)*, "as understood in the passover celebration at the time of Christ," is taken up as the clue to "the Church's effectual proclamation of God's mighty acts" in the eucharistic memorial. Through the eucharistic prayer, members both participate in benefits "and enter into the movement of his self-offering."

"The presence of Christ" occupies six of the twelve sections (6–11). The Windsor Statement affirms real presence but without use of substantiationalist language. "Communion [supply *koinonia?*] with Christ in the eucharist presupposes his true presence, effectually signified by the bread and wine which, in this mystery, *become* his body and blood" (section 6, italics added). At this point a note appears on transubstantiation: it "should be seen as affirming the *fact* of Christ's presence and of the mysterious and radical change which takes place. In contemporary Roman Catholic theology it is not understood as explaining *how* the change takes place." "Christ is present and active, in various ways, in the entire eucharistic celebration . . . through the proclaimed word . . . and . . . sacramentally in the body and blood of his pascal sacrifice," offering "the special gift of himself" (section 7). "When this offering is met by faith, a lifegiving encounter results." There is a sacramental sign, personal relationship, and sacramental eating (sections 8–9). Through the prayer of thanksgiving *(anaphora)*, "the bread and wine *become* the body and blood of Christ by the action of the Holy Spirit" (section 10, italics added), "the transforming action of the Spirit of God" (section 11).

This Windsor Statement was then considered in national ARC dialogues in England, Canada, Japan, the United States, and elsewhere. To comments and criticisms from these and other sources, ARCIC offered further exposition in its 1979 *Elucidation,* completed at its Salisbury (England) meeting after a drafting process of over a year. It had to be emphasized that the Windsor Statement was no "comprehensive treatise on the eucharist" but took up only what "divided our two communions." The meaning of "substantial agreement" was defined by a sentence from the 1973 ARCIC Statement on Ministry: agreement by all dialogue members "on essential matters where . . . doctrine admits no divergence." The *Elucidation* on the Eucharist had to face the question of whether "new theological language . . . evades unresolved differences" in the two "breakthrough" areas (section 4).

Does use of *anamnesis* paper over old disputes about eucharistic sacrifice? Evangelical Anglicans feared "reintroduction of the theory of a repeated immolation" of Christ or "an eternal sacrifice in heaven." On the other hand, traditionalists of both Roman and Anglo-Catholic persuasion "doubted whether *anamnesis* sufficiently implies the reality indicated" by language to which they were accustomed (section 3). Lurking behind whatever ARCIC might say was a long debate over "offertory" or "oblation," what the worshipers offer to God, including bread and wine, in the course of the eucharistic liturgy. In the *Book of Common Prayer,* wording going back to what Cranmer said in the invocation, after reference to "these thy holy gifts, which we now offer unto thee," "here we offer and present unto thee, O Lord, ourselves, our souls and bodies, to be a reasonable, holy, and loving sacrifice unto thee." Dom Gregory Dix later contrasted Cranmer with what he described as the "old concept of the oblation,"

that Christ offers His perfect oblation of Himself to the Father, and that the earthly church as His Body enters into His eternal priestly act by the eucharist. *(The Shape of the Liturgy* [London: Dacre Press, 1945], p. 666)

Discussion within the Church of England had in 1970 answered the question, "What *can* we offer at the Eucharist?" with the words,

> Not mere bread and wine—even the term "offertory" sounds an odd note; not merely "the fruit of the lips" [Heb. 13:15]; . . . not merely ourselves . . .; not even ourselves in Christ, if that is seen in separation from our feeding on Christ; but ourselves as reappropriated by Christ. If the sacrament . . . communicate[s] . . . benefits . . . it also communicates . . . demands. . . . It may be good liturgically to express our self-offering as responsive to God's grace (by putting the prayer of self-oblation after communion). *(Growing Into Union,* pp. 59–60)

The Windsor Statement had handled this area by the idea of *anamnesis* as understood in Jesus' day and by a reference to how members of Christ "give thanks for all his mercies, entreat the benefits of his passion on behalf of the whole Church, participate in these benefits and enter into the movement of his self-offering" (section 5). Is this list just quoted all part of the eucharistic prayer (with Dix) or are at last two items "related especially to reception of communion" (thus Charley speaking for Evangelical Anglicans, *Anglican–Roman Catholic Agreement,* p. 18, n. 2) so that our "movement into [Christ's] self-offering" comes as communicants go from the church building to "serve the Lord" through a self-giving ministry to others in the world (Rom. 12:1)?

The Salisbury *Elucidation* responded to this matter by sticking to its position on "the Semitic background" of *anamnesis* and by citing examples of the Greek term in 1 Cor. 11:24–25, Luke 22:19, Justin Martyr, and subsequent use of the Latin equivalents, *commemoratio* and *memoria,* down to appearance of the term in Faith and Order's *One Baptism, One Eucharist and a Mutually Recognized Ministry.* One wishes for more on how scholarship today understands the "Semitic sense in Jesus' day." There is this helpful statement:

> In the New Testament sacrificial language refers primarily to the historical events of Christ's saving work for us. The tradition of the Church . . . used similar language to designate . . . the *anamnesis* of this historical event. *(Elucidation,* section 5; ARCIC *Final Report,* p. 20)

But we are left with a reiteration of the Windsor Statement:

> In the celebration of the memorial, Christ in the Holy Spirit unites his people with himself in a sacramental way so that the Church enters into the movement of his self-offering.

Thus, what "many Anglicans and some Lutherans believe" (but not all) and what had been stated as one opinion in the Pullach Report (see pp. 118ff., below) is here asserted as this dialogue's position (so G. Kretschmar, *Ökumenische Rundschau* 29 [1980]: 15–16).

What of the other problem area of Christ's presence in the Eucharist? Here Catholic critics wondered whether "the *permanence* of Christ's eucharistic presence" was "sufficiently acknowledged." Evangelicals were "unhappy" about language of *change* and statements that bread and wine "*become* the body and blood of Christ" (section 3). Salisbury elucidated Windsor's meaning by recalling what had earlier been affirmed: the glorified Lord, through the action of the Holy Spirit, encounters us, "appropriating bread and wine so that they become the food of the new creation already inaugurated by the coming of Christ." "*Becoming* does not here imply material change," it is now added. It is not presence in the same manner as "in his earthly life," nor is it limited to "consecrated elements." What is involved? "Sacramental presence." "Before the eucharistic prayer . . . 'It is bread.' After the eucharistic prayer . . . 'It is truly the body of Christ, the Bread of Life.'" "In the eucharist the human person encounters in faith the person of Christ in his sacramental body and blood. . . . The ultimate change intended by God is the transformation of human beings into the likeness of Christ." In a closing sentence that sounds like a eucharistic version of a dictum on the incarnation by Irenaeus, "The bread and wine *become* the sacramental body and blood of Christ in order that the Christian community may *become* more truly what it already is, the body of Christ" (section 6).

What does ARCIC think of "receptionism," it had been asked. Two "movements" are recognized as complementary: presence in the elements, and presence in the heart by faith.

Beyond what Windsor said, the *Elucidation* was asked also to say more on reserving the sacrament. In the post–Vatican II spirit it could be said that to reserve the sacrament—for example, for sick communion or for adoration of the Father and even of Christ—accords with the purpose of the Eucharist, though "veneration . . . wholly dissociated from the eucharistic celebration of the community" contradicts it. But others, it was reported, find "adoration of Christ in the reserved sacrament unacceptable" (section 9; cf. Article 28 of the Thirty-Nine Articles: "The Sacrament of the Lord's Supper was not by Christ's ordinance reserved, carried out, lifted up, or worshiped"). Answer: "Differences of theology and practice may well coexist with a real consensus on the essentials of eucharistic faith" *(Elucidation,* section 9).

Issues like intercommunion were set aside pending later statements on authority and ministry (section 10). When *The Final Report* was completed in 1981, its Introduction to the statements on all three topics made *koinonia* (communion) fundamental to all three—*koinonia* as the mystery of the church, centered in "union with God in Christ Jesus through the Spirit." Thus, the Eucharist is "the effective sign of *koinonia"; episcopē* ("oversight") serves the *koinonia;* "primacy" is "a visible link and focus of *koinonia."* ARCIC's most recent word on Holy Communion (1981 Introduction, section 6) is this: the Eucharist is

> the sacrament of Christ, by which he builds up and nurtures his people in the *koinonia* of his body. By the eucharist all the baptized are brought into communion with the source of *koinonia*. He is the one who destroyed the walls dividing humanity (Eph 2:14); he is the one who died to gather into unity all the children of God his father (cf. John 11:52; 17:20ff).

In 1977 Archbishop Donald Coggan journeyed from Canterbury to Rome and met with Pope Paul VI. In 1983 Pope John Paul II paid a much-publicized visit to Canterbury. But in spite of warm personal gestures of reconciliation, no dramatic announcement about eucharistic fellowship in light of the ARCIC dialogue was forthcoming. The *Common Declaration* of the two leaders in 1977 speaks of the "communion with God in Christ through faith and through baptism and self-giving to Him that stands at the centre of our witness to the world." It is acknowledged that "many in both communions are asking themselves whether they have a common faith sufficient to be translated into communion of life, worship and mission." But for the present, "between us communion remains imperfect" *(The Final Report,* pp. 121–22).

Evaluation

Tribute has already been paid to the preparation for, and far-reaching impact of, the work of ARCIC. New approaches and terms are employed to deal with old impasses. The U.S. Anglican–Roman Catholic dialogue, in a 1972 report on "Doctrinal Agreement and Christian Unity: Methodological Considerations" *(Journal of Ecumenical Studies* 9/2 [Spring 1972]: 445–48), observed that "within a single Church one and the same formula often receives different theological interpretations." That truth is applied by the Catholic Theological Society review to ARCIC's work in

this way: "insufficient attention" has been paid "to the doctrinal pluralism within the Anglican communion itself"; "theological differences"
exist "not only between . . . but also within the Anglican and Roman
Catholic delegations." Further, "the statements in general are biblically
and historically thin." But the members of the Anglican and Roman Catholic dialogue are commended for having and explaining relationships
between the American dialogue and the international one (Proceedings,
1979, pp. 257–62, 284).

Lutheran-Episcopal Relations: An Agreement

Given their separate dialogues with Roman Catholics as background
and their own common Western and Reformation heritages—whereby
each claims to be in some sense both "evangelical" and "catholic"—
Lutherans and Anglicans could be expected to enjoy considerable commonality in beginning discussions on the Lord's Supper and other topics.
Further, each world family of churches—centered respectively in the
Lutheran World Federation and the Lambeth Conferences—had a long
history of interrelationships in Europe, North America, Africa, and the
Far East. Both are liturgical communions. Both had long been involved
in Faith and Order, Life and Work, and other ecumenical agencies. Each
had experience with ministry in lands of the other faith—Anglicans
through English-speaking churches on the continent, Germans and Scan-
dinavians through holding services in their mother tongues in the British
Isles for business people, students, travelers, and seafarers.

Historic differences that could, however, affect eucharistic understanding included the Lutheran passion, far beyond that of Anglicans, for
doctrine and confessional statements (though both emphasize the ancient
creeds) and the Anglican embodiment of episcopacy and threefold ministry (though Lutherans stress an ordained ministry and in some European
churches long have termed their leaders "bishops" and even can in the
Church of Sweden claim the historic episcopate).

Amid the proliferating course of the bilaterals, Anglican-Lutheran
conversations began early in the 1960s, blossomed in the 1970s and led
to results of a striking sort in the early 1980s. We shall look first at the
international and European conversations and then dialogues in the
United States, though American agreement on "Interim Sharing of the
Eucharist" in 1982 was to have positive influence in other parts of the
world.

Internationally and in Europe

As early as 1964, upon the initiative of the archbishop of Canterbury, representatives of the Church of England met with those of the Evangelical Church in Germany (EKD), a federation of Lutheran, Reformed, and Union churches. The aim was simply to achieve greater knowledge and understanding of each other. At the second of three meetings, that at Bethel, West Germany, in 1966, the topic dealt with was "Word and Eucharist."

What became the Anglican-Lutheran International Conversations had been set afoot, however, by even earlier events, namely, the negotiations for church union in South India and East Africa. It was sensed that in these discussions issues of more than regional concern were being raised, and so by 1963 there were plans within the Lutheran World Federation for beginning wider talks about the Lutheran and Anglican concepts of the ministry and episcopacy. By 1967 a memorandum was worked out by the LWF and the Lambeth Conference for the commission to discuss "the general mission of the Church in the world and only afterwards proceed to questions of doctrine and order." The nineteen participants who came from all parts of the world, plus a Presbyterian observer from the World Council of Churches, were to meet four times between 1970 and 1972. The final meeting at Pullach, near Munich, dealt with "Word and Sacrament" and also put together *The Report* of these *Anglican-Lutheran International Conversations.*

Treatment of the Lord's Supper in the Pullach Report comes in the central section on "The Word and the Sacraments," after "Sources of Authority" (Scripture, creeds, confessional formularies, tradition, and theology) and "The Church." It is followed by sections on "Apostolic Ministry" (where the historic episcopate remains the area of least agreement) and "Worship." Both Word and Sacrament, while differing in "the mode of Christ's action," are termed "occasions of his coming in anamnesis of his first advent and in anticipation of his parousia. The Word imparts significance to the Sacrament and the Sacrament gives visible embodiment to the Word" (section 63).

"In the Lord's Supper," it was agreed, "the Church obediently performs" what Christ commanded and "receives . . . the body and blood of Christ, . . . forgiveness of sins and all the other benefits of his passion." The real presence is affirmed, but without defining how: "the bread and wine, while remaining bread and wine, become the means whereby Christ is truly present and gives himself to the communicants" (sections 67–68). The final paragraph on the Lord's Supper takes up sacrifice: "Christ's sacrifice was offered once and for all for the sin of the whole world. Yet without denying this fundamental truth . . . the Eucharist in some sense involves sacrifice." The last four sentences, with their agreements and relative contrast, deserve to be quoted in full:

> We offer our praise and thanksgiving, ourselves and all that we are, and make *(begehen)* before God the memorial of Christ's sacrifice. Christ's redemptive act becomes present for our participation. Many Anglicans and some Lutherans believe that in the Eucharist the Church's offering of herself is caught up in his one offering. Other Anglicans and many Lutherans do not employ the concept of sacrifice in this way. (section 64)

On this last point Georg Kretschmar once proposed adding descriptively, "There are Anglicans and Lutherans who not only do not use this concept but regard such a way of speaking as subject to misunderstanding and improper" *(Ökumenische Rundschau* 29 [1980]:6).

Under "Worship" it is added that "in both Churches, the Holy Communion is coming back into the centre of the picture as the principal worship service of each Sunday." Lutherans are reappropriating traditional liturgical forms; in Anglicanism there is use of the sermon now in many more celebrations of Holy Communion. The recommendations in the report include one for "a greatly increased measure of intercommunion," including extension of existing arrangements by the Church of England with the Churches of Sweden and Finland (and the "hospitality rights" extended to other Scandinavian Lutherans) now "to include all Lutheran Churches in Europe" (sections 96 and 97; cf. p. 27).

As a follow-up to Pullach, three "regional dialogues" were proposed, in the United States, Europe, and Tanzania. The dialogue in the United States between 1976 and 1980 (see pp. 121ff., below) proved "the most important Anglican-Lutheran dialogue on a national level" and influenced the work of the Anglican-Lutheran European Regional Commission (ALERC) and its 1982 report.

The European Regional Commission of twelve persons from the British Isles, Germany, and Scandinavia took up "Worship and Eucharist" at its first meeting in Edinburgh 1980, discussed sacraments further at Pullach 1981, and then dealt with Holy Communion in its report *Anglican-*

Lutheran Dialogue, completed in Helsinki in 1982. One finds input in the final document not only from Lutheran-Episcopal talks but also from conversations with Roman Catholics (ARCIC and RCLJC) and Faith and Order on the Eucharist.

In the historical survey (sections 8–16) of Anglican and Lutheran relationships in Europe, Puritanism and then the Oxford movement are singled out for bringing about a "parting of the ways" from a common Reformation heritage. In a later section on "The Present Situation of the Anglican and Lutheran Churches in Europe" (sections 52–61), secularization and social changes are discussed as factors confronting both groups.

Under "Doctrinal Issues: Agreements and Convergences" (sections 17–51) Eucharist is treated as one of six areas. The three paragraphs (sections 26–28) come after Justification (the relevance and "fundamental" nature of which is asserted, along with a mini-overview of the gospel of grace) and just after Baptism. As in the Pullach Report of 1972 there are also treatments of Spiritual Life and Liturgical Worship (including rites as expression of doctrine—*lex orandi, lex credendi),* Ordained Ministry and Episcopacy (the longest section, 32–43), and The Nature of the Church (here *koinonia* enters as a term).

What Pullach, Roman Catholic dialogues, and *BEM* had said is noted (section 26) as a "wider ecumenical consensus on the eucharist" within which Anglicans and Lutherans have "a basic identity of understanding" about this sacrament that nurtures and deepens the relationship with God and "fellow members of Christ's Body." It is—to take up the first of two issues that we find in so many statements, namely, sacrifice—"the memorial of the crucified and risen Christ . . . not simply the calling to mind of an event in the past" but "the sacrament of Christ's sacrifice . . . still operative on behalf of all . . . the Church's effectual proclamation of God's saving acts in Christ." Phrases now familiar from the history of doctrine and other bilateral statements (cf. ARCIC especially) are there, but worded a bit differently: sacraments are "instruments and means . . . from Christ . . . by which, through 'outward and visible' signs, we truly receive Christ's grace. It is through this contemporary application of Christ's salvation, particularly in the eucharist, that the Church becomes truly itself and the other means of grace find their place" (section 27). A later statement (section 29) should be placed alongside this one: "the living Christ is encountered in different ways in the Church," in proclamation, sacraments, and personal and corporate worship.

The other issue, namely, "presence," is treated by affirming (section 28) that "Christ is present and active in the entire eucharistic celebration," but there is "a particular sacramental presence." For "in virtue of the living Word of Christ and by the power of the Holy Spirit the bread and wine are the sacrament of Christ's body and blood. . . . Under these elements Christ comes." Traditionally, both churches say Christ effects forgiveness; today both stress also the building up of community, strengthening of faith and hope, witness and service. The future eschatological note is struck by a closing reference to "a foretaste of the eternal joy of God's kingdom."

The ALERC report, while acknowledging a difference that remains over the question of historic episcopacy in any organic church union (section 43), finds its chief recommendations in the area of the Eucharist: to "welcome communicants from the other Church and encourage their own communicants to receive Holy Communion in Churches of the other tradition"; and to "make provision for a fuller mutual participation in eucharistic worship . . . by allowing Lutheran pastors and Anglican priests to celebrate the eucharist together, subject to the tradition and law" of each church (p. 30).

When this is put into effect, Lutherans and Anglicans will have advanced to celebration by clergy who are in some sense mutually recognized. Such was the level of sharing begun in the United States in an interim way by Episcopalians and Lutherans in 1982.

U.S. "Interim Sharing of the Eucharist"

The First Series of dialogues between the Episcopal Church and the three major Lutheran bodies in the United States began in 1969 (thus prior to the start of the Anglican-Lutheran International Conversations) and stretched over six meetings until 1972. Elements of commonality and historic difficulties were much like those outlined above in introducing discussions between these two world communions. However, a study booklet that grew out of the Second Series of U.S. meetings, *Traditions Transplanted: The Story of Anglican and Lutheran Churches in America*, by William H. Peterson and Robert J. Goeser (Cincinnati: Forward Movement Publications, 1981), was able to point to many similarities in the American experience of emigrants from mostly state churches in Europe and Britain as they adjusted to the religious pluralism of the New World.

The mandate for the 1969–72 talks was limited: to define "possibilities and problems for a more extended dialogue having more specific fellowship or unity or union goals" *(Lutheran-Episcopal Dialogue,* 1973, p. 13). But in the course of considering such topics as Scripture, Worship, Baptism-Confirmation, and Apostolicity, the group of eighteen found itself centering attention "more and more upon the concept of *communio in sacris*—that is, intercommunion, or pulpit and altar fellowship." Their recommendations called for not only "commendation of communicants of each communion to the Eucharistic celebrations and gatherings around the Word of the other" but also "intercommunion between parishes or congregations" where understanding and trust allowed (pp. 23–24). Most strikingly, the Lutheran-Episcopal Dialogue, First Series (LED I), argued that each church could sufficiently "affirm the presence of the Gospel and apostolicity" in the other so as to let shared Eucharists be a *means* to unity (and renewal) rather than be a *goal* of unity (pp. 13–14). Thus, LED I rather daringly suggested that "contrary to orthodox Lutheran opinion, a full *consensus de doctrina* is thus not held to be a precondition for increased eucharistic sharing and other forms of ecclesial fellowship" (Ehrenström-Gassmann, *Confessions in Dialogue,* p. 56), and contrary to Anglican opinion that possession of the historic episcopate is no prerequisite. In the words of the Lutherans' *apologia* to the Lutheran audience, the question had become " 'why not?' rather than 'why?' " (p. 37).

As regards the Eucharist, the summary statement from the 1970 session on "Christian prayer and worship" included in the final *Report,* is quite brief: "the proclamation of the Gospel and the celebration of the Holy Eucharist constitute the distinctive and central act of Christian worship." But more attention should be given to "what the Eucharist means and how it is to be celebrated." As for practice, unity "is to be found more in the 'shape' of Eucharistic liturgies [cf. Dom Gregory Dix?] than in fixed texts" (pp. 16–17). As for "Eucharistic Sacrifice," further discussions would also be helpful," as to "what is meant and not meant." Nonetheless, intercommunion—especially on the local level—is desirable as a means to unity. To support this, an LWF Consultation on Bilateral Conversations in 1971 was quoted, that "communicatio in sacris and its acknowledgment may properly *precede* the attempt to state doctrinal consensus in the form of agreed statements" (p. 34).

The proposals of LED I scarcely "carried the day" on either side. Indeed the summary statements of the dialogue sometimes point to new, unresolved questions that loom larger than traditional problems. For example, under "Baptism-Confirmation," voices in both camps were noted urging "delay of infant Baptism" until a personal confession of faith could be made (p. 18). But overall LED I's notion of enough agreement to warrant eucharistic fellowship, thereby providing "a matrix out of which more complete unity could develop" *(Ecumenical Methodology,* ed. P. Højen [Geneva: LWF, 1978], p. 114), would eventually find more sympathetic ears.

But more work was needed, especially on the ministry, including the place of bishops. As the "Statement addressed to Episcopalians" delicately put it, "First, we propose that the apostolicity of the Lutheran ministry be acknowledged by the Episcopal Church" (p. 41). Further, "as an implementation of this acknowledgment, we are proposing that Lutherans who are communicants in good standing in their own churches be admitted to our altars" and that "Episcopalians be likewise encouraged to receive communion at Lutheran altars on appropriate occasions, subject to individual conscience" (p. 42). But "what we are proposing is neither full communion nor structural reunion. We still believe that all four points of the [Lambeth] quadrilateral must be met" (p. 43; so R. H. Fuller, writing in LED I as an individual, but presumably for the Episcopal delegation). The appeal was to the four articles approved by the Lambeth Conference of 1888 (originally from the Protestant Episcopal Church in the U.S.A., 1886) as essentials for a reunited Christendom: Scripture, Creeds, "the two Sacraments ordained by Christ Himself— Baptism and the Supper of the Lord—ministered with unfailing use of Christ's Words of Institution, and of the elements ordained by Him," and the Historic Episcopate.

Accordingly, the Second Series of talks (1976–80) in the U.S. Lutheran-Episcopal Dialogue focused on providing "more historical and theological documentation" *(The Report of the Lutheran-Episcopal Dialogue,* 1981, p. 5). This was done through papers by participants, especially for our topic by two papers on "The Eucharistic Presence" at the August 1979 meeting, and, as the *Report* volume shows, by use of documents from other dialogues, notably U.S. Lutheran–Roman Catholic and international Anglican-Lutheran. The discussions of LED II recognized, almost as a starting point, that LED I had gone beyond its original mandate in proposing "mutual ecclesial recognition and limited communion" at least locally. LED II decided to pursue the route of "joint confessional statements in matters that have separated" Lutherans and Episcopalians *(Report,* pp. 14–15). In a sense, Gospel and Episcopacy were the starting themes. Eventually joint statements were produced on Justification, the Gospel, Eucharistic Presence, the Authority of Scripture, and Apostolicity (pp. 22–42). The section on Apostolicity, including succession and *episcopē* (oversight), is the longest; "serious divergence in the actual ordering of the Pastoral Office in the two Communions" and over the historic episcopacy is admitted, but the two sides declare together "that both the Lutheran Church and the Episcopal Church stand in Apostolic Succession" (p. 41).

Perhaps one should not expect much new to be said in the "Joint Statement on Eucharistic Presence," but the understanding of these five pages (25–29, including notes) as a joint confession makes them significant. In fairness, one should assess what is said within a diagrammed concept, Figure 3 below, in the Theological Methodology section of the 1981 *Report* (p. 20). If, admittedly (pp. 14–15), the statement on Justification is not all that Lutherans would want to say and the statement on Apostolicity not "all that Anglicans would want to say," perhaps the statement on the Eucharist shows a greater area of central agreement but is not all that either would want to say. Or is it that there are diversities *within* each group, not necessarily indicated, so that one could chart greater overlap of Evangelical Anglicans with Lutherans or of "catholic Lutherans" with

FIGURE 3

U.S. Lutheran–Episcopal Dialogue

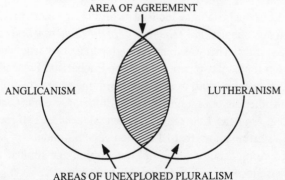

Episcopalians, and less of Anglo-Catholics with "strongly confessional" Lutherans (p. 16)?

The Joint Statement begins with the Reformation period (section 1) and its Western church heritage (section 3), mentioning what both traditions rejected (for example, transubstantiation as a "metaphysical explanation of the Real Presence") and what both affirmed (Christ as "both the gift and giver"). But the distinctive emphases of each tradition as it developed are also noted. For example, "in light of the recovery of the gospel of justification by faith, Lutherans rejected any notion of sacrifice which obscured the sufficiency and finality of Christ's sacrifice upon the cross," and they "defended the Real Presence" by the formula of "Christ's body and blood 'in, with, and under' the forms of bread and wine," implying "a two-fold eating of the sacrament, spiritually and orally (Formula of Concord, Solid Declaration VII:60–61). Anglicans, on the other hand, followed the Reformed emphasis on the spiritual eating by faith, thus denying that the wicked and unbelievers partake of Christ (*Articles of Religion* 28–29)." It was Richard Hooker who "gave Anglicanism its normative approach to eucharistic doctrine by teaching that the elements of bread and wine are the instruments of participation in the body and blood of Christ" *(Report,* pp. 25–26, section 1).

Here we are confronted with a classic difference between Anglican and Lutheran confessional documents concerning the *manducatio impiorum,* or "eating," of the bread by the "unworthy or unrighteous." The Thirty-Nine Articles of the Church of England said (28 and 29, though 29 with its Reformed position seems lacking in printed texts before 1571),

> to such as rightly, worthily, and with faith, receive the same, the Bread which we break is a partaking of the Body of Christ; and likewise the Cup. . . . The Body of Christ is given, taken, and eaten, in the Supper, only after an heavenly and spiritual manner. And the mean whereby the Body of Christ is received and eaten in the Supper, is Faith. . . . (29) The Wicked, and such as be void of a lively faith, although they do carnally and visibly press with their teeth (as Saint Augustine saith) the Sacrament of the Body and Blood of Christ; yet in no wise are they partakers of Christ: but rather, to their condemnation, do eat and drink the sign or Sacrament of so great a thing.

The Lutheran Formula of Concord a bit later (1577) argued, however,

> that not only godly, pious, and believing Christians receive the true body and blood of Christ orally in the sacrament, but also the unworthy and godless hypocrites, like Judas and his ilk. . . . There is therefore a twofold eating

of the flesh of Christ. The one is spiritual, of which Christ speaks in John
6:48–58. This occurs, in no other way than with the spirit and faith, in the
preaching and contemplation of the Gospel as well as in the Lord's Supper. . . .
This spiritual eating, however, is precisely faith. . . . The other eating . . . is
oral or sacramental, when all who eat . . . partake of the true, essential body
. . . of Christ orally. Believers . . . unbelievers . . . too . . . not, however, in a
coarse, carnal, Capernaitic [cf. John 6:52–65] manner [i.e., transubstantia-
tion], but in a supernatural, incomprehensible manner. (Solid Declaration
VII: 60–64, Tappert ed., pp. 580–81)

LED II deals with these "classical affirmations of *manducatio impiorum*
and *manducatio oralis*" and the fact that the Thirty-Nine Articles take "a
somewhat different stand" by asserting, "Anglicans today have no interest in these particular doctrinal affirmations. Rather, they tend to express
their belief in the Real Presence in ceremonial action, by the reverence
with which they treat the consecrated elements outside of Communion"
(Report, p. 17, under "Theological Methodology," a revealing section
that should be read alongside the Joint Statement). Instances like this help
explain why representatives of the Lutheran Church—Missouri Synod
offered "dissenting statements" (in LED II, on Scripture, p. 31) or
issued their own recommendations (pp. 12, 58–59), and why that body
has not pursued recommendations of this and similar U.S. dialogues.

To return to the Joint Statement by LED II, "the eucharistic celebration
of Word and Sacrament is the heart and center of the life and mission of
the Church," nourishing the community's corporate life for service in the
world, enlivening the church, and strengthening oneness with Christ
(section 2, p. 26). Only later (section 5, p. 27) is the "individual" side
hinted at: the Lord " 'in, with, and under' the forms of bread and wine
enables all Christians to avail themselves of the benefits" of his death and
resurrection, in a "sacramental transformation of the called and gathered
people of God into the image of Christ, that we may be, in Luther's
words, 'Christ to our neighbor.' "

Concerning old debates on presence and sacrifice, LED II methodo-
logically holds, "Modern New Testament exegesis offers a way to cut
through all these dilemmas, inherited as they are largely from the Middle
Ages. In most contemporary exegesis the words 'body' and 'blood' are
interpreted increasingly not as substances but as saving event *(Heils-
ereignis).* And with the biblical notion of *anamnesis* being brought into
play, the once-for-all saving event can be understood as rendered

present" (p. 17), as in ARCIC's Windsor Statement. Hence sections 3 and 4. "The presence of Christ in the Church is proclaimed in a variety of ways." Christ "presides at each assembly," and Christ is proclaimed in the scriptural readings (cf. *Eucharist as Sacrifice,* Lutherans and Catholics in Dialogue III, p. 192). Then LED II adds (p. 26), Christ "is represented by each of the baptized members and in a special way by the ordained ministers." But only after reference to "the presence of the Holy Spirit" do we get the christological-eucharistic statement that "Christ's very body broken on the cross and his very blood shed for the forgiveness of our sins are present, distributed and received, as a means of partaking here and now of the fruits of that atoning sacrifice." And it is immediately added, "This is also the presence of the risen and glorified Christ who pleads for us before the throne of God" (p. 27). Faith does not effect this presence but, seemingly, seals the blessings involved.

LED II on the Eucharist also includes a reference to the growth of weekly celebrations of the sacrament and extension of the distribution to sick and homebound persons (while disavowing veneration of reserved elements). There is a closing section (6) on the "eschatological dimension" of participating in "the joys of the age to come." Because the Eucharist "manifests unity," therefore "communion among separated Christians is to be sought wherever sufficient agreement on Word and Sacraments can be reached" (p. 29).

In 1982 the Episcopal Church and three Lutheran bodies (The American Lutheran Church, the Association of Evangelical Lutheran Churches, and the Lutheran Church in America) agreed, by convention action, that that stage had been reached among them—in spite of a footnote in LED II that not all Lutherans and Episcopalians necessarily agree that "such 'sufficient agreement' " had been achieved. Indeed, five topics were listed *(Report,* p. 29, n. 3) for the agenda of LED III.

The route to the resulting *Lutheran-Episcopal Agreement* lay through the approval of the work of the dialogue by the Standing Commission on Ecumenical Relations of the Episcopal Church and its decision to bring recommendations to the Triennial General Convention in September 1982; and then, upon communication of this to Bishop James R. Crumley, Jr., of the LCA, through a study process in the LCA, leading to recommendations shared further and developed by a joint committee of Lutherans and Episcopalians. The resulting "agreement" went before each of the four conventions, meeting at about the same time in four different U.S. cities in September 1982. To the surprise of some observers, the agreement was approved in each church by large to overwhelming votes.

What was approved is not identical to the recommendations of either LED I or II or the international Anglican-Lutheran Conversation. In affirming "Interim Sharing of the Eucharist," the participating churches made these points:

1. Each church rejoices that the three dialogues have made "substantial progress" and each looks to "the day when full communion is established." This means a judgment that the dialogues have made a credible case for the actions proposed, but that "full" or "inter-" communion does not exist as yet, that further stage when members and ministers can freely communicate and officiate sacramentally in the other church.

2. Each recognizes the other "as a church in which the Gospel is preached and taught." This marks the first time that American Lutherans have officially so spoken about "a group not subscribing to the Lutheran Confessions" and the first time the Episcopal Church has "officially accorded such recognition to any church" with which they have not "already been in full communion" *(The Lutheran-Episcopal Agreement: Commentary and Guidelines*, 1983, p. 7).

3. Prayer, Bible study, programs together of all sorts, and "joint use of physical facilities" are encouraged.

4. The teaching of each church "is consonant with the Gospel and is sufficiently compatible with" that of the other church "that a relationship of Interim Sharing of the Eucharist is hereby established between these churches." The guidelines that follow reflect existing statements of each body:

a. The welcome of members of the other church "constitutes a mutual recognition of Eucharistic teaching," though not "formal recognition of each other's Eucharists or ministries."

b. Common, joint celebration of the Eucharist may be permitted by bishops/church presidents, using a eucharistic prayer from the *Lutheran Book of Worship* or *Book of Common Prayer,* with "an ordained minister of each participating church at the altar," thus showing both unity and division that is yet to be overcome. Again, "rejection or final recognition of either church's Eucharist and ministry" is not implied.

c. The experience of this Interim Sharing is to be communicated regularly to other Lutheran and Anglican churches and the dialogues in which they are involved.

Two details call for comment. The Episcopal Church's General Convention did not wish to suggest that there would be agreement on the doctrine of Eucharist separate from agreement on the ordained ministry. Hence it inserted between 4a and 4b a declaration that "or" in the phrase "recognition of each other's Eucharists *or* ministries" is to be taken conjunctively, as "and." There is as yet no final recognition of either, for the two interrelate.

Lutherans have asserted in their *Guidelines* (pp. 11–12) that 4b does not imply "concelebration," that is, the recitation of the eucharistic prayer *together* by two or more ministers. While there are ancient and Eastern examples of such a practice and Vatican II restored it for certain occasions, neither the *Book of Common Prayer* nor Lutheran statements employ the term. Indeed the ALC–LCA *Statement on Communion Practices* (1978) insists, "Only one minister shall preside over the entire celebration," so as to avoid notions of priests concelebrating with a bishop or a "corps of clergy" or the necessity of all the ordained present to join in during the prayer. Both Episcopalians and Lutherans had a further reason for avoiding the term in their agreement, namely, the modern practice of ministers from different denominations standing together and reciting the Words of Institution; in such a case, each group can assume the communion is "valid," but there has been no necessary core of agreement on doctrine and praxis concerning the Lord's Supper or ministry.

So U.S. Lutherans and Episcopalians began in the fall of 1982 the experiment of lived fellowship in the Eucharist as a step toward "full intercommunion." In late 1983 an international Anglican-Lutheran working group of leaders from Europe, Africa, and the United States recommended moving beyond the first two stages of dialogue statements of "agreement in the faith" and "interim sharing of the eucharist" to "full communion." The further stage would require "consensus" on authority, gospel, justification, sacraments, and ministry. It would mean "autonomous" but "interdependent" churches engaged in common tasks, sharing of the sacraments, and bishops of one church taking part in consecrating bishops of the other church. The Cold Ash report (named for the center in Berkshire, England, where the fifteen persons involved met) thus looks forward to stages moving toward full communion (*Anglican-Lutheran Relations* [London: Anglican Consultative Council,

Geneva: Lutheran World Federation, 1983]; Appendix III lists seventeen
countries outside Great Britain, Canada, and the United States where
Anglicans and Lutherans have more than ten thousand members each).

Evaluation

If "nothing succeeds like success," this is a premier bilateral, for it has
led to official, if interim, eucharistic sharing in the U.S. (1982), and it
has been a model for Europe (1983 statement) and could be a model
elsewhere. The results are being watched, far beyond Anglican and
Lutheran circles, as a way of bringing together, by the stage of shared
sacraments, churches of the word and an episcopal communion. How do
gospel and ministry, faith and order, fit together? Perhaps this way.

The Lutheran-Episcopal dialogues are to be commended for a certain
boldness; for example, LED I for proposing at an early stage local, selective intercommunion between parishes, and for beginning to popularize
the Greek word *episcopē* ("oversight") as a way to talk of a necessary
function in all churches without necessarily having bishops *(episcopoi)*
in historic succession, for "succession" can also refer to apostolic mission, Scriptures, creeds, and sacraments, as well as ministry (LED II).

On the other hand, there has been a persistent criticism since LED I
(cf. *Lutherans in Ecumenical Dialogue*, pp. 23–24) that "there is yet
much work to be done." The Summary Statements (LED I) or Joint Statements (LED II) are quite brief, and the accompanying statements by participants (LED I, pp. 29–46; LED II, pp. 58–63) reveal the unsolved
difficulties on both sides. Lutherans in 1977 found "disturbing" the 1972
statement by an Episcopalian to Episcopalians: "if we edge forward to a
closer relationship . . . , it will help us come closer to our Lutheran
brethren and prepare the way for restoration among them of the episcopate in historical succession" *(Progress Report, p. 43)*. Do Lutherans
after 1982 feel the same way as the 1977 assessment did?

Yet the fellowship is underway. Have U.S. Lutherans raised to a sacramental level the "Lund Principle," that "we do *everything together* which
we can do practically and in good conscience" (1981 *Report*, p. 61, referring to a thesis framed at the Lund Faith and Order meeting of 1952)?

Other Examples and Evaluations
of the Bilaterals

While these four case studies may present us with the premier bilateral
results on the Eucharist, they are by no means the whole story.

As already indicated, bilaterals provide little evidence of Radical Reformation, Free Church, or Pentecostal thinking about the Lord's Supper and relatively little of Eastern Orthodox views on the Sacrament. An interesting exception, however, on the one hand is the U.S. Disciples of Christ–Roman Catholic consultation (cf. *An Adventure in Understanding: Roman Catholic/Disciple Dialogue 1967–1973* [Washington, D.C.: U.S. Catholic Conference Publications Office, 1974]), since the Disciples stress both Holy Scripture (as exclusive authority, rejecting all creeds) *and* congregational celebration of the Lord's Supper as the chief act of worship *every Sunday*. Yet the 1979 Catholic Theological Society critique *(Proceedings*, 34, pp. 262–64) faulted this dialogue for not being "biblical enough" and "critically" so, while recommending here the development of a "biblical theology of the Eucharist."

On the other hand, even, for instance, in the Anglican-Orthodox Joint Doctrinal Discussions (1966 and following; see Ehrenström-Gassmann, pp. 19–22), conferences dealt only in passing with the "Anglican Understanding of the Holy Eucharist" (1969). Early agenda turned on whether "union of the Anglican Church with the Orthodox is possible," given the intercommunion which "the Anglican Church . . . is now practising with certain Lutherans" and "with the Confessions which took part in the South India Scheme" (p. 20). A 1972 recommendation urged that dialogue include, besides questions of church life and worship, "all the truths of Christian faith, in the hope that . . . members will achieve unity of faith" (p. 21). This is a high view of doctrinal agreement. But of direct discussion of the "synaxis," there has been little. The one essay on the Eucharist in the volume resulting from the Orthodox-Reformed dialogue in the United States, "The Eucharistic Community and the Catholicity of the Church" by John D. Zizioulas (in *The New Man* [Valley Forge, Pa.: Agora Books, 1973], pp. 107–31, originally *One in Christ* 2 [1971]), deals with local community and catholicity. Of greater specificity is "The Eucharist as Sacrifice: A Roman Catholic-Reformed Dialogue," by Christopher Kiesling and Ross McKenzie *(Journal of Ecumenical Studies* 15 [1978]: 415–40).

Beyond these examples, perhaps the most significant of recent dialogues on the Eucharist are those involving Roman Catholics and the Reformed (1977, in Figure 2, above), Anglicans and the Orthodox (1976), and the EKD–Russian Orthodox meeting in 1976.

The document on "The Presence of Christ in Church and World," which resulted from the dialogue between the World Alliance of

Reformed Churches and the Secretariat for Promoting Christian Unity (Rome) over the years 1970–77, has a section on "The Eucharist" (##67–92). The Reformed participants particularly included a number of New Testament scholars (Markus Barth, George Caird, W. C. van Unnik, and Eduard Schweizer), and there is considerable reference to New Testament verses in these paragraphs. While new ground cannot be said to have been broken, there were widespread agreements, in light of which it was suggested that further discussions are needed on the meaning of "agape-celebrations" and on the "rich contents" of anamnesis. To quote a major insight from the document: "The specific mode of Christ's real presence in the Eucharist is thus to be interpreted as the presence of the Son who is both consubstantial with us in our human and bodily existence while being consubstantial with the Father and the Holy Spirit in the Godhead (John 17:21–23). It is important to see that Calvin's Christology was mainly inspired by the theology of St. Cyril of Alexandria and St. Athanasius" (section 84). The evaluation paper by Paul J. Achtemeier in *Reformed World* (36 [1981]: 212–20) reported that Reformed Churches in different parts of the world, in their responses, "found the most agreement" in the discussion on the Eucharist, these churches expressing gratitude for "a new perception of the presence of Christ in the Lord's supper" (p. 213; cf. 223). The next round of Reformed–Roman Catholic dialogue is to include, under its general theme of "The Church in the World of Today," a section on "perseverance of the communio by the celebration of the Eucharist."

The Anglican-Orthodox statement of 1976 builds upon earlier work, notably an agreement in Bucharest in 1935 (see *Documents on Christian Unity, Third Series 1930–48,* ed. G. K. A. Bell [London: Oxford University Press, 1948], pp. 44–45). *Anglican-Orthodox Dialogue: The Moscow Statement Agreed by the Anglican-Orthodox Joint Doctrinal Commission 1976* (ed. K. Ware and C. Davey; London, 1977) can be called a "consensus document" even though Orthodox teaching comes frequently to the fore (so G. Kretschmar, *Ökumenische Rundschau* 29 [1980]: 15). "Western" questions such as "real presence" and "sacrifice" do recede. The Eucharist is given an ecclesial setting. The *epiclesis* is emphasized but from a broader perspective than that of the sacrament. Thus it is said, "The Church is that Community which lives by continually invoking the Holy Spirit" (section 32). "The Eucharistic understanding of the Church affirms the presence of Jesus Christ in the Church, which is his Body, and in the Eucharist."

Figure 2, above, lists Protestant (Lutheran) dialogues with the Orthodox involving German and Finnish churches (Roumania could also be added; cf. G. Kretschmar, *Ökumenische Rundschau* 29 [1980]: 14, n. 23). Perhaps the most significant recent conference on aspects of the Eucharist was the one held at Arnoldshain, West Germany, 6–10 June 1976, involving the Russian Orthodox and the Evangelische Kirche in Deutschland. It focused on the "sacrifice" of Christ and of Christians *(Das Opfer Christi und das Opfer der Christen,* Beihefte zur *Ökumenischen Rundschau,* 34 [Frankfurt: O. Lembeck, 1979]).

But even all these examples do not provide us with the comparable amounts of material on the Eucharist for the Free churches and the Orthodox that one gets from the bilaterals on Anglican, Lutheran, and Roman Catholic views.

The bilaterals are further limited in pointing out what is happening between certain other confessional groups like Anglicans and the Presbyterians and Reformed family. Here one must look to church merger negotiations, both successful (like South India) or unsuccessful (Church of England, Church of Scotland, or, somewhat similarly, Anglican-Methodist talks in Great Britain). The talks in the United States within COCU (the Consultation on Church Union, later "the Church of Christ Uniting") have in their documents both reflected other ecumenical discussions and sometimes contributed to them, as in the Lutherans and Catholics in Dialogue III, *The Eucharist as Sacrifice* (p. 188, n. 3).

One way of both verifying the picture presented above and extending it is to look at what a given church has been doing in bilaterals beyond those examples already noted. To illustrate with the Lutherans in America, there have been other bilateral involvements, but not dealing with the Holy Communion. For example, Lutheran-Methodist dialogue, both internationally and regionally, has dealt with topics other than the Lord's Supper. The U.S. Lutheran–United Methodist first round (1977–79) concentrated on baptism *(Perkins Journal* 34 [1981]: 1–56). But it was observed at its initial consultation in 1977 that Luther's insistence on Christ's real and bodily presence in the Supper (with the result that "every metaphor and metonymy" is rejected in interpreting the Words of Institution) has probably taken a back seat amid American pluralism in religion. Such an observation about modern content can be undergirded by the claim that—while American Lutherans have, especially in the last twenty years, put greater emphasis upon frequent Communion services as the center of church life (as have other denominations)—they now stress less than before a "real, corporeal presence" in the elements, at least according to a sociological survey of five thousand Lutherans (M. P. Strommen, et al., *A Study of Generations* [Minneapolis: Augsburg Publishing House, 1972], chapter 5). The Lutheran-Conservative Evangelical dialogue (reported in *The Covenant Quarterly* 41 [1983]: 1–99) does not, as one might expect, deal with the Eucharist. So, from this sample profile, we are probably justified in concluding that examination of other dialogues adds little on the Eucharist.

But attention must also be given to other types of dialogue work by "professional ecumenists," for example, in groups of responsible theologians who are not necessarily appointed by their hierarchies or respective church authorities. In France for some years, under the leadership originally of Abbé Paul Couturier (1881–1953), Roman Catholics and Protestants (Reformed and Lutheran) gathered periodically to discuss theological issues. (Cf. Geoffrey Curtis, *Paul Couturier and Unity in Christ* [London: SCM Press, 1964].) In 1972 this "Group of Les Dombes" (so called because of sessions at the Trappist monastery of Notre Dame des Dombes near Lyon) produced a statement containing both doctrinal and pastoral agreements on the Eucharist. Their emphases—the Lord's Supper; Act of Thanksgiving to the Father; Memorial of Christ; Gift of the Spirit; Sacramental Presence of Christ; Communion in the Body of Christ; A Mission in the World; and Banquet of the Kingdom—catch up very systematically themes found in other statements, including those of Faith and Order. (Frère Max Thurian, president of the steering group that drafted *BEM,* was one of the fourteen Protestants involved in the Group of Les Dombes text in 1972.)

A final example is the volume on *The Eucharist in Ecumenical Dialogue* (New York: Paulist Press, originally published as a special issue of the *Journal of Ecumenical Studies* 13, 2 [Spring 1976] in connection with the International Eucharistic Conference in Philadelphia in 1976). The idea was to focus on Roman Catholic dialogues with the Orthodox, Anglicans, Lutherans, Reformed, Methodists, and Baptists, and even the Jews, on the topic of the Eucharist. Of course, in only some cases could the essayists point to actual bilateral attention to the topic. The editor, Professor Leonard Swidler, argues that (1) the Second Vatican Council intended the Eucharist as a means of grace to foster unity among Christians, but (2) the *Directory Concerning Ecumenical Matters* published in Rome after the Council (1972) reversed that direction by making no provision for ecumenically shared Eucharists as a means of promoting Christian unity; but (3) the bilaterals have shown "quite startling general agreement" on the ministry, Eucharist as sacrifice, real presence, and intercommunion. As evidence for the first point, the Decree on Ecumenism *(Unitatis Redintegratio,* 1964) is cited, that *communio in sacris* is not "to be used indiscriminately for the restoration of unity among Christians." Does that mean it is to be used "discriminately"? (The point is reiterated, from the same source, in the U.S. Roman Catholic–Presbyterian-Reformed Consultation Statement, "The Unity We Seek" [Washington, D.C., 1975], pp. 81–82.) If so, Lutheran-Episcopal Interim Sharing of the Eucharist is the application of a Vatican II idea.

Even if the commonalities laid out in this symposium, *The Eucharist in Ecumenical Dialogue,* are somewhat overstated, the similarities of bilateral after bilateral are impressive. What might all these Christians be able to say together? *BEM* is, of course, a multilateral effort to answer that question.

Before turning to that statement, however, it is necessary to remind ourselves of two notes of reality lest Faith and Order's achievement seem to have been too easily accomplished. First, for all its dialogue and Faith-and-Order involvement, the Eastern Orthodox Church has affirmed the "ecclesial status" of other Christian churches by no official act; even where the Roman Catholic Church has offered Communion to the Orthodox, there has been no reciprocal Orthodox move or even "permission to the Orthodox faithful to accept the offer of Roman Catholic communion" (M. Aghiorgoussis, in *The Eucharist in Ecumenical Dialogue,* pp. 13, 15, 19). Second, many of the ecumenists who labor in the bilaterals are also Faith and Order participants. There is therefore a kind of "outsider's" fear in some quarters that "professional experts" have been calling the shots who may not represent their church constituencies, at least not the rank and file.

The feeling that a church in bilateral dialogues might "talk out of both sides of its mouth" has been officially perceived. There is a fear that there could be "convergence" with almost *anyone,* as long as the right "pussy-footing theologians" (to echo the tag often wrongly pinned on Melanchthon) were named to the right dialogues! Catholics were concerned enough about this matter to do a review and critique of their bilaterals in 1972 *(Proceedings of the Catholic Theological Society of America,* vol. 27). Lutherans in the United States did a blue-ribbon committee study in

1977, *Lutherans in Ecumenical Dialogue.* The LWF has done studies on "the interrelations between the various bilaterals" (1977) and, more broadly, on "Ecumenical Methodology" (1972–78). U.S. Roman Catholics repeated their review-and-critique process in 1979 *(Proceedings* 34).

In general, it may be said, these attempts to thoroughly examine the ecumenical discussions have concluded that there is a high degree of internal consistency within them.

> The positions taken by Lutherans in the various dialogues do not in any overt way contradict one another, but whether they are fully consistent in every sense would be hard to demonstrate. *(Lutherans in Ecumenical Dialogue, p. 30)*

Specifically, on the Lord's Supper as discussed in the Malta, Leuenberg, and Anglican-Lutheran International ("Pullach") reports, it is said:

> Lutherans have been bearing witness to their confessional heritage and have adapted it to the present day situation of ecumenical debate. *(Ecumenical Relations, LWF, p. 18)*

Nonetheless, as the same report goes on, criticisms can be made. The tendency in dialogue has been, necessarily, to go back over past problems. But "an honest facing up to the problem of the Eucharist in the context of the present secularized world might transcend the historical burden of theological problems we carry with us" (p. 19). Moreover, each bilateral speaks in a specific context but does not seek "a comprehensive treatment" of the whole topic, theologically or for praxis; hence the tasks of the systematician (and of liturgiologists and the parish pastor as local synthesizer, theologian, and practitioner) continue nonetheless. Carl E. Braaten, in an independent assessment of ten years of bilaterals (1974), spoke of the overemphasis on "retrieval operations" and salvage of sacred (Catholic) words on which "our forefathers stubbed their toes" and which are now given Lutheran meanings. A higher level of hermeneutic is therefore needed. What is really happening, he suggested, is that each side has come to see "a real and genuine grasp of the truth of Christ" in the other side and "the provisional status of all religious experience," including one's own. But, Braaten asks, why press for language about "sacrifice" when New Testament studies emphasize the "eschatological horizon"?

The analysis by U.S. Roman Catholics in 1972 of documents from four dialogues (Anglican, Lutheran, Disciples of Christ, and Orthodox) found "surprising unanimity," showing a "dramatic advance" over past polemics. Of course, each dialogue accents "what Catholics share in common" with the other tradition: with the Christian Church (Disciples of Christ), "religious experience"; with Lutherans, "the primacy of Christ"; "ARC[IC] emphasizes sacrifice, and Orth[odox] Cath[olic] emphasizes the role of the Holy Spirit." But this provides "a healthy mutual complementarity" (p. 215). The 1979 report does not reach any different view on the matter but does chide "most of the consultations" for not taking "into explicit account the works of the other bilateral groups" (p. 281).

If there has thus been progress two by two, it is by no means an automatic matter or even an easy task to bring *all* the many churches of Christendom together with reference to the Lord's Supper.

FAITH AND ORDER: EUCHARIST IN *BEM* (1982)

The development of a statement on the Eucharist on the part of the Faith and Order Commission along with one on Baptism, together with the inevitably interrelated question of Ministry, was noted on pp. 80–85, above. The task was the work of several decades, first under Lukas Vischer and then under William Lazareth (1979–83). Probably the highlight of the Commission's long history, the text of *Baptism, Eucharist and Ministry* was completed at its triennial meeting in Lima, Peru, 2–16 January 1982, where it was unanimously voted that *BEM* was ready for transmission to the churches. We now focus on its eight pages of text and commentary on Eucharist (pp. 10–17).

The Background and Future of the *BEM* Statement
Development

It has already been indicated that the Faith and Order text on the Eucharist has a fifty-five-year history. The process began with the Lausanne (Switzerland) Conference, the first of that movement in 1927, and was furthered at the second conference in Edinburgh 1937 and at the third in Lund 1952 (see Figure 1, above). By that time ecumenism had begun to advance beyond simple comparison of traditions. A foundation never to be overlooked in the whole process was the Fourth World Conference on Faith and Order (Montreal 1963), where there was a fundamental agreement regarding Scripture, Tradition (with a capital), and the traditions (lower-case and plural) whereby

> we can say that we exist as Christians by the Tradition of the Gospel (the *paradosis* of the *kerygma)* testified in Scripture, transmitted in and by the Church through the power of the Holy Spirit. *(Montreal Report,* Section II, par. 45, p. 52, cited in *Ecumenical Perspectives,* p. xvi, and in part in *BEM,* p. ix)

That is to say, one seeks to return to the "primary sources" in Scripture and in Tradition as "the Holy Spirit explaining the Gospel to the Church" *(Ecumenical Perspectives,* p. xvi), behind our separate Orthodox, Roman, Lutheran, Anglican, or other traditions.

It is a praiseworthy feature of the Faith and Order movement that it seldom pursued one topic in isolation from other topics. Christology, ecclesiology, worship, and the world or creation were constantly interwoven with the themes that became the focus of *BEM* during commission meetings in the 1960s and 1970s. "Hope" was a topic even as the commission dealt with the latest draft on *BEM* at Bangalore in 1978.

A point of considerable significance came at the Bristol meeting of the Commission in 1967. At that time Roman Catholic theologians were participating, as a result of Vatican II, and a plan was being developed to speak on the sacraments and ministry, employing material from existing reports, liturgies, and practice, with the ultimate aim of churches mutually recognizing each other in these areas. Already at the Louvain meeting of the Commission in 1971 a report was presented on *Baptism, Confirmation and the Eucharist.* The road to Accra and Lima had begun.

Actually, however, each section of *BEM* has a history of its own. The story of the Baptism section has, for example, been recounted by such participants as Geoffrey Wainwright (originally in *Studia Liturgica* 12 [1977]: 67–68, and revised in his *Ecumenical Moment,* pp. 31–53) and Gunter Wagner ("Baptism from Accra to Lima," in Faith and Order Paper No. 116, pp. 12–32). In broad terms, a first draft on the Eucharist was produced after the Bristol meeting in 1967 (where a section of the Commission's work was devoted to "The Eucharist, A Sacrament of Unity"). The first draft on Baptism was ready by 1970, and by 1972 the draft was ready on Ministry. In the words of William Lazareth, the Director of the Secretariat when Faith and Order completed *BEM,* and Max Thurian, Study Advisor and head of the steering group in that statement's final stages, the section on Eucharist "evolved in a fairly consistent way from 1967 to 1982"; however, the section on Baptism underwent "fairly radical recasting," and the original draft on Ministry was replaced by a "much longer" one that was then "skimmed down" (Paper No. 116, p. xv).

While there was some development in the section on the Eucharist, comparison of the 1967 Provisional and Second Drafts (reprinted in Paper No. 116, pp. 198–209), of the Accra Statement of 1974, and of *BEM* in 1982 shows that the development was "homogenous," the first draft containing "all the elements later made explicit and specified" (ibid., p. 197). In other words, *BEM* on the Eucharist was basically complete in the late 1960s and early 1970s. One may verify this through the remarks by Lukas Vischer in the Accra Statement on how the three statements came into existence (Paper No. 73, pp. 58–61); he emphasizes even more how the Baptism and Eucharist portions draw on previous conference agreements, but the Ministry section derives from then-current debate and emerging perspectives.

The 1974 versions could be described in their subtitles as "agreed statements." No such phrase appears with the Lima text of 1982. Instead, one hears of the unanimous decision of the Commission to transmit the text to the churches. But one should not make more of either point than is warranted. For the three reports from Accra "do not represent a consensus in the fullest sense of that word" but rather "a summary of shared convictions and perspectives"; nor do they give "a complete theological treatment," let alone one in "the language of our time" (Paper No. 73, pp. 6–7). The Lima unanimity has to do not with every item in its contents but with a feeling across the group that the Commission had perfected *BEM* as fully as it could; it was now time for the churches to react. Therefore, one ought to look at the material not as a ukase from a world court of theologians voting 9–0 but as an agreed survey of the terrain, where problems are indicated on which representatives could not always agree but which stare the churches in the face.

One way to perceive this nature of *BEM* is to distinguish the "main text," which shows the theological convergence, and the "commentary," where one finds indicated "historical differences that have been overcome" or "disputed issues still in need of further research and reconciliation" (p. ix). Another way is to note the "extra" consultations before Lima where particular concerns could be heard. Of signal importance for

Baptism was the special consultation in Louisville, Kentucky, in 1978, where the views of adherents of believers' baptism, especially U.S. (Southern) Baptists, were enunciated to churches that traditionally baptize infants (Paper No. 79; cf. *BEM*, Baptism IV.A). With regard to episcopacy, there was a special Geneva consultation in 1979 (Paper No. 102), and "the draft text was also reviewed by representatives of Orthodox Churches" that same year *(BEM*, p. viii). Though no similar conference on the Lord's Supper is listed in *BEM*, a consultation did take place in 1980 at Bad Sagerberg, near Hamburg, Germany, on "eucharist with children" (Paper No. 109, *". . . and do not hinder them": An ecumenical plea for the admission of children to the eucharist,* ed. Geiko Müller-Fahrenholz, 1982).

If "infant baptism" versus "believers' baptism" is an ecumenical issue of controversy in Part I of *BEM,* then, presumably, child or infant communion is an issue in Part II. To no one's surprise, episcopacy, historic episcopate, and threefold office of ordained ministry are the issues in Part III.

Toward A.D. 2000

BEM itself (p. x) indicates that its text relates to a long-range "research project" called "Towards the Common Expression of the Apostolic Faith Today." The roots for this ambitious undertaking lie partly in the celebration in 1981 of the sixteen hundredth anniversary of the Council of Constantinople (with Faith and Order Paper No. 103, *Spirit of God, Spirit of Christ* [London: SPCK, 1981], aimed at settling East-West controversy over the *Filioque* in the Creed, over whether the Holy Spirit "proceeds from the Father *and the Son")* and discussion of the disputed christological dogma of the Council of Chalcedon, A.D. 451. (The Monophysite churches of the East—Coptic, Abyssinian, Syrian Jacobite, and Armenian—never accepted the Chalcedonian Formula. Out of unofficial consultations [1964-71], an Eastern Orthodox–Oriental Orthodox dialogue has grown up; see Ehrenström-Gassmann, pp. 46–47. Faith and Order published a paper in 1981, *Does Chalcedon Divide or Unite?)* There have also been initiated by Faith and Order some consultations on the nature of faith and confessing the faith; cf. *Giving Account of the Hope Today* [that is within us, 1 Peter 3:15] (Paper No. 81, 1976); *Towards a Confession of the Common Faith* (Paper No. 100, 1980); and the collection of contemporary confessional statements, *Confessing Our Faith*

Around the World (Paper No. 104, 1980). A brief account of the whole study process on "the Apostolic Faith today" is given in *Towards Visible Unity* (Vol. II, pp. 4–12). In addition there has been attention in the work of Faith and Order to "conciliar unity," that is, the quest for reunion through ecumenical councils (Bangalore, 1978).

It needs to be said that this project on contemporary expression of the apostolic faith, as well as another on the "Unity of the Church and the Renewal of Human Community," was on the agenda of the Lima meeting of Faith and Order along with the *BEM* text (see *Towards Visible Unity*, Vols. I, Minutes, and II, Papers). Further, it has become apparent that in ecumenical circles the Nicene Creed (traditionally dated A.D. 325 and 381 but more likely fifth century and customarily recited at the Eucharist) provides the preeminent expression of the church's faith in the post–New Testament "building period," before the "time of divisions" (Chalcedon and beyond) (cf. *The Nicene Creed: Our Common Faith* by Emilianos Timiadis [Philadelphia: Fortress Press, 1983]). Finally, it is recognized that "a common contemporary statement of faith," interpreting the Nicene Creed for today, is much desired, but that must be the work of a future council. *BEM*, "A Common Account of Hope," and the Bangalore text (1978) could, however, all be steppingstones to such a "new creed" (see U. Kuhn, in *Towards Visible Unity*, Vol. II, pp. 13–23). Committees have been at work, for example, examining *BEM* for its contents and implications on almost every major doctrine in the Christian faith.

It is no surprise, therefore, that some have suggested the year 2000 might be the proper time, if we rightly planned ahead, for a "truly ecumenical gathering of Christians." At that pivotal date, a new creed might be worked out. (Cf. Michael Fahey, "Christian Unity by 2000?" *One in Christ* 19 [1983]: 2–13; or William Boney, "Christian Responsibility and the Year 2000," *Ecumenical Trends* 9 [1980].) Toward all this *BEM* could point.

Outline and Structure of the 1982 Statement

There are several ways to get at the meaning of the thus crucial *BEM* text and appreciate what it is saying and is not saying.

Baptism and Eucharist

One method is to examine *BEM* as a document "as is," comparing each part in it with the other two. Here it readily becomes apparent that the section on Ministry differs from the others in structure, as might be expected from the contents and from the way in which this section evolved within Faith and Order (see above). However, the first two sections of *BEM* do exhibit a comparable outline:

Baptism (pp. 2–7)	*Eucharist (pp. 10–17)*
I. The Institution of Baptism (#1)	I. The Institution of the Eucharist (#1)
II. The Meaning of Baptism (#2)	II. The Meaning of the Eucharist (#2)
A. Participation in Christ's Death and Resurrection (#3)	A. The Eucharist as Thanksgiving to the Father (##3–4)
B. Conversion, Pardoning and Cleansing (#4)	B. The Eucharist as Anamnesis or Memorial of Christ (##5–13)
C. The Gift of the Spirit (#5)	C. The Eucharist as Invocation of the Spirit (##14–18)
D. Incorporation into the Body of Christ (#6)	D. The Eucharist as Communion of the Faithful (##19–21)
E. The Sign of the Kingdom (#7)	E. The Eucharist as Meal of the Kingdom (##22–26)
III. Baptism and Faith (##8–10)	(cf. Eucharist II.D)
IV. Baptismal Practice	
A. Baptism of Believers and Infants (##11–13)	(cf. Eucharist, Commentary #19)
B. Baptism-Chrismation-Confirmation (#14)	
C. Towards Mutual Recognition of Baptism (##15–16)	
V. The Celebration of Baptism (##17–23)	III. The Celebration of the Eucharist (##27–33)

The common outline runs "institution, meaning, celebration." Under Part II there is a certain paralleling with the terms "Spirit," "faith(ful)"

(Eucharist ##19–21; Baptism ##8–10), and "kingdom." But there is also an unexpected lack of parallel; why, for example, is there nothing on the "mutual recognition of Eucharist"? Is the best to be hoped that *"some* churches" may "attain a greater measure of eucharistic communion among themselves" (#33, italics added)? In the parallelism that does exist one should probably not, however, assume any notion of an *Ursakrament* or common notion of "the sacramental" behind each specific topic with its own historical profile.

Evolution of the Drafts on Eucharist

A second method involves tracing out historically the evolution of the Eucharist section, from first draft in 1967, based as it was on Faith and Order statements at Lund (1952), Montreal (1963), and Bristol (1967), through the Accra "agreed statement" (1974), to the text with commentary (1982) now before the churches. For the section on Baptism an interesting example of such textual and tradition criticism has been provided by the Baptist New Testament scholar in Switzerland, Gunter Wagner (in Paper No. 116, pp. 12–32, "Baptism from Accra to Lima"). In such a study historians can further call attention to influences from, or reciprocated in, the bilaterals during the course of development of the Faith and Order drafts.

Wagner's essay is helpful in examining the development of a *BEM* section over an eight-year period. He points out omissions and additions and changes in outline and arrangement of Baptism from Accra to Lima. He even awards medals—gold, silver, and bronze—for sections least changed in the process. (Lima #17 remains verbatim the same as Accra #9, the only paragraph to survive intact, but then it consisted of just a single sentence.) For our purposes, perhaps Wagner's most interesting observation is that Accra on Baptism, #6, about "Eucharistic Sharing" as an implication of baptism, has been entirely omitted in *BEM*. Accra had called attention to the point thus:

> There is a necessary relationship between our understanding and practice of baptism and our understanding and practice of the Lord's Supper. We must learn afresh the implications of baptism for our sharing in the eucharist. (#6) Our failure to share in the one Table of the Lord, to live and act as one visible and united body appears to many a contradiction of the baptismal gift that we all claim to have received.

This "thrust" at Accra toward "mutual acceptance at the Lord's Table on the basis of our common baptism" has been replaced in *BEM* by one simply "towards the mutual recognition of baptism" (Lima, Baptism ##15–16; Wagner, Paper No. 116, p. 14).

While Wagner writes (p. 13), "as far as I can see, the Lima text on the 'Eucharist' does not repair the damage" of this omission of eucharistic sharing interdenominationally as an implication of baptism, one must note the Lima Commentary to its Eucharist #19,

> there is discussion in many churches today about the inclusion of baptized children as communicants at the Lord's Supper. *(BEM, p. 15)*

That is an implication for "eucharistic sharing from baptism," but applied to children, not divided denominations.

Those interested in the most neuralgic issue raised in *BEM* about baptism—the issue of infant versus believers' baptism and whether the solution is for the churches to accept both as "equivalent alternatives" (Lima, Baptism #12, especially the Commentary on it)—should especially examine Wagner's "Baptist response" (pp. 24–28). Here he compares three models of baptism suggested in the Lima text:

A. The Baptist model: "baptism upon personal profession of faith" (Lima #11);
B. The (Eastern) Orthodox model: baptism "with the gift of the Holy Spirit and participation in holy communion" (Lima #20);
C. The Process model: where baptism at an early age is followed later by personal confession and commitment (Lima #15).

Wagner's own analysis is that models A and B are the true competitors, with the deepest difference being between "sacramental objectivism" (in B) and "emphasis on the faith-reception of the sacrament" (in A); he regards model C as "the bridge leading eventually to an ecumenical understanding of Christian initiation" (p. 27). In a process of initiation, confession-of-faith/confirmation would have such a role that infant baptism could then parallel believers' baptism as "equivalent alternatives." So Wagner maintains. Once again we see the interrelatedness of topics like baptism and Eucharist and the ecumenical challenge of different models or sacramental systems.

An analysis of Eucharist in *BEM*, tracing its development from earlier drafts, is definitely one way to ascertain the meaning and nuances of the section. However, it would have to take into consideration stages prior to

Accra, because so much of the section on the Lord's Supper had been drafted at an earlier stage than the Baptism section.

We shall use both the method of internal comparison among *BEM*'s three parts and the method of historical development of the 1982 document, together with attention to the bilateral statements and to Scripture as prime source, in discussing the contents on the Eucharist.

Outlines on the Eucharist

Before delving into the major subdivisions of the Eucharist section of *BEM*, it will be helpful to lay out one more matter, the skeleton outline of the 1982 statement and its predecessor drafts (see page 146).

The point, previously stated, that what becomes explicit in the Lima document was already implicit in the 1967 draft, is generally true. In some ways what appear to be changes in the outline turn out not to be when the text itself is examined, for the contents that seem missing at one point appear elsewhere in *BEM*. To explain this, here are further comments about additions, deletions, and shifts in structure.

1. The 1967 "Preamble" provided a setting in "the Word" for the two sacraments of baptism ("never repeated") and the Lord's Supper ("constantly repeated"). God makes present through the Holy Spirit the unique events of Christ's incarnation, life, death, resurrection, and ascension (cf. Lima #6). Accra #1 retained most of this material, and Accra #2 carries over verbatim a paragraph from the Second Draft of 1967. All this material is dropped in the Lima statement.

Thus, Lima lacks any overall reference to "the Word" such as occurred in the *Anglican-Lutheran International Conversations* ("The Word and the Sacraments"), or U.S. LED II ("Justification, the Gospel, Eucharistic Presence"), or even an overall theme as in ARCIC's *Final Report* where such a theme appeared in terms of *koinonia*. This makes it all the more important to assume for *BEM* a background in earlier statements of Faith and Order—like the one at Montreal—on Scripture or on gospel or in its concurrent work on confessing the faith.

2. The paragraphs on "Institution" first appeared in the Accra version and are expanded in the Lima text. This is perhaps the most difficult section to find prefigured in the 1967 drafts, for example in the reference to the Passover of Israel and the many names the meal has acquired *(BEM,* end of #1, p. 10). On names for the Supper, cf. ARCIC Windsor Statement, section 1 (*The Final Report*, p. 12; above, p. 111).

3. The material under the first point in the 1967 versions, about the

1967 Provisional Draft	*Accra 1974*	*Lima 1982*
Preamble: Word, Baptism and Eucharist (Second draft: Preamble)	Preamble (##1, 2)	
	I. The Institution of the Eucharist (##3–5)	I. The Institution of the Eucharist (#1)
	II. The Meaning of the Eucharist (#6–22)	II. The Meaning of the Eucharist (##2–26)
1. The Eucharist, as a meal and as the Lord's Sacrament (Second draft: The Eucharist, the Lord's Supper)		
2. The Eucharist, thanksgiving to the Father	A. The Eucharist: thanksgiving to the Father (##6–7)	A. The Eucharist as Thanksgiving to the Father (##3–4)
3. The Eucharist, the memorial of Christ (Second draft adds "anamnesis" after "memorial")	B. The Eucharist: Anamnesis or Memorial (Representation and Anticipation of Christ) (##8–13)	B. The Eucharist as Anamnesis or Memorial of Christ (##5–13)
4. The Eucharist, the invocation of the Spirit (Second draft: "gift of the Spirit")	C. The Eucharist: Invocation and Gift of the Spirit (##14–18)	C. The Eucharist as Invocation of the Spirit (##14–18)
5. The Eucharist, communion of the body of Christ	D. The Eucharist: Communion within the Body of Christ (##19–22)	D. The Eucharist as Communion of the Faithful (##19–21)
		E. The Eucharist as Meal of the Kingdom (##22–26)
	III. Implications of the Eucharist	
(Second draft: 6: The Eucharist, mission to the world)	A. The Eucharist: Mission to the World (##23–26)	
(Second draft: 7. The Eucharist, end of divisions)	B. The Eucharist: Ending of Divisions (#27)	
6. The celebration of the Eucharist	IV. The Elements of the Eucharist (##28–30)	III. The Celebration of the Eucharist (##27–33)
	V. Recommendations (##31–36)	

Eucharist as "Meal" and "Lord's Sacrament or Supper," appears in the 1974 draft as Accra ##3–5. Very little of this material survived in the Lima text, where #1 on "Institution" is quite different from anything in the prior drafts.

4. The heart of the section on the meaning of the Eucharist, about Father, Christ, Spirit, and communion with one another in the church (*BEM*, Eucharist, II.A, B, C, and D), comes very much out of the Accra statement, which in turn rested squarely and often verbatim on the 1967 drafts, especially the second one. The earlier versions indicate the source of each quotation in previous Faith and Order statements, either by footnotes or (in the 1967 Second Draft) by quotation marks. The Lima text, we may observe, has been more careful to use inclusive language (men *and women;* human beings) and to drop words like "anamnetic" (an adjectival form of "anamnesis") from its paraphrase of such statements from fifteen to almost thirty years before.

5. *BEM* II. E on the "Meal of the Kingdom" (##22–26), while appearing new, draws on Accra's section about "mission to the world" (##24–25). The Accra paragraphs (which came in turn from the Second Draft in 1967 but were seemingly fresh creations then, not drawn from earlier Faith and Order statements) are introduced in *BEM* by an eschatological note, "the vision of the divine rule which has been promised as the final renewal of creation," but this future aspect is immediately followed by a present eschatological reference to Eucharist as "foretaste" amid "signs of this renewal" in the world (#22) and to the "new reality" the Eucharist brings, "which transforms Christians into the image of Christ." But it is then added, ". . . and therefore makes them his effective witnesses" (#26). The mission note is also struck by #25, an improved rewriting of Accra #23 (see analysis below).

6. The emphasis in earlier drafts on the Eucharist as an "end of divisions" finds a pale reflection in Lima #26, again in connection with witness, in the statement that the inability of Christians "to unite in full fellowship around the same table" weakens their "missionary witness." Accra #27, quoting Bristol 1967, *New Directions in Faith and Order* (3, III, 3, p. 63), had been much more blunt in deriving eucharistic rights from baptism:

> When, therefore, the right of the baptized members and their ministers to participate in and preside over eucharistic celebration in one church is called into question by those who preside over and are members of other eucharistic congregations, the catholicity of the eucharist is obscured.

BEM preserves this only in its Commentary on Eucharist #19. The Second Draft from 1967 had also been bold to say, concerning the world, "The Eucharist is also the feast of the continuing apostolic harvest, where the Church rejoices for the gifts received in the world *and welcomes every man of good will"* (p. 207, italics added). Accra #26 excised the last seven words, and the whole paragraph has disappeared in the Lima text.

The heady hopes of 1967 seem to have evaporated in light of subsequent hard experience, as in the bilaterals, that recognition of each other's baptism does not readily translate into agreement on Eucharist and ministry, let alone a *communio in sacris* with all persons (unbaptized?) of good will. Lima seems to have backed away from hopes about intercommunion (1967, Second Draft, pp. 208–9), keeping a mild tone of rebuke about the weakening of "missionary witness" at a divided table, all under the heading of the "meal of the kingdom" (cf. also Lima #33 with Accra #36).

7. What earlier statements said about "the celebration of the Eucharist" or elements that make up the eucharistic liturgy appears in the Lima text (#27) in an expanded form. Such a listing appeared already on the Provisional Draft and occurred in the Preamble of the Second Draft. Lima puts into an itemized list what Accra (#28) distinguished as elements "usually" occurring and those which this list "is not meant to exclude" (but of less wide use in Christendom and therefore of less importance?).

8. The "Recommendations" at Accra appear in the Lima statement in ##28, 31, and 32. In general, this is a movement from "commands" to "requests to consider":

> 1967 (p. 208): "The question of intercommunion demands. . . . The Churches . . . should address themselves to the following questions: . . ."
> 1974 (Accra #35): "it is desirable. . . ."
> 1982 *(BEM #32):* "it is worthwhile to suggest. . . ."

A Thesis to Be Tested

From this analysis, a preliminary conclusion emerges: in *BEM* the Eucharist section is a text rewritten, partly in light of responses of the churches to the Accra statement (cf. Paper No. 84, *Towards an Ecumen-*

ical Consensus on Baptism, Eucharist, and Ministry), but it stems basically from earlier drafts in 1967; these, in turn, rest on Faith and Order statements (occasionally, the Group of Les Dombes, cf. Accra, notes 9 and 18) which date from 1967 (Bristol), 1963 (Montreal), and 1952 (Lund). Put another way, the foundations of *BEM*'s Eucharist are, to a great extent, pre-bilateral dialogues and only beginning to be informed by Vatican II (often in the most optimistic period, immediately after the Council). In terms of biblical scholarship, this means by and large the exegetical approach and biblical theology positions are from the era of Joachim Jeremias and Oscar Cullmann, for example, and the position of historical liturgiology from Dom Gregory Dix especially. We shall bear these possibilities in mind in examining the actual contents, section by section, of the Lima text and commentary.

Assessing the Text and Commentary on Eucharist

Aware of the structure and background of *BEM,* we now move from source and tradition criticism of its Eucharist section to redaction criticism of the finished composition. We turn to analysis of its thirty-three paragraphs and half-dozen "Commentary" sections, examining the document as it has been presented to the churches for reaction. We follow its own outline.

I. The Institution of the Eucharist

BEM's text begins with an important thematic statement: "The Church receives the eucharist as a gift from the Lord." First Corinthians 11:23-25 is then quoted, with its reference to *anamnesis;* in the Bible passage, "from the Lord" refers to a tradition Paul received, not the sacrament itself. The Synoptic parallels are cited. Then in a second, long paragraph the roots of the Lord's Supper are mentioned: meals Jesus shared during his earthly ministry, including "the feeding of the multitudes," his last meal, and "the breaking of the bread" after his resurrection (cf. pp. 2-5, above, including the reference to the Cullmann-Leenhardt *Essays*). The past, present, and future are joined together in Israel's Passover memorial, Christ's new covenant, and anticipation of the Supper of the Lamb. The (Jewish) "liturgical meal" (actually, family worship) that Jesus celebrated with symbolic words and actions is linked to the "sacramental meal" of the church where "visible signs" communicate God's love to us. Some of the many names of the meal are noted (with no preferred one stated), and the note is struck of its celebration "as the central act of the Church's worship."

This section (#1), basically new since the Accra statement, broadens the picture there that tied the dominical institution to the Upper Room (Accra #3) so as now to include other meals of Jesus before and after Easter. This position reflects New Testament scholarship as it already existed in the 1950s.

The criticism by G. Wagner (Paper No. 116, p. 14) regarding *BEM* on Baptism, about the first section "including sentences which seem to belong under the heading of the *meaning* of Baptism, rather than its *institution*," could also apply here. But his answer there also applies on Eucharist: "one's understanding of the meaning of the rite determines also one's description of its institution."

More pointedly in the Baptism section, *BEM* faced a problem in how to use the Bible. To refer to the sacraments being "instituted by Jesus Christ" (Accra #1) runs into the problem, when citing Matt. 28:18–20 (as Lima #1 does), of differences between "theologians strongly advocating the 'trinitarian approach' and exegetes with their historical-critical interpretation" of the Matthean verses (p. 15). In the case of the Lord's Supper, *BEM* has, in effect, moved beyond the traditional position of a direct and sole line of influence from the Upper Room to a view of multiple origins.

Perhaps, some may feel, the Words of Institution deserve more prominence amid the triple listing of meals in Eucharist #2, but then the tradition of 1 Cor. 11:23–25 has been quoted, though without any kind of development of the meal within the New Testament period. The most interesting treatment of this matter in the predecessor documents to Lima is in *Bristol 1967* (Paper No. 50, pp. 64–66) which seeks to distinguish and relate "Eucharist and Agape" in the early church while keeping the "agapeic character of the Eucharist."

II. The Meaning of the Eucharist (Five Aspects)

An introductory paragraph (#2) to what is the heart of the text on Eucharist (##3–26)—namely its five meanings—reiterates in a trinitarian structure the point of the lead sentence in #1: "The eucharist is essentially the sacrament of the *gift* which *God* makes to us in *Christ* through the power of the *Holy Spirit*" (italics added). This gift comes to every Christian through the eating and drinking. Communion has, seemingly, results both corporate ("giving life to the body of Christ") and individual ("renewing each member"—forgiveness of sins, eternal life). Before listing the five aspects under which the statement will proceed, the paragraph insists "the eucharist is essentially one complete act," a point perhaps better stated in #27, "The eucharistic liturgy is a single whole," a phrase used in the Preamble of Accra (#2).

Before looking at the five aspects which for purposes of analysis must be listed separately, attention may be given to their structure and sequence:

The Eucharist as	key theological theme	key Greek term
A. Thanksgiving to the Father	Father	*eucharistia*
B. Memorial of Christ	Christ	*anamnesis*
C. Invocation of the Spirit	Spirit	*epiklesis*
D. Communion of the Faithful	ecclesiology	*koinonia* (?)
E. Meal of the Kingdom	eschatology, mission, and world	

The trinitarian sequence of aspects A, B, and C is reasonably clear, especially in light of #2. As for the key New Testament words, "Eucharist" derives, of course, from the Greek word for "thanksgiving," *eucharistia,* a point further suggested by use of the Hebrew *berakah* in #3 (though it is translated there as "benediction," and the point will turn out to be not quite so simple). *Anamnesis* is the word behind "memorial" or "remembrance" (as in 1 Cor. 11:24, 25; cited in #1). The noun *epiklesis* ("invocation") is not a New Testament occurrence, though the verb is— "to 'call on' the name of our Lord," as in 1 Cor. 1:2. While Lima uses *epiklesis* only in its Commentary on C #14, it employs the adjective "epikletic" in #16, and Accra had said, for better or for worse, "The *anamnesis* leads to *epiklesis*" (#14). All this simply follows Bristol's section, "The Anamnetic and Epikletic Character of the Eucharist" (Paper No. 50, pp. 61–62). Readers can be grateful that the drafting process has minimized such language.

Aspect D, Communion of the Faithful, is more problematic. "Communion" is obviously the key word (#19), with Christ and with one another in the body of Christ. Behind the Latin *communio,* one can posit the Greek New Testament term *koinonia,* as in ARCIC's *Final Report.* In some ways, therefore, the section is about ecclesiology, and references to "the church" should be noted.

Aspect E, Meal of the Kingdom, uses Accra material on the mission of the church to the world within an eschatological setting. Some of the Accra material (#21) goes back to Bristol on "agapeic implications of the Eucharist" (Paper No. 50, p. 64), but the material has been reworked several times; while often biblical in terms, it has no obvious Greek term behind it.

Are these five aspects adequate for summing up what needs to be said about the Lord's Supper? The bilaterals are of little help here, for they have been concerned chiefly with points disputed between two traditions, not in articulating a comprehensive view.

BEM is, of course, well advised not to follow the structure of a theology on this sacrament found in any one later tradition. The framers of the Eucharist section were well aware that they were not setting forth an absolutely full account; as Accra (#2) put it, "No document could be a complete exposition of every aspect of eucharistic thought."

Measured by New Testament standards, the *BEM* treatment may be weak on eschatology (cf. pp. 23–26, above; G. Wainwright, *Eucharist and Eschatology,* especially pp. 128–53, and his *The Ecumenical Moment,* pp. 120–33). What *BEM* says is not uneschatological, though aspect E seems a late and mixed appendage, more on "realized" than "future" eschatology.

Some might want "covenant" stressed more, or "faith," or "judgment" and "discernment" (see above, pp. 34ff.), but *BEM* touches on all these items (the last pair perhaps least).

Measured by later disputes in the history of eucharistic doctrine and practice, the statement does well. It touches on "presence" and "sacrifice" under B, the memorial aspect. It raises some classic questions from East-West theological debate and within Western Christianity in the Commentary on aspect C, the *epiklesis* of the Spirit. The Commentary in #19 touches on the relation of baptism to Eucharist, noting briefly the matter of recognition of the "authenticity" of other churches' communions and more specifically the question raised by longtime praxis of the Eastern Orthodox, "the inclusion of baptized children as communicants at the Lord's Supper." The final Commentary section (#28) raises the problem of whether "local food and drink" can be substituted for bread and wine; that is, what was "unchangeably instituted by Jesus" and what can the church decide to change?

Until proven otherwise, the list of aspects may be termed adequate, if not complete. A further question is whether the items under each aspect belong there or do justice to the topic.

A. The Eucharist as Thanksgiving to the Father

The outline of ##3 and 4 about the church's thanksgiving to God is clear (the arrangement of lines to bring this out is my own):

#3. The Eucharist "is the great thanksgiving to the Father
    for everything accomplished in creation, redemption and sanctification,
    for everything accomplished by God now in the church and in the world . . . ,
    for everything that God will accomplish."
#4. "The eucharist is the great sacrifice of praise by which the Church speaks on behalf of the whole creation."
    The world "is present at every eucharist: in bread and wine," in the faithful and their prayers.
    "Christ unites the faithful with himself and . . . their prayers within his own intercession, so that the faithful are transfigured and their prayers accepted."
    "This sacrifice of praise is possible only through Christ."
    Bread, wine, fruits of the earth and of human labor "are presented to the Father in faith and thanksgiving."

The whole is prefaced by a new introductory sentence, not in Accra #6: "The eucharist, which always includes both *word* [Scripture reading? preaching?] and sacrament, is a *proclamation* and a celebration of the work of God" (#3, italics added). Here, at last, is the "word" mentioned in the 1967 Provisional Draft's "Preamble."

Finally, two conclusions are drawn: #3, "The eucharist is the benediction *(berakah)* by which the Church expresses its thankfulness for all God's benefits." #4, "The eucharist thus signifies what the world is to become: an offering and hymn of praise to the *Creator,* a universal communion in the body of *Christ,* a kingdom of justice, love and peace in the *Holy Spirit"* (italics added; the last phrase echoes Rom. 14:17).

The section is built around the terms "thanksgiving" (see above, "A Note on Terms," pp. 1–2) and "sacrifice of praise" (Heb. 13:15; see above, p. 12), developed as in much subsequent eucharistic theology. In *BEM* the structure of Eucharist #3 is "everything accomplished" in past, present, and future; in #4, the sequence is logical and argumentative. Originally the material in the latter paragraph was put together to demonstrate "the catholic character of the eucharist" *(Bristol 1967,* Paper No. 50, p. 63); here it seems used to explain the church's sacrifice of praise and what is offered to the Father in thanksgiving.

It may be noted that a somewhat different impact is made if, with the *Study Guide to BEM* (Paper No. 114), the parallel thematic phrases in ##3 and 4 are taken to be "the *work of God"* and the church's *"sacrifice of praise."* Then divine accomplishment and human response are the sequence.

Some will ask whether the line between "thanksgiving" and "thankoffering" (to God) has been blurred (cf. also #20, first sentence). The *Anglican-Lutheran International Conversations* (section 69) pointed up the question over the belief of "many Anglicans and some Lutherans" that in the Eucharist "the Church's offering of herself is caught up into his [Christ's] one offering" and the rejection of such a concept by "other Anglicans and many Lutherans." In terms of classic British hymnody, it is the difference between

> We offer to Thee of Thine own
> Ourselves and all that we can bring,
> In Bread and Cup before Thee shown,
> Our universal offering.
> > (V.S.S. Coles,
> > *Hymns Ancient and Modern*
> > [Oxford: Oxford University Press, 1909],
> > 264, v. 2)

or

> And having with us Him that pleads above,
> We here present, we here spread forth to Thee
> That only Offering perfect in Thine eyes,
> The one true, pure, immortal Sacrifice.
> > (William Bright, *Hymns Ancient and Modern* [1909], 267, v. 1)

and

> Nothing in my hand I bring;
> Simply to Thy Cross I cling.
> (Augustus Toplady, *Hymns Ancient and Modern*
> [1909], 467, v. 3)

Others ask how the opening emphasis in #2 on the Eucharist as "proc-lamation" (italicized when quoted above) and main points on thanksgiving and praise to God, especially when conceived as "benediction" *(berakah),* fit together. J. M. R. Tillard, a Roman Catholic participant in Faith and Order, has been critical here (see his "The Eucharist, Gift of God," in Paper No. 116, pp. 104–18):

> The Lima text would certainly have been improved had it paid more atten-tion to the distinction between blessing *(berakah, eulogia)* and thanksgiv-ing. To translate *eucharistein* as "to bless," without qualifications, is impossible as serious studies have shown. The term *eucharistia* in its verbal connotation refers basically to confession, to proclamation in the form of praise. (p. 115)

Precisely in Ignatius of Antioch and Justin Martyr the Eucharist

> proclaims the heart of the faith (cf. 1 Cor. 11:26). . . . It is far more, there-fore, than "the benediction *(berakah)* by which the Church expresses its thankfulness to God for all his benefits." (Tillard, in Paper No. 116, p. 116, citing #3; a similar inexactness with *berakah* occurs in #27)

There is a final, more pointed question. By beginning with "the Father" in its trinitarian sequence, *BEM* has thereby placed "thanksgiv-ing" first in its admittedly interrelated list of aspects of the Eucharist. Does this, along with the constant use of the term "eucharist" itself, create an impression in the statement that would be different if the aspect of thanksgiving came later? In other words, does aspect A tend to counter the strong opening emphasis on the gift character of the Lord's Supper? Tillard's essay proceeds from "gift of God to the church" to "gift received in thanksgiving."

B. The Eucharist as Anamnesis or Memorial of Christ

This longest of all aspects of the sacrament treated in *BEM* (##5–13, with two comments) takes us into the now-familiar territory of *anamnesis* and the questions of "presence" and "sacrifice." The section is lengthy, somewhat repetitive, and filled with links to other aspects of the Eucharist. The structure of the paragraphs is hard to discern or at least open to several possibilities. Paragraphs 5, 13, and the second part of #8 seem added to a core (##6–12) of the Accra statement.

The opening paragraph (#5) introduces the theme of "the biblical idea of memorial as applied to the eucharist," which is said to be "the memorial of the crucified and risen Christ, i.e., the living and effective sign of his sacrifice accomplished, once and for all on the cross and still operative. . . ." It refers to the "present efficacy of God's work when it [the Eucharist] is celebrated by God's people in a liturgy." This is explained to mean (#6) that he "is present in this *anamnesis,* granting us communion with himself" (see aspect D, pp. 162–64, below) and "the foretaste of his *parousia* and of the final kingdom" (an anticipation of aspect E). Here in #6 the emphasis is placed on all Christ accomplished, from incarnation to the sending of the Spirit, not on his suffering and sacrifice alone.

In #7 *anamnesis* is termed "both representation [no hyphen] and anticipation" and is defined as "not only calling to mind of what is past" but (also) "the Church's effective proclamation [nota bene!] of God's mighty acts and promises." So it *is* "remembering" but *also* something more.

"Representation and anticipation," we are then told (#8), "are expressed in thanksgiving [cf. aspect A] and intercession [aspect C]." "Thanksgiving" is defined in a phrase that aspect A had not employed, "recalling God's mighty acts of redemption" (here, Accra #9 had *"proclaiming* before God"). "Intercession" emphasizes Christ as "great High Priest," in communion with whom "the Church offers its intercessions." It is in this paragraph that *BEM* makes the point Christ's sacrifice was "unique," as are the events from incarnation to ascension which "God does not repeat"; indeed, they "can neither be repeated or prolonged."

The *anamnesis* of Christ is next presented as "basis and source of all Christian prayer" (#9), Christ empowering us "to pray through him."

In Christ, nourished in the Eucharist, "we offer ourselves as a living and holy sacrifice in our daily lives (Rom. 12:1; I Peter 2:5)" and are "renewed in the covenant" (##10, 11).

Another short paragraph (#12) adds the strongest word on preaching in the section: "Since the *anamnesis* of Christ is the very content of the preached Word as it is of the eucharistic meal, each reinforces the other. The celebration of the eucharist properly includes the proclamation of the Word" (cf. #27).

The final, longer paragraph (#13) moves from "the words and acts of Christ at the institution of the eucharist" to the "real presence" and "mode of presence" (which is termed "unique") in the Eucharist: "This is my body . . . this is my blood." The presence is "real, living and active." Christ's presence "does not depend on the faith of the individual," but "to discern the body and blood of Christ, faith is required."

There is surely a cluster of major ideas here at the center of this central section of aspects of the Eucharist. But as to how they fit together, other readers may see other patterns.

The statement itself helps us see the crucial issues for today by posing several questions in the Commentary on ##8 and 13.

(1) "Sacrifice"—"there is only one expiation," the cross, but it is "made actual in the eucharist and presented before the Father in the intercession of Christ and of the Church for all humanity." In

FIGURE 4
The Anamnesis of Christ involves

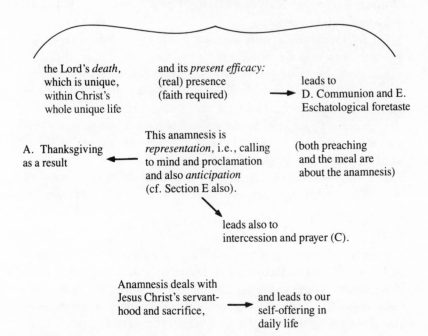

the Lord's *death*, which is unique, within Christ's whole unique life

and its *present efficacy:* (real) presence (faith required)

leads to D. Communion and E. Eschatological foretaste

A. Thanksgiving as a result

This anamnesis is *representation,* i.e., calling to mind and proclamation and also *anticipation* (cf. Section E also).

(both preaching and the meal are about the anamnesis)

leads also to intercession and prayer (C).

Anamnesis deals with Jesus Christ's servant-hood and sacrifice,

and leads to our self-offering in daily life

light of "the significance of the eucharist as intercession," the
eucharist as "propitiatory sacrifice" may be understood (#8).
(2) "Presence"—Many churches hold the bread and wine "become
. . . the body and blood of the risen Christ"; "some other
churches . . . do not link that presence so definitely with the signs
of bread and wine" (#13).

Both questions appeared frequently in the bilateral dialogues. As to
(1), "expiation" implies "atone for" or "cover over" sin; "propitiatory" may mean "appease or placate" an angry deity (cf. Lutherans
and Catholics in Dialogue III, *Eucharist as Sacrifice,* p. 190, n. 7, and
from the same dialogue, *Righteousness in the New Testament* [Philadel-
phia: Fortress Press; New York: Paulist Press, 1982], p. 37). Prescinding
from that terminological question, the Commentary makes the appeal to
all churches to "deepen their understanding of the reasons why other
traditions than their own have either used or rejected this term," sacrifice.
As for (2), the decision is whether the differences of opinion over presence "under the signs of bread and wine" can be accommodated within
the formulation in *BEM* #13 on the Eucharist: "real presence . . . unique
. . . living and active"; "what Christ declared [in the *verba*] is true." An
affirmative answer on (2) is easier for many groups than for the Reformed
and Free Church traditions.

The final somewhat cryptic statement in #13 (quoted above) is *BEM's*
apparent answer to the problem of "receptionism" (cf. pp. 107, 109,
115, above), that is, the role of faith (see pp. 46–47, above).

An underlying question which confronts this section of *BEM* is one
common to so many of the bilaterals: has "the biblical idea" of *anamnesis* been correctly understood and applied? (Cf. pp. 27ff, above.) With it
goes the feeling that perhaps too much is being attached to this Greek
word for "memorial." What appears in the *verba* only in 1 Corinthians
and the longer text of Luke, not in Mark or Matthew, namely "in memory
of me," has become the linchpin by which much else is held in place.

C. The Eucharist as Invocation of the Spirit

The trinitarian-structured portion of the five aspects of the Eucharist in
BEM concludes with a section (##14–18) on the Spirit, using *epiklesis,* or
"invocation," as the key term. The underlying principle, *"anamnesis
leads to epiklesis"* (Accra #14), means that recalling/representing/pro-
claiming today all that Christ did, especially in his cross, depends upon

"the work of the Holy Spirit" *(BEM* #16) and so "the Church prays to the Father for the gift of the Holy Spirit in order that the eucharistic event may be a reality" *(BEM* #14). The section thus turns out to be about "the presence of Christ" which "is clearly the centre of the eucharist." The terms "presence" and "present" occur four times in #14, in addition to the words "effective," "alive," and "reality" thus linking #14 closely with the last paragraph in aspect B, #13 on "real presence." The study guide on *BEM* (Paper No. 114) actually treats #13 together with ##14–17 under Invocation of the Spirit.

The opening sentence in #14 successfully conveys the point the section wishes to make: "The Spirit makes the crucified and risen Christ really present to us in the eucharistic meal, fulfilling the promise contained in the words of institution." Therefore the church prays to the *Father* for the gift of the *Spirit* that *Christ* may be present.

The trinitarian pattern is firmly embedded in #14:

the Father is origin and fulfillment of the eucharistic event;
"by and in" the Son of God "it is accomplished in its living center";
the Holy Spirit is the "strength of love which makes it possible and
continues to make it effective."

Hence the stress on the "Triune God." (Cf. also #18, the Holy *Spirit,* kingdom of *God,* the *Lord's* return.)

By the Holy Spirit, then—the remaining, shorter paragraphs go on— "bread and wine become the sacramental signs of Christ's body and blood" and "remain so for the purpose of communion" (#15; cf. #32); "the whole action of the eucharist has an 'epikletic' character," depending on the Spirit (#16); the church is thus "sanctified and renewed, led into all justice, truth, and unity" and empowered for mission (#17; this is anticipation of aspect E); and the church, having a foretaste of the kingdom, also "receives the life of the new creation and the assurance of the Lord's return" (cf. aspect E also).

In thus mounting these claims about the Spirit, the section also once parallels "the living *word* of Christ" with "the power of the Holy Spirit" (#15) and lays emphasis on the concept of *promise* (three times in #14, plus noun and verb in the Commentary on that paragraph).

What we are to make of all this is explained, at least in part, in the two Commentary paragraphs. The first Commentary states, "There is an intrinsic relationship between Christ's promise, the words of institution, and the *epiklesis,* the invocation of the Spirit." The church's "prayer

action" brings about "the reality promised by Christ," invocation of the
Spirit on both the community and on the elements of bread and wine
(Commentary #14). The second Commentary states that Christ's presence in the Eucharist, "in virtue of the living word of Christ by the power
of the Holy Spirit" (#15), has been variously explained in the history of the
church. Emphasis on the Spirit should help us understand both this presence and the oft-debated question of "a special moment of consecration"
(because, presumably, the Spirit is invoked upon the whole eucharistic
action and is not limited to a precise moment, *Bristol, 1967*, Paper No.
50, p. 62).

The importance of these agreements announced in *BEM* can scarcely
be underestimated. Behind the statement lies a long dispute between
Eastern and Western Christianity. Though *epiklesis* meant originally
prayer in general, it came to be used for the calling upon God to send the
Holy Spirit in the eucharistic liturgy. Though the exact details are subject
to scholarly controversy, the practice likely appeared by the time of the
Apostolic Tradition of Hippolytus (early third century) and certainly by
the time of Cyril of Jerusalem (A.D. 347) and likely referred, in some
instances, to Spirit-wrought transformation in the communicants, rather
than—or as well as—in the bread and wine. The prayer, in the former
case, was for sanctification and (ethical) fruits in the faithful. In any case,
the East presumed and stressed such invocation. The West did not, and
the canon of the Roman Mass did not stress an epiclesis. The Reformation, in its reaction to the canon, placed its emphasis in the Words of
Institution of Jesus. The matter is complicated by another stream of liturgies, as in Egypt, where the Word *(Logos)* was regarded as the agent to be
invoked in the epiclesis. (Cf. for example, H. Lietzmann, *Mass and
Lord's Supper* [1926, Eng. trans., Leiden: E. J. Brill, 1953–79], chaps. 4
and 7). One has the options, in thinking of, or praying to God for, Christ's
presence, of viewing this as coming about

A. through the Word   or through the Spirit   (or both),   and
B. in the elements   or in the people of
   of bread and wine,   the congregation   (or both).

Thomas Cranmer's prayer in the 1549 *Book of Common Prayer* is a
classic example that has been in and out of Anglican liturgies, "With Thy
Holy Spirit and *Word* vouchsafe to bless and sanctify these thy gifts and
creatures of *Bread and Wine*."

The *BEM* statement, with great emphasis, presents the Spirit (once, the "word," in #15) as effecting the relationship between the Words of Institution and "presence" here and now. The *anamnesis* of the *verba* is brought about by *epiklesis*. The importance of this is stated in these words by a Dominican participant in Faith and Order:

> By restoring the Holy Spirit to its essential place . . . in the entire eucharistic celebration and what makes it the event of grace . . . , the text makes possible an enrichment of the Western traditions. . . . The approval by the Faith and Order Commission—and this with absolute unanimity!—of a doctrinal statement on the eucharist which once more restores the function of the Holy Spirit to its leading role is indubitable evidence of the fecundity of the ecumenical movement . . . [Western churches] are becoming receptive to the totality of the trinitarian mystery. (J. M. R. Tillard, in Paper No. 116, pp. 107–8)

It may be added that this emphasis on the Spirit could also be a way of transcending later Western disputes over "spiritual" versus more "literal" concepts of "presence" (cf. Reformed-Lutheran dialogue).

To probe this ecumenical "breakthrough" a bit further, however, *BEM* does it in part through use of "promise" language. Earlier, #7 had spoken of "God's promises" and #13 of Christ's "promise to be always with his own even to the end of the world" (Matt. 28:20; cf. 18:20, though the presence here is scarcely eucharistic). By "Jesus' promise in the words of institution," a phrase found three times in #14, is meant his promised presence, "This is my body, this is my blood" (cf. #13), though #2 also uses "Christ's promise" to include "forgiveness of sins (Matt. 26:28) and the pledge of eternal life (John 6:51–58)."

Closer examination of the biblical texts, however, confronts us with an embarrassing problem: none of the New Testament versions of the Words of Institution refers to the Spirit. That should not surprise us with the Synoptics, for those Gospels have a paucity of references to the Spirit. But 1 Corinthians 10 and 11 do not refer to the Spirit either. John 6, however, does. If that chapter is eucharistic (cf. p. 12, above), it makes the certainly climactic point, "It is the *spirit* [Spirit?] that gives life, the flesh is of no avail; the *words* that I have spoken to you are *spirit* and life" (6:63). If we go the route that "spiritual" food and drink in 1 Cor. 10:3–4 means "conveying the Spirit" (see p. 46, above), we seem to have food providing the Spirit—but not invocation of the Spirit to make Christ present.

The most likely possibility of a link in New Testament material between the Lord's Supper and invocation of God for the Spirit may lie in a textual variant in Luke 11:2. Instead of "thy kingdom come," as the second petition in the Lord's Prayer, two eleven-to-twelfth-century Greek manuscripts have, "Thy Holy Spirit come upon us and cleanse us." There is some patristic evidence, notably in Gregory of Nyssa, for earlier use of this phrase in the Lord's Prayer, perhaps even as early as the second century. Textual editors and commentaries on Luke relegate the variant to the critical apparatus, for it is very unlikely that Luke wrote it. But it could be an early variant, for liturgical use, possibly at the Lord's Supper. If an epiclesis, it deals with people, not elements: "come *upon us.*"

All in all, the argument presumed for *BEM* must run in the following way. The New Testament *verba* imply Jesus' "presence" ("This is . . ."), though not only at the meal ("Lo, I am with you always . . . where two or three are gathered in my name").In the post–New Testament period, the developing doctrine and experience of the Spirit made invocation of the Spirit upon Christians and upon "elements" a means of "presence." The Jewish idea of "remembering," for example, at Passover, cannot be said to have involved the (holy) Spirit. It is when biblical *anamnesis* (representation) of Christ, combined with promised "presence," is associated with patristic *epiclesis* that the pattern behind *BEM* emerges; but as the Lima text at times recognizes there is also a pattern, even stronger in the Old and New Testaments, at times in patristic thought and very pronounced in the Reformation, of "the word"—in all its nuances as "words of Jesus," utterance of God, and Christ himself—as the means by which God communicates.

D. The Eucharist as Communion of the Faithful

Once Part II of Eucharist leaves its trinitarian structure, the flow of the argument may become more difficult to perceive in aspects D and E. The general line of development is that the presence of Christ, brought about by the invoked Spirit, upon the church's prayer of thanksgiving and praise to the Father, results in communion. This communion is with Christ and within the body of Christ. In the bread and cup there is "oneness of the sharers with Christ and with their fellow sharers." Section 19 abounds with English words that could come from the Greek root of *koinonia*: "communion," "*common* cup," "(fellow) *sharers.*"

"Although *koinonia* is never equated with 'Church' in the New Testament" (ARCIC's *Final Report*, p. 5), in patristic Greek it came to mean, among other things, "sacramental fellowship." In modern ecumenical jargon it has been widely used to designate "community, fellowship" and therefore church. *BEM* in #19 makes this transition in the sentence, "It is in the eucharist that the community of God's people is fully manifested," and then goes on to speak of the Church and the world.

Local eucharistic celebrations have to do with "the whole Church." Therefore "a church" (local? or "denomination"?) "will take care to order its own life in ways which take seriously the interests and concerns of other churches" (#19). Later, "the obstinacy of unjustifiable confessional oppositions within the body of Christ" is condemned (#20).

References to the world are introduced by the statement that "the eucharist embraces all aspects of life" and is "thanksgiving and offering [compare and contrast #4] on behalf of the whole world" (#20). The Eucharist is said to involve "the believer in the central event of the world's history" (the cross or the whole Christ-event?), and therefore "we are" actively to participate in the "ongoing restoration of the world's situation."

The theme of "reconciliation" also runs through the lengthy #20. "Eucharistic celebration demands reconciliation and sharing" *(koinonia?)* among "all those regarded as brothers and sisters in the one family of God" (church? or the bigger human family?). The Eucharist shows what is inconsistent in our behavior with "the reconciling presence of God in human history." Hence the challenge to overcome injustice, racism, and lack of freedom, and the note of "continual judgment" on unjust relationships, pride, materialism, and power politics. But "through the eucharist the all-renewing grace of God penetrates and restores human personality and dignity."

The final #21 in the section begins, "Solidarity in the eucharistic communion of the body of Christ and responsible care of Christians for one another and the world find specific expression in the liturgies." Then follows a list of examples: "in the mutual forgiveness of sins; the sign of peace," and so forth. Such manifestations of love are given a christological basis (Christ's servanthood) and incarnational analogy ("as God in Christ has entered into the human situation, so eucharistic liturgy is near to the concrete and particular situations of men and women"). We are back in ecclesiology and ministry in the final two sentences about how deacons and deaconesses in the early church expressed "this aspect of the eucharist," and "such ministry between the table and the needy properly testifies to the redeeming presence of Christ in the world."

If parts of #21 seem less than lucid, it is because material is here employed from *Bristol 1967* (Paper No. 50, p. 64) that once described the "agapeic implications" of the Eucharist. The 1967 concern was about the agape ("love feast"), or communal meal, in early Christianity. There was an interest at that time in reviving it or at least transferring features of it to the eucharistic celebrations. Lima speaks of "manifestations of love," but omits from its list what in the 1967 version was the immediate antecedent of "the ministry between the table and the needy," namely, "the bringing of gifts for the communal meal and for distribution to the poor brethren." Even where the list of examples in 1967 was pertinent to deacons (and deaconesses), in the reference to "taking of the Eucharist to the sick and those in prison," the 1982 text has changed it to read, "the taking of the elements to the sick and those in prison or *the celebration of the eucharist with them.*" The italicized addition reflects the alternative position of those who prefer a "private communion service" with *verba* to carrying previously consecrated elements to the sick; the former would be conducted by an ordained person, the latter done by a deacon.

The length and sprawling nature of #20 make it difficult to grasp. It is the longest paragraph in Part II of Eucharist, and only #1 exceeds it in the entire Eucharist section of *BEM*. Part of the obscurity may lie in the difficulty of distinguishing when and how the document refers to "church" and when and how to "world." It may be an improvement, as in the Study Guide on *BEM* (Paper No. 114), to make the sequence #19 followed by #21 (on the church community) and then #20, lines 1–15 (on believers' involvement in the world).

Theological questions that some would flag in this section involve the use of "grace" (a relatively little-used word in the text) and the reference to "judgment," both in #20. Grace "penetrates and restores"; does that conceive of grace as a substance or existentially? As for "judgment" ("sin" is a relatively rare term, but cf. #3), it is "continual" (not "at the end") and involves societal sins (not offenses against God) (cf. also #21, "*mutual* forgiveness of sins," that is, a horizontal, not a vertical relationship). We may note in passing the servant Christology (cf. also #6), a favorite in 1950s biblical theology.

Section D advances the document as a whole most of all in #19. One might overlook the aspect of communion with Christ and with each other, if it were not thus brought out. Both in the New Testament and Christian experience this aspect is prominent.

E. The Eucharist as Meal of the Kingdom

Three themes have already been suggested as appearing under this final aspect of the Eucharist, namely, eschatology, mission, and world. The three are interrelated, and each has been signaled in earlier paragraphs. The clear sequence present in the Accra statement (#23) and indeed since the 1967 Second Draft through the heading "Mission to the World" as an implication of the Eucharist has been somewhat blunted by the present order of paragraphs, which is "world," then "mission."

The eschatology is asserted flat-out at the beginning of #22:

> The eucharist opens up the vision of the divine rule which has been promised as the final renewal of creation, and is a foretaste of it. Signs of this renewal are present in the world wherever the grace of God is manifest and human beings work for justice, love and peace [cf. #4, "a kingdom of justice, love and peace in the Holy Spirit"]. The eucharist is the feast at which the Church gives thanks for these signs [cf. #3] and joyfully celebrates and anticipates the coming of the Kingdom in Christ (I Cor. 11:26; Matt. 26:29) [cf. #3, everything "God will accomplish in bringing the Kingdom to fulfillment"].

Besides the obvious reflection of #3 and #4, this paragraph, new at the Lima stage, picks up #6 ("foretaste of Christ's *parousia* and of the final kingdom"), #18 ("foretaste of the Kingdom of God"), #17 (renewal of the church for its mission in the world), and #20 (restoration of the world). It makes reference to the world directly and as "creation," though "mission" is not mentioned as yet. The two scriptural references point to *future* fulfillment, as do the words "vision" and "foretaste." However, the *present* aspect of eschatology is found not only in the Eucharist itself but in the graced efforts of, apparently, non-Christians as well as the faithful for "justice, love and peace"—qualities, referred to in earlier sections of *BEM*, in connection with the kingdom that the world "is to become." That we have here "realized eschatology"—as well as an emphasis, quite common in the 1960s and 1970s, on the Eucharist as celebration of signs and accomplishments in the world—is suggested by the other clearly eschatological statement in the section: "the eucharist brings into the present age a new reality which transforms" (#26). But here the object is "Christians" being transformed "into the image of Christ" for witnessing.

The world, which has already been mentioned in #22, is prominent in #23: "the world, to which renewal is promised, is present in the whole

eucharistic celebration. The world is present in the thanksgiving to the
Father . . . in the memorial of Christ . . . in the prayer for the gift of the
Holy Spirit." This trinitarian development appeared already in Accra
#24. Lima #4 says that the world "is present at every eucharist" and
defines that presence as bread, wine, the faithful, and their prayers. The
wording of #23 about the *anamnesis* "where the Church . . . prays for the
world" is an advance beyond anything said previously (cf. ##3 and 8;
though #27 includes "intercession for . . . the world" in its outline of the
liturgy; cf. also #21, "intercession for all"). The attitude toward the
world established in ##22 and 23 is very different from that toward the
kosmos in the Gospel of John: *"not* concerning the world do I pray"
(17:9). But the Johannine note of oneness "that the world may believe"
finds reflection in what follows.

The theme of witness or mission is noted in ##24, 25, and 26. Using
"reconciliation language" (cf. #20), #24 calls members of Christ's body
to be "witnesses" of resurrection joy, like Jesus "in solidarity with the
outcast" as "signs of the love of Christ" (cf. #21). In #25 "God's mission
to the world" is mentioned, with "the very celebration of the eucharist"
viewed as "an instance of the Church's participation" in it. "This participation" *(koinonia?),* it is then said, "takes everyday form in the proclamation of the Gospel, service of the neighbour, and faithful presence in
the world." This attempt to reflect Rom. 12:1 (cf. #10) I find to be the
most "evangelistic" statement in the Eucharist section, oriented to proclamation as well as service but aware that, in some situations, the "faithful presence" of Christians in the world is all that they can provide.

BEM is not quite finished here with the mission theme, for #26 speaks
of how the Eucharist brings "a new reality," transformation into Christ's
image, which makes Christians "his effective witnesses." Thus "the
eucharist is precious food for missionaries, bread and wine for pilgrims
on their apostolic journey. The eucharistic community is nourished and
strengthened for confessing by word and action the Lord Jesus Christ."
Any "eucharistic assembly must be concerned for gathering also those
who are at present beyond its visible limits." There is a final jab at church
divisions: "missionary witness" is weakened when "Christians cannot
unite in full fellowship around the same table" (#26).

After speaking of "the faithful" in aspect D, E never quite comes
around to expressing the need "that the world may believe (come to
faith)," for the view of the world in ##22–23 is rather positive and the

hope in context is to gather at the table all who are beyond the eucharistic assembly's "visible limits." But the emphasis on "mission to the world" is strong. "The world" receives full due, as God's creation for whose salvation Christ gave his life, and all this is set within a vision of "the final renewal of creation"—signs of which are already seen in human work for justice, love, and peace and in Christians' signs of love for those outside.

Is the right title for all this, "the Meal of the Kingdom"? "Meal-language" is prominent: "feast" (##22, 26), "celebration" (##23, 25), "table-fellowship" (#24), "food" (#26), and "the meal of the one Lord" (#26). The Kingdom is mentioned only in #22 in a future sense (Matt. 26:29) and as "the divine rule which has been promised." But Kingdom (of God) has been mentioned before in ##1, 2, 3, 4, 6, and 18. One would not want to see either term less prominent in the document, for both are venerably biblical. In the Isaianic vision (Isa. 25:6–9, which stretches on into the New Testament, till the great eschatological "Supper of the Lamb [Rev. 19:9]," cited in #1), we have the picture of "wine on the lees" at the "mountain of the Lord" for "all peoples," according to the promise of God.

We may note before moving on into the third and final main section of Eucharist that there will continue to be connections between the "aspects" in Part II and the suggestions in Part III (##27–33). The *BEM Study Guide* (Paper No. 114) has interestingly rearranged the aspects thus:

A. Thanksgiving to the Father (##3–4) and
B. Meal of the Kingdom (##22, 25, plus ##30–31);
C. Memorial of Christ (##5–8, plus commentary on #8);
D. Invocation of the Spirit (##13, 14, 15, 16–17, plus #33);
E. Communion of the Faithful (##19, 21 and 20 first half).

The Study Guide relates Part III material so that, for example, the idea of the deepening of faith by celebration and reception of the Eucharist (##30–31) is tied directly to the eschatological vision and missionary impact of the meal.

III. The Celebration of the Eucharist

While the Accra statement had concluded with "Recommendations" in both the Baptism and Eucharist sections, the Lima text concludes its treatment of each sacrament with the heading "Celebration." This does not mean that advice is not given or hopes are not expressed, but rather that, in connection with "liturgy" or celebration (the real topic that appears in virtually every paragraph), we have first a list of liturgical elements for a service of the Lord's Supper or the Mass, and then a series of descriptive admonitions on unity and diversity, the minister, frequency of Holy Communion, and what to do with the "consecrated elements" after the service. This format allows *BEM* both to state desired convergences and to uncover problem areas in a way that is not alarming about differences that still exist.

All drafts of Eucharist since 1967 included a list of elements found in Communion liturgies. The lists have grown longer and longer. The original Provisional Draft said simply that "Orders of Holy Communion usually include" two parts:

(a) a service of the word, and
(b) a service of the sacrament, with the "shape of taking, blessing, breaking, and giving"

(cf. Dom Gregory Dix and pp. 4–5, above). But even by the Second Draft of 1967, a shift has been made: "The Eucharist is essentially a single whole, consisting *usually* of . . . ," and then a list of nine items follow, to which is appended five more things which the list "is not meant to exclude" (Paper No. 116, pp. 200–201, 203). Accra retained the same introductory words and the distinction between the two sorts of items, but expanded its lists to twelve items and six appended things. Lima #27 has twenty-one items, all in one list. In the Lima text as printed below words are italicized that are significant for comparison. Two asterisks are added after each entry also occurring in Accra's first list of "usually" found items, and one asterisk is added for Accra's "other items."

The eucharistic liturgy is *essentially a single whole*, consisting *historically* of the following elements in varying sequence *and of diverse importance:*

–hymns of praise [*];

–act of repentance [* Accra: contrition];

–declaration of pardon [* forgiveness of sins];

–proclamation of the Word of God, in various forms [** cf. #12];

–confession of faith (creed) [*];

–intercession for the whole Church and for the world [** cf. ##4, 8, 23];

–preparation of the bread and wine;

-thanksgiving to the Father for the marvels of creation, redemption and sanctification (deriving from the Jewish tradition of *berakah*) [** cf. ##3, 8];

-the words of Christ's institution of the sacrament according to the New Testament tradition [** cf. ##1, 13];

-the *anamnesis* or memorial of the great acts of redemption, passion, death, resurrection, ascension and Pentecost [cf. #6], which brought the Church into being [** cf. ##5-9];

-the invocation of the Holy Spirit *(epiklesis)* on the community, and the elements of bread and wine [cf. #14 Commentary and #16] (either before the words of institution or after the memorial or both; or some other reference to the Holy Spirit which adequately expresses the "epikletic" character of the eucharist) [** cf. ##14-16, and #14 Commentary];

-consecration of the faithful to God [* Accra: self-dedication];

-reference to the communion of saints [*];

-prayer for the return of the Lord and the definitive manifestation of his Kingdom [** cf. ##1, 3, 6, 18, 22];

-the Amen of the whole community [**];

-the Lord's prayer [**];

-sign of reconciliation and peace;

-the breaking of the bread [**];

-eating and drinking in communion with Christ and with each member of the Church [** cf. ##19, 21];

-final act of praise [**];

-blessing and sending.

As the number of components in a single list grows longer (doubtlessly justified by examination of actual examples of liturgy), it is important to insist on variations in arrangement and in the relative weight placed on a given part in different traditions. To say the elements occur "historically" means "in this historical example or that," not that all of them classically occurred together at one specific time in the past. One of the bilaterals to treat the "basic pattern" or "form" of "constitutive elements" in Holy Communion/the Mass was the international Lutheran–Roman Catholic volume, *The Eucharist* (German 1978); it mentions (#76)—to use key words from the list above—proclamation, thanksgiving, the Words of Institution, invocation, intercession, the Lord's Prayer, and eating and drinking (Communion). But, then, the Lutheran/Roman Catholic Joint Commission extracted it from Accra #28.

The remaining paragraphs (##28–33) in *BEM* are framed by a concern for unity among the churches at the Lord's Table (italics added).

The best way towards *unity* in eucharistic celebration and communion is the renewal of the eucharist itself in the different churches in regard to teaching and liturgy. (#28)

The increased mutual understanding expressed in the present statement may allow some churches to attain to a greater measure of eucharistic communion among themselves and so bring closer the day when Christ's divided people will be visibly *reunited* around the Lord's Table. (#33)

That note picks up the aim of the Faith and Order Commission itself in its By-Laws, "to call the churches to the goal of visible unity in one faith and one eucharistic fellowship" *(BEM,* p. viii).

"Teaching" in #28 refers to the entire statement on Eucharist, and "liturgy" relates to the elements listed in #27 and the Comments that follow: "churches should test their liturgies in the light of the eucharistic agreement now in the process of attainment" (#28). "The liturgical reform movement has brought the churches closer together in the manner of celebrating the Lord's Supper. However, a certain liturgical diversity compatible with our common eucharistic faith is recognized as a healthy and enriching fact." This tension between unity (how much?) and diversity (within what bounds?) sets the tone for the remaining topics.

We leave to further study, as *BEM* does, the question of whether "local food and drink"—for example, in Hong Kong, rice and "Green Bamboo Leaf" wine—may serve better as elements than bread and wine in some parts of the world (Commentary #28).

In all the bilaterals, any agreement about the Eucharist ran into the problem of the involvement of the officiating minister, that is, the (mutual) recognition of ordained ministers or priests. Lima #29 addresses this area of celebration christologically:

> *Christ* gathers, teaches, nourishes, invites, presides, as shepherd, prophet, and priest.

Link: "In most churches, this presidency [a semi-technical term meaning 'the function or act of presiding,' not to be interpreted in a U.S. political sense as referring to one elected for a term by the people to head the executive branch, or as in the Federal Republic of Germany where the president is a state 'master of ceremonies' and protocol figure] is signified by an ordained minister," whose role makes clear that "the rite is not the assemblies' own creation or possession" but is "a gift from Christ." Therefore,

the ordained *minister* of the eucharist is the ambassador who represents the divine initiative and expresses the connection of the local community with other local communities in the universal Church [italics added].

To follow up on this point, one must turn to *BEM*'s Ministry section where in #14 the ordained ministry is called "the visible focus of the deep and all-embracing communion between Christ and the members of his body." In addition (#17), ordained ministers "may appropriately be called priests because they fulfil a particular priestly service . . . through word and sacraments." The Commentary on Ministry #17 specifies further by saying "priest" came to be used to designate the minister "as presiding at the eucharist."

Frequency of Communion is examined in Eucharist ##30–31. Because "faith is deepened" by the Lord's Supper, the Eucharist "should be celebrated *frequently*" (#30). Because the Eucharist "celebrates the resurrection of Christ," #31 continues, "it is appropriate that it should take place *at least every Sunday.*" "As it is the new sacramental meal of the people of God, every Christian should be *encouraged* to receive communion *frequently*"(italics added).

It is helpful here to have acknowledged the important distinction between celebration and reception. The closing statement represents a change from what Accra #33 had said, it "seems *normal* that every Christian should receive communion *at every celebration*" (italics added).

In regard to the frequently/every Sunday issue flagged in the statement itself, we note the reasons advanced for the conclusions. First and most impressive is the argument that the Lord's Supper is "the *new* sacramental meal of the people of God." For all the appeal to Jewish antecedents, there is something to the claim that Holy Communion emerged as the particularly Christian type of worship, especially in the shift from annual Passover celebration within the family to the more-frequent agape–Lord's Supper in the gathered assembly. However, pagan meal analogies in the Greco-Roman world ought not to be completely overlooked as a factor in development, lest we make the Christian meal too uniquely new.

Joining communion "at least every Sunday" with "the resurrection of Christ" is a less satisfactory argument. Its rootage in "biblical theology" can be said to be in the conclusions reached by a pupil of Oscar Cullmann, Willy Rordorf *(Sunday: The History of the Day of Rest and Worship in the Earliest Centuries of the Christian Church* [Philadelphia: Westminster Press, 1968; trans. of the 1962 German original], especially pp. 303-7): by "instituting the Lord's Supper afresh on Easter evening" (cf. pp. 231-37; Acts 10:41 and John 20:19-23 are especially in view), Jesus "also 'instituted' the day on which it should henceforth be celebrated: on Sunday." Rordorf argued indeed that the Lord's *Supper* likely gave rise to the term "the Lord's *Day*" (cf. Acts 20:7). His own epigrammatic conclusion is, "no Lord's Supper without Sunday, no Sunday without the Lord's Supper" (p. 303). Partly on his supposition that "the sermon *alone* is not able to build up the community" (p. 306, italics his), Rordorf states that "in the ancient Church . . . Sunday was absolutely nothing without the Lord's Supper" (p. 305). Quite apart from how in detail these propositions have subsequently fared (cf. especially for literature, W. Stott, "Sabbath, Lord's Day," in *The New International Dictionary of New Testament Theology,* Vol. 3 [Grand Rapids: Zondervan Publishing House, 1978], pp. 411-15), the case is overstated and the dogmatic connection of "Supper" and "Sunday" makes the "at least" in *BEM* problematic (Accra had said, "not less frequently than every Sunday"). Moreover, the Lord's Supper has ties not merely to Easter but also to Good Friday (1 Cor. 11:26, though cross and resurrection belong together) and to "Holy Thursday." And, finally, *all* Christian worship can be similarly tied to the "first day of the week" (1 Cor. 16:2, the collection!; cf. the noneucharistic list of elements in a "service of the word" [W. Bauer] at 14:26).

The third underlying reason (actually the first, in #30) for celebrating the Eucharist frequently is that this deepens Christian faith. ("Reception" must be assumed.) The argument is of a piece with that in #28, that "renewal of the eucharist itself" is "the best way towards unity in eucharistic celebration." It seems an expression of the view, now exemplified in the 1982 U.S. Lutheran-Episcopal agreement on interim eucharistic hospitality, that such sharing is a stage toward full fellowship. However, the sad truth from experience is that frequent, even weekly, celebration within a church, while no doubt deepening the faith of its communicants, has also called attention to and sometimes reinforced dividedness from others.

The final problem area taken up in *BEM* is the question of how long the presence of Christ "perdures," or carries through, in the Lord's Supper. The U.S. Lutheran-Catholic dialogue in 1967 found this an area where "historical divergencies" were being overcome but where that bilateral could not yet speak "with one voice" *(Eucharist as Sacrifice,* Lutherans and Catholics in Dialogue III, pp. 19–94):

> We are further agreed that as long as Christ remains sacramentally present, worship, reverence and adoration are appropriate.
>
> Both Lutherans and Catholics link Christ's eucharistic presence closely to the eucharistic liturgy itself. Lutherans, however, have not stressed the prolongation of this presence beyond the communion service as Catholics have done.

The statement then went on to note, however, that "opposition on this point is not total." For "Lutherans may distribute the elements from the congregational communion service, in some cases as an extension of this service, in some cases with the words of institution spoken either for their proclamatory value or as consecration." For Roman Catholics, the then-recent *Instruction on Eucharistic Worship* was cited that the "primary and original purpose" of reserving the host was for "communicating the sick," though a note observed the meaningfulness of adoration of the reserved sacrament for Catholic devotion. In the work of the Anglican–Roman Catholic International Commission, a section of the 1979 *Elucidation* on the Eucharist was devoted to the same topic. The ARCIC treatment contrasted but seemingly allowed coexistence between those who practice such eucharistic devotion (while not dissociating the reserved sacrament from administration of Communion, even if reception is not immediate) and those who find such adoration unacceptable *(Final Report,* pp. 23–24).

BEM's treatment is first descriptive, then hortatory. "Some churches stress that Christ's presence in the consecrated elements continues after the celebration." Others emphasize "the act of celebration itself" and "consumption of the elements in the act of communion." "Regarding the practice of reserving the elements, each church should respect the practices and piety of the others." Given diversity and yet convergence, remember "the primary intention of reserving the elements is their distribution among the sick and those who are absent," and that "the best way of showing respect for the elements served in the eucharistic celebration is by their consumption, without excluding their use for communion of the sick" (so Accra #35, echoing the Group of Les Dombes).

Given such problems and differences, perhaps the best expectation *is* that "some churches" will attain, through *BEM,* "a greater measure of eucharistic communion among themselves." But the hope remains for that "day when Christ's divided people will be visibly reunited around the Lord's Table."

Evaluation

The real testing of the Lima text will come as churches respond to it officially, and we see what happens as a result, and as individuals and groups of all sorts wrestle with what it has said.

As this evaluating is done, some of the problems noted above from the text itself, possible tensions and ambiguities within the Lima draft, and downright points of disagreement will emerge, often guided by the tradition and experiences of each individual church. Orthodox, Roman Catholic, Anglican, Reformation, Free Church, or Pentecostal perspectives may each see issues not even mentioned above. There may be objections over omissions as well as what is said.

Let us note two places where questions might crop up. As a discussion of *Holy* Communion, stressing the *Holy* Spirit, is "holiness" underplayed? Is there an absence of the implications from the ancient cry, "Holy things for holy people" (cf. the application of Matt. 7:6, about not giving "what is holy to dogs," in *Didache* 9.5)? Is the "sanctity" of the sacrament too readily related to "the world?"

Behind *BEM*'s references to "the world" should be noted not only the theological trend in the 1960s and 1970s to emphasize a "worldly theology" but also the centuries-old Orthodox emphasis on God's creation and the Eucharist. In addition, there is the drive, from biblical theology and other sources, not to rend asunder "the sacred" and "the secular."

More significant may be how Eucharist does refer to aspects of holiness under an array of terms. These include "sanctification" (##3, 23, 27), "sanctified" (##10, 17), "communion of saints" (#27), "ourselves as a living and holy sacrifice" (#10), perhaps "justified sinners, joyfully and freely fulfilling his will" (#9), and "consecration of the faithful to God (#27) and "consecrated elements" (#32).

Readers and churches will have to judge whether such explanations and examples suffice for their concern. They might, of course, carry out similar reconnaissances in *BEM* looking for themes of interest to them.

The other probe we make here involves "Christian initiation." *BEM* focuses, not improperly, on the two great and widely acknowledged sacraments and on the ministry. As indicated earlier, each section—Baptism, Eucharist, and Ministry—had a history of its own development, and only in the 1970s were they combined. An earlier formulation of topic had been "Baptism, *Confirmation,* and Eucharist" (italics added), as in a draft document of 1968 *(Study Encounter* 4,4 [1968]: 194ff.) and 1970 Faith and Order consultations in Czechoslovakia and Geneva *(Studia Liturgica* 8,2 [1971/1972]). The significance of the shift, between 1971 and 1974 (Accra), to treat baptism and Eucharist but not a fuller initiation process into Christianity is described thus by the Baptist Gunter Wagner (who, it may be recalled, is expressing in the context a personal interest in the model of a process of initiation involving baptism/confession of belief or confirmation/Eucharist):

> The trend toward such a comprehensive view of *Christian initiation* was strong between 1968 . . . and 1971, when the Faith and Order Commission met in Louvain; at the latter meeting E. Schlink called this concept of "initiation" a *breakthrough* provided it does not ignore the once-for-all nature of baptism [Paper No. 60, 1971, p. 31]. However, already in Accra 1974, the concept of "initiation" does not receive the full attention it deserves, and in the Lima text the potential ecumenical significance of confirmation has certainly not been highlighted. (Paper No. 116, p. 27)

For all churches a theory and praxis of continuing initiation with deepening of faith is needed. In the face of competing models of baptism-chrismation-Eucharist (see p. 144, above), clarity is needed on each. By focusing just on baptism and Eucharist, *BEM* has sidetracked the matter of "confirmation" or of other "stages" after baptism, including "first Communion." Churches that regard baptism and Eucharist—but not confirmation—as sacraments, should not necessarily feel a victory in the perimeters of *BEM;* churches that regard all three—baptism, confirmation, and Eucharist—sacramentally, should not simply feel that *BEM* is two-thirds complete; churches that practice baptism of believers and regard the Lord's Supper as "an ordinance of the Lord," while perhaps feeling only partially represented in *BEM*'s positions, should not simply concentrate on its three parts. At stake for all is the further question of a comprehensive and comprehensible system of ongoing initiation into Christian faith and life.

We have paid tribute to the way *BEM* does not treat one topic in isolation, as can be a danger in a bilateral. But in focusing on baptism and

Eucharist *BEM* may overlook the initiation question.

We may now return to our preliminary conclusion (see pp. 148–49, above). The Eucharist in *BEM* is a text rewritten after Accra especially in the following sections:

I. Institution (#1)
II. Meaning (#2)
    B. Anamnesis (##5, 8b, 13)
    C. Invocation of the Spirit (##14, 17)
    D. Communion (##19b and 20)
    E. Meal of the Kingdom (##22, 25–26)
III. Celebration (##28b, 29, 30, 33).

But elsewhere, and even in some "new sections" where ideas are drawn from earlier drafts, it was basically shaped by 1967 and rests on even earlier Faith and Order statements.

Eucharist shows little direct reflection of the bilateral dialogues (exception: the Group of Les Dombes). But in that the bilaterals and *BEM* drafting processes often took cognizance of each other (the bilaterals more so of Faith and Order materials) and involved some of the same personnel, it cannot be said that the results are widely divergent.

If Roman Catholic involvement since Vatican II is apparent, it can only be seen in a general way, seldom in specific issues (perhaps "propitiatory sacrifice," #8 Commentary). Any earlier extreme "optimism" after the Council seems tempered by subsequent ecumenical realities (cf. #33). Perhaps Eastern Orthodox positions have had a more-pronounced impact on the statement (for example, *epiklesis,* communion of baptized children).

Finally, the biblical scholarship does seem to rest on views of the "biblical theology" approach popular as Vatican II was beginning. The J. J. von Allmen monograph, *The Lord's Supper* (1966, English 1969), written originally for the Faith and Order Commission and providing the background for *Bristol 1967* (Paper No. 50, see p. 60), remains the foundational study of *BEM* exegetically on Eucharist. And it is built on such assertions as "it was when He instituted the Supper that Jesus instituted the Church"; the paucity of records in the early church is to be explained by "liturgical secrecy"; and the Reformation marked "the first time men dared to separate the Lord's Day and the Lord's Supper" (pp. 12, 13, 17).

BEM, however, is beginning to develop a life of its own, quite apart from how the churches officially respond to it. The "Lima liturgy" of Faith and Order was based on it and has occasionally been used elsewhere, and the installation service of the Commission's former director, William Lazareth, was built around it ecumenically when he became pastor of a Lutheran congregation in New York City in 1983.

In an imaginative article entitled "Story and Eucharist," S. W. Sykes, of Durham University in England, has analyzed the Eucharist statement as "story" with its four components:

Setting:	A. Thanksgiving to the Father (creation);
Theme:	B. Memorial of the Son (redemption);
Plot:	D. Communion of the faithful (church);
Resolution:	E. Meal of the kingdom (eschatology).

If that leaves out the doctrine of the Holy Spirit (C. *epiklesis)* as "spare wheel," that is because, Sykes says, he is little inclined to see the Spirit as agent of "eucharistic 'change'"; rather, the Spirit should be correlated with the act of *anamnesis* and the response of gratitude that gives the Christian life its characteristic shape as "eucharistic." Sykes's article, in *Interpretation* (37 [1983]: 365–76), insists, as it explores Gese's *todah-*theory (see p. 22, above), that in order "to realize the true force of the relationship between story and Eucharist, one needs the theological category of sacrifice. To preserve the eucharistic sacrifice from cultic distortion, one needs the force of the concept of story" (p. 376).

FOR FURTHER READING AND REFERENCE

GENERAL:

Quanbeck, Warren A. *Search for Understanding: Lutheran Conversations with Reformed, Anglican, and Roman Catholic Churches.* Minneapolis: Augsburg Publishing House, 1972. For the general reader, by a dialogue participant.

Ehrenström, Nils, and Günther Gassmann. *Confessions in Dialogue: A Survey of Bilateral Conversations among World Confessional Families, 1959–1974.* Faith and Order Paper No. 74. Geneva: World Council of Churches, 3d rev. and enlarged ed. by N. Ehrenström, 1975. 1st ed., 1972, reprinted 1973.

Empie, Paul C. *Lutherans and Catholics in Dialogue: Personal Notes for a Study.* Edited by Raymond Tiemeyer. Philadelphia: Fortress Press, 1981. Personal reminiscences by Lutheran chairman of the U.S. dialogue.

Meyer, Harding, and Lukas Vischer. *Growth in Agreement: Reports and Agreed Statement of Ecumenical Conversations on a World Level.* Faith and Order Paper No. 108. New York: Paulist Press, 1984.

FAITH AND ORDER (UNLESS OTHERWISE NOTED, GENEVA: WORLD COUNCIL OF CHURCHES):

Vischer, Lukas, ed. *A Documentary History of the Faith and Order Movement 1927–1963.* St. Louis: Bethany Press, 1963.

Roger, P. C., ed. *The Fourth World Conference on Faith and Order: Montreal, 1963.* London: SCM Press, 1964.

Allmen, Jean-Jacques von. *The Lord's Supper* (see above, chap. 1). The French, *Essai sur le Repas du Seigneur* (1966), was written for the Commission's study on the Eucharist authorized in 1964 after Montreal.

Paper No. 50. *New Directions in Faith and Order: Bristol 1967. Reports–Minutes–Documents.* 1968.

Paper No. 59. *Faith and Order: Louvain 1971. Study Reports and Documents.* 1971.

Paper No. 73. *One Baptism, One Eucharist and a Mutually Recognized Ministry: Three agreed statements.* 1975. "Accra Statement."

Paper No. 84. *Towards an Ecumenical Consensus on Baptism, the Eucharist and the Ministry: A Response to the Churches.* 1977.

Paper No. 92. *Sharing in One Hope: Bangalore 1978.* 1979.

Paper No. 111. *Baptism, Eucharist and Ministry.* 1982.

Paper Nos. 112 and 113. *Towards Visible Unity: Commission on Faith and Order, Lima 1982.* Edited by Michael Kinnamon. Vol. I: *Minutes;* Vol. II: *Study Papers and Reports.* 1982.

Paper No. 114. *Growing together in baptism, eucharist and ministry: A study guide.* By William Lazareth. 1982.

Paper No. 116. *Ecumenical perspectives on baptism, eucharist and ministry.* Edited by Max Thurian. 1984.

Hicks, F. C. N. *The Fullness of Sacrifice: An Essay in Reconciliation.* London: Macmillan, 1938.

Wainwright, Geoffrey. *Eucharist and Eschatology.* London: Epworth Press, 1971; 2d. ed. 1978. U.S. ed., New York: Oxford University Press, 1981.

———. *The Ecumenical Moment: Crisis and Opportunity for the Church.* Grand Rapids: Wm. B. Eerdmans, 1983.

LUTHERAN-REFORMED:

Skibbe, Eugene M. "Discussion of Intercommunion in German Protestantism." *Lutheran Quarterly* 11 (1959): 91–111. Arnoldshain Theses, pp. 108–11.

———. "Reaction to the Arnoldshain Theses on the Lord's Supper." *Lutheran Quarterly* 12 (1960): 249–55.

_____. *Protestant Agreement on the Lord's Supper.* Minneapolis: Augsburg Publishing House, 1960.

Bretscher, Paul M. "The Arnoldshain Theses on the Lord's Supper." *Concordia Theological Monthly* 30 (1959): 83–91.

Empie, Paul C., and James I. McCord, ed. *Marburg Revisited: A Reexamination of Lutheran and Reformed Traditions.* Minneapolis: Augsburg Publishing House, 1966. Papers from the first series of American dialogue.

"Leuenberg Agreement." *Lutheran World* 20 (1973): 347–53. Further discussion in *LW* 21 (1974): 328–48, 376–87. Also in *Reformed World* 32 (1973): 256–74.

Mannermaa, Tuomo. *Von Preussen nach Leuenberg. Hinterground und Entwicklung der theologischen Methode der Leuenberger Konkordie.* Arbeiten zur Geschichte und Theologie des Luthertums, Neue Folge, 1. Hamburg: Lutherisches Verlagshaus, 1981. As one would expect, the most detailed work on the Leuenberg Agreement has been done in Europe, as this and the next title indicate. This study begins with the Prussian Union of Lutheran and Reformed Churches in 1817–21.

Schieffer, Elisabeth. *Von Schauenburg nach Leuenberg. Entstehung und Bedeutung der Konkordie reformatorischer Kirchen in Europa.* Konfessionskundliche und kontroverstheologische Studien, 48. Paderborn: Bonifacius-Druckerei, 1983. Covers the Arnoldshain Theses (1955–60), the conferences at Bad Schauenburg (1964–67), and the Leuenberg meetings (1969, 1970, 1971), leading to the Agreement (Konkordie) of 1973. Includes texts, drafts, and summaries of papers and discussions.

Andrews, James E., and Joseph A. Burgess, eds. *An Invitation to Action: The Lutheran-Reformed Dialogue, Series III, 1981–1983.* Philadelphia: Fortress Press, 1984.

LUTHERAN–ROMAN CATHOLIC:

Lutherans and Catholics in Dialogue. Edited by Paul C. Empie and T. Austin Murphy.

III. *The Eucharist as Sacrifice.* New York: U.S.A. National Committee of the Lutheran World Federation; Washington, D.C.: Bishops' Committee for Ecumenical and Interreligious Affairs, 1967. Reprinted with Vols. I and II, Minneapolis: Augsburg Publishing House, 1975.

IV. *Eucharist and Ministry.* New York and Washington, D.C., as above, 1970.

"Report of the Joint Lutheran/Roman Catholic Study Commission on 'The Gospel and the Church'" (Malta Report). *Lutheran World* 19 (1972): 259–73. Widely reprinted elsewhere.

The Eucharist. Lutheran/Roman Catholic Joint Commission. Geneva: Lutheran
World Federation, 1980. German, *Das Herrenmahl.* Paderborn: Bonifacius;
Frankfurt: Lembeck, 1979.

"Eucharistic Hospitality—A Statement by the Institute for Ecumenical
Research. Strasbourg, France, on Lutheran-Roman Catholic Intercommu-
nion." *Lutheran World* 20 (1973): 353–60, cf. 22 (1975): 149–57. *Journal of
Ecumenical Studies* 10 (1973): 856–58.

ANGLICAN–ROMAN CATHOLIC:

ARCIC (Anglican–Roman Catholic International Commission):
  An Agreed Statement on Eucharistic Doctrine. London: SPCK, 1972. "The
    Windsor Statement." 1971.
  Elucidations: Eucharistic Doctrine, Ministry and Ordination. London:
    SPCK, 1979. Completed at Salisbury, 1979.
  The Final Report, Windsor, 1981. London: SPCK; Cincinnati: Forward Move-
    ment Publications; and Washington, D.C.: U.S. Catholic Conference,
    1982. The above texts, plus those from ARCIC on *Ministry and Ordination*
    and *Authority in the Church,* to which are appended "The Malta Report" of
    the Joint Preparatory Commission, 1968, and the Common Declarations of
    the pope and the archbishop of Canterbury in 1966 and 1977. All these
    documents have also been published in other Anglican and Catholic sources.
Charley, Julian W. *The Anglican–Roman Catholic Agreement on the Eucharist.*
  Grove Booklet on Ministry and Worship 1. Bramcote, Notts.: Grove Books,
  1971, 2d ed. 1972. Includes historical introduction and theological commentary by an Evangelical Anglican member of ARCIC.

LUTHERAN–EPISCOPAL:

*Anglican–Lutheran International Conversations: The Report of the Conversa-
tions 1970–1972 authorized by the Lambeth Conference and the Lutheran
World Federation.* London: SPCK, 1973. "The Pullach Report."
*Anglican–Lutheran Dialogue, The Report of the Anglican–Lutheran European
Regional Commission, Helsinki, August-September 1982.* London: SPCK,
1983.
*Anglican-Lutheran Relations. Report [of the] Anglican-Lutheran Joint Working
Group, Cold Ash, Berkshire, England, 28 November–3 December 1983.* London: Anglican Consultative Council; Geneva: Lutheran World Federation,
1983.
Lutheran-Episcopal Dialogue: A Progress Report. Cincinnati: Forward Movement Publications, 1973. "LED I." Three of the papers in the volume were
previously published in the *Concordia Theological Monthly* 43 (1972).
The Report of the Lutheran-Episcopal Dialogue Second Series 1976–1980. Cincinnati: Forward Movement Publications, 1981. "LED II."

The Lutheran-Episcopal Agreement: Commentary and Guidelines. New York: Lutheran Church in America, Division for World Mission and Ecumenism, 1983.

OTHER DIALOGUES AND EVALUATIONS:

Modern Eucharistic Agreement. London: SPCK, 1973. Includes the ARCIC "Windsor Statement" (1971); LRC/usa (1967); the World Council of Churches statement at the Faith and Order meeting, *Louvain 1971;* and the statement of the Group of Les Dombes (1972), originally published in *Documentation catholique* nr. 1606 (2 April 1972): 334–38.

Swidler, Leonard, ed. *The Eucharist in Ecumenical Dialogue.* New York: Paulist Press, 1976. Also published as *Journal of Ecumenical Studies* 13, 2 (special issue, Spring 1976): 191–344, but with the book pages (cited above) also given.

Catholic Theological Society of America:
  "The Bilateral Consultations Between the Roman Catholic Church in the United States and Other Christian Communions . . . . Report of July 1972." *Proceedings of the Catholic Theological Society of America* 27 (1973): Appendix A, 179–232.
  "The Bilateral Consultations Between the Roman Catholic Church in the United States and Other Christian Communions (1972–1979). A Theological Review and Critique by the Study Committee Commissioned. . . ." *Proceedings* 34 (1979): Appendix C, 253–85.

Lutherans in Ecumenical Dialogue: An Interpretive Guide. "Studies" series. New York: Lutheran Council in the U.S.A., Division of Theological Studies, 1977.

Lutheran World Federation, Secretariat for Interconfessional Research and Dialogue, Geneva:
  Ecumenical Relations of the LWF: Report of the Working Group on Interrelations between the Various Bilateral Dialogues. 1977.
  Ecumenical Methodology: Documentation and Report. Edited by Peder Højen. 1978.

Braaten, Carl E. "A Decade of Ecumenical Dialogues." *Dialog* 13 (1974): 142–48.

Kretschmar, Georg. "Konvergenz- und Konsenstexte als Ergebnis bilateraler Dialoge über das hl. Abendmahl." *Ökumenische Rundschau* 29 (1980): 1–21. Expanded version of the survey presented in English at the Forum on Bilateral Conversations, sponsored by the Faith and Order Commission, 6 June 1979. It examines Lutheran-Reformed, Anglican-Lutheran, Anglican–Roman Catholic, Lutheran–Roman Catholic, Methodist–Roman Catholic, Reformed–Roman Catholic, and Anglican-Orthodox dialogues.

Schöpsdau, Walter. "Eucharistie," pp. 60–105, in *Kommentar zu den Lima-*

Erklärungen über Taufe, Eucharistie und Amt. Edited by Konfes-
sionskundliches Institut, with E. Geldbach and R. Frieling. Bensheimer
Hefte, 59. Göttingen: Vandenhoeck & Ruprecht, 1983. An analysis of *BEM*,
from a German Protestant Ecumenical Institute. Schöpsdau points up the considerable Eastern Orthodox influences in the document.

4

Some Conclusions
and Comments

THE MOTIFS made prominent by modern biblical studies and by ecumenical discussions concerning the Lord's Supper are powerful factors in most understandings of this sacrament today. They are often also factors for change of long-inherited views.

All churches in Christendom are being asked to respond to the 1982 Faith and Order statement *Baptism, Eucharist and Ministry* as an initial step in a process of "reception." The New Testament, of course, speaks of "receiving" the Gospel of Christ's death and resurrection (1 Cor. 15:1) and of "receiving" basic traditions about that kerygma (1 Cor. 15:3-5) or about the Lord's Supper (1 Cor. 11:23-25). It also enjoins "receiving" (RSV, "welcoming") one another—the "strong" and the "weak" parties, Gentiles and Jews—"as Christ has welcomed [or received] you" (Rom. 15:7), in one body. While historians can point to how the decisions of councils through the centuries were "received," or Reformation confessions accepted, there is relatively little in the way of modern ecumenical precedent of "receiving" documents from bilaterals or multilaterals. (Cf. Ulrich Kuhn, "Reception," in *Ecumenical Perspectives on Baptism, Eucharist and Ministry,* Paper No. 116 [Geneva: WCC, 1984], pp. 165-71). The formal acceptance of the Leuenberg Agreement by Lutheran, Reformed, and Union churches in Europe is, however, one example. "Interim sharing of the Eucharist" by U.S. Lutherans and Episcopalians in 1982 provides another.

As a result of the ecumenical findings and their biblical foundations, as viewed today, each Christian is also, in a sense, being asked to decide about these matters. When their churches act on such agreements, Christians are individually called upon to affirm (or reject) those actions by the way they carry them through in local congregations. Where their churches have not formally "received" a dialogue agreement or *BEM,* individuals may nonetheless react by the way they deal with other Christians, above all by inviting or going with each other to share together at the Table of the Lord. Whatever churches as a whole do or do not do officially, people will continue to vote—often with their feet!—on altar fellowship, in some cases by going to places where greater ecumenical inclusiveness is possible and in others by pulling out of churches where intercommunion has begun to occur.

It is therefore imperative that churches and Christians grasp some of the changes that have been taking place regarding the Eucharist and the revolutions in attitude that may be ahead in faith and practice. The potential changes are enough to require what Nikos Nissiotis has called "a conversion of heart and mind" (Preface to *Ecumenical Perspectives,* Paper No. 116, p. xii).

The two main chapters of this book have sought to sketch some of the currents in the biblical and ecumenical streams of thought today about the Eucharist, with briefer attention to the centuries of development between the New Testament and modern church discussions. From these descriptions now emerge some conclusions, options, and comments that may be of help in guiding assessment of where things are in connection with this sacrament.

1. There has obviously been great *progress* in reversing the scandal that the sacrament of one bread and one cup (1 Cor. 10:16–17, 21) had become Christianity's most denominationally segregated moment. Regardless of how limited actual results are as yet, more and more Christians are thinking more and more about the need to be one at the table that belongs not to their denominations but to Christ, who is not divided into parties (1 Cor. 1:13).

2. While it is possible to concentrate on the Lord's Supper as the particular focal point of unity, *BEM* is correct that Eucharist *interrelates* with baptism and the ministry, not to mention the gospel, Scripture and the Word of God, among other things.

a. The bilateral dialogues—in that they concentrate on what has been divisive in the past and often take up a single topic at a time—tend, however, to *isolate* subjects or at best deal with them *sequentially.* The U.S. Lutheran–Roman Catholic dialogue, for example, took up baptism, then Eucharist, then ministry, but never with the parallelism of Faith and Order's treatment of the three. Or is the way *BEM* draws parallels, even in its outline for Baptism and Eucharist, somewhat forced?

b. Oddly enough, Scripture studies may be the worst offender in *not* seeing the Eucharist, baptism, ministry, and other topics *holistically*. There are a number of New Testament monographs on each subject individually, but rarely are they treated together. The treatment in biblical theology is an exception but there the analysis seldom goes beyond first-century documents. An exception here was Alan Richardson's *An Introduction to the Theology of the New Testament* ([London: SCM Press, 1958], especially pp. 364–87), where, however, the patristic solutions were often read back into the New Testament (for example, pp. 380–81).

3. *Biblical theology* and its results have been of considerable import in recent, cooperative progress in views about the Lord's Supper. However, one senses at least *two* different types of biblical theology or ways of proceeding in this much-debated discipline.

There was an *older* style, stressing the *unity* of the New Testament writings and resting on the view that scholarship can recover a great deal about *the historical Jesus* and his intentions about, for example, a church and continuation of the Last Supper as a Lord's Supper. This approach flourished until the early 1960s and is exemplified in the writings of Oscar Cullmann, Joachim Jeremias, J. J. von Allmen, and others.

The alternative view came to the fore later, stressing *variety* in New Testament thought, casting doubt on our ability to work back to *Jesus* "as he really was and thought," and presenting at best a careful tracing of the *lines of development* in the New Testament period. J. D. G. Dunn's *Unity and Diversity* exemplifies this trend.

a. The *BEM* statement on Eucharist seems to rest on the earlier type of biblical theology, though there is little doubt that contemporary studies have moved away from that approach.

b. With the bilateral dialogues it is harder to tell where they are in the use of "biblical theology" and exegetical findings. Some dialogues show little reflection in their statements of what type of biblical analysis, if any, was employed. The U.S. Lutheran-Catholic volumes may be the most significant here because they include the essays by Scripture scholars from which their discussions proceeded. But their scriptural input seems heavier in the studies on Peter and papal primacy and on justification than on the Lord's Supper.

4. It is necessary to record a certain *cleavage* among churches *over Scripture and its use*. For one thing, in spite of statements like the Lambeth Quadrilateral for Anglicans on the need to agree upon an essential role for the Bible in the reunion of the churches, there is probably some

difference of opinion over the exact *place of the Bible* in theology, especially on the part of Protestant liberals or of churches placing strong emphases on ecclesiastical tradition. For another, there is probably an even-greater division over the degree to which one is to use the various *methods of modern historical criticism* in interrogating the Bible about what it says on any issue. Here the Orthodox, the Fundamentalist churches (or wings of churches), and some Third World churches line up against Protestant churches in the North Atlantic countries generally, many Roman Catholics, and some Third World theologians (for example, in Latin America, Japan) on the usage of "tradition criticism" and its subdisciplines. A vivid example, with regard to the Eucharist, would be a position which takes the Gospel texts as presenting a unified picture of Jesus in the Upper Room instituting the Eucharist, in contrast to a position that sees a number of roots for the Lord's Supper in the early church, with the Gospels reflecting stages in this development, not Jesus' "very words."

Where rapprochement has occurred about the Lord's Supper in ecumenical discussion, it comes where participants either share a noncritical approach to Scripture or where they agree generally on the propriety of the use of the historical-critical method. In the case of Leuenberg, New Testament analysis actually helped pave the way for agreement. Where historical-biblical studies are rejected in principle or practice, the way to agreement is likely more difficult (for example, inter-Lutheran relations in the United States, on which cf. *Studies in Lutheran Hermeneutics* [Philadelphia: Fortress Press, 1979]; obviously discussions with the Orthodox may face peculiar problems here).

5. The *centuries of development* of eucharistic doctrine and practices between New Testament times and today saw decisive steps in the understanding of the sacrament: in the second to sixth centuries, including the fixing of its place within a sacramental system (or systems) of priestly ministry; in the ninth and eleventh centuries, with sharp controversies over "symbolic meaning"; and in the sixteenth century, in certain Reformation emphases. A new stage has come since the 1960s with the ecumenical attempts to resolve old divisions that have grown up over the past centuries.

6. The way has been prepared for these recent rapprochements not only by biblical studies but also by the *liturgical movement*. This movement has often rolled back denominational emphases from the sixteenth

or other centuries by seeking to locate a consensus point in some earlier century, often in the work of a third-century figure like Hippolytus. We may note that writers like Dom Gregory Dix often combined both liturgical and biblical interests. But we may also note that an earlier emphasis on a characteristic fourfold "form," or shape, to the sacrament in the action of taking, giving thanks, breaking, and giving the bread (such as Dix espoused) is now less heard and has become in *BEM* an emphasis on (five) motives connected with the Eucharist (von Allmen's seminal essay for Faith and Order saw six: *anamnesis* and *epiklesis;* the church; Communion; living bread and sacrifice; prayer and fulfillment; Mass and Eucharist [*The Lord's Supper,* p. 20]).

7. The *bilateral dialogues* have especially and repeatedly tackled the longtime problems of Christ's presence and the understanding of sacrifice to be connected with the Eucharist. While only time will tell how convincing their arguments are, the dialogues among Roman Catholics, Anglicans, Lutherans, and Reformed and Presbyterians have found common agreement on the *presence* of the whole Christ in the Eucharist, indeed with the elements, from consecration until the use of the bread and wine in eating and drinking—and, with varying emphasis, a presence beyond that time (still disputed). There has also been widespread agreement on the uniqueness of Jesus' *sacrifice* in his death upon the cross but then also on its continuing availability to people today as a means for forgiveness and life—something with which believers themselves are united in sacrifice (though expression of this point remains under debate). Variously nuanced, the agreements in the dialogues claim to transcend the old divisiveness at these two critical points.

Such agreements are reflected in *BEM,* and some of the following emphases in the agreed statement of Faith and Order were likewise sometimes employed in subsequent bilaterals.

Whether *BEM* is accepted or rejected as a whole, or, as is more likely, is widely accepted in part, the bilateral agreements may provide the most specific arenas of agreement in the next few years and therefore of actual advance.

8. The Eucharist statement from Faith and Order, in setting forth the first three of its five motifs, follows a *trinitarian arrangement* of thanksgiving to *the Father,* memorial of *Christ,* and invocation of *the Spirit.* This arrangement is both fitting and attractive, though not without its questions (see below), for the sequence of the motifs requires consider-

ation of each in terms of content and should not simply be assumed on the basis of the traditional order in doctrine of "Father, Son, and Holy Ghost." Not only do the remaining *BEM* motifs (see pp. 191–92, below) then hang somewhat loosely in the outline but other (New Testament) motifs like "covenant" and "Jesus' death" or "faith" have perhaps been somewhat blunted by the five themes thus stated and elevated into prominence.

9. Though several bilaterals and *BEM* indicate the many names by which this "meal" or "Sacrament of the Altar" has been known since New Testament times, the term "Eucharist" has apparently become, out of certain historical concerns and for reasons of convenience, *the* name in a common ecumenical language today. Thus, terminology that certain traditions may have little used twenty or thirty years ago has come to be the widespread—if unreflectively adopted—parlance.

One result of this development is, almost instinctively, in order to explain the term "Eucharist," the assertion of *thanksgiving to the Father* as the initial motif for emphasis. In its favor as an initial emphasis is the example of Jesus, at the Last Supper—in accord with the practice of Jews at all meals: to bless God and give thanks, in a *berakah*. This mealtime feature became in time a thanksgiving in the Communion service for all God's beneficent acts in the great drama of salvation history, from the creation, through Israel's experiences, to Jesus' death and resurrection, stretching till the hoped-for time of his Parousia. Yet this notion of blessing or "benediction *(berakah)* by which the Church expresses its thankfulness to God for all his benefits" *(BEM,* Eucharist #3) is open to the criticism that it mistakenly strikes this note of blessing for *eucharistein* (the Greek verbal root giving us Eucharist) when praise, confession, and proclamation of God is what ought to be heard (J. M. R. Tillard, *Ecumenical Perspectives,* Paper No. 116, pp. 115–16, though Eucharist #3 does speak of the Eucharist as "a proclamation and a celebration of the work of God").

When giving thanks merges into "thank-offering," and the device of getting bread and wine to the altar through an offertory procession suggests an initial human contribution that "primes the pump" for the celebration, the way is open to criticism from an evangelical point of view: the thanksgiving stands in danger of becoming a vehicle for expression of human merit alongside Christ's, a way of putting our contribution as an addition to God's saving work. Of course, an answer to all this, even for the staunchest evangelical, is a reminder that all that believing Christians do is within a diastolic-systolic rhythm: "freely ye have received, freely give" (Matt. 10:8, KJV). What is offered to God for use in this meal comes from the bounty God has already granted in creation and salvation, along with God's gift of faith.

There is also the fact to be noted that thanksgiving—to God, Father, Son, and Spirit—runs through all the Communion service. It is especially often expressed at the close of many liturgies, upon reception of the gift of Christ himself and all that gift means, by further prayer.

10. The christological aspect in a trinitarian outline of eucharistic motifs appears in the emphasis, so dominant in recent ecumenical discussion, on *anamnesis, or memorial of Christ*. It is rooted in the Pauline and Lukan forms of the Words of Institution (1 Cor. 11:24, 25; Luke 22:19, "in remembrance of me"). What once seemed a battleground between Reformed (and Anglican) concepts of the communicants' thinking upon Jesus in contrast to a more realistic view of Christ's presence has been transcended in almost all recent ecumenical statements on the basis of earlier biblical and liturgical scholarship. The Semitic concept of "remembering," so that a past event like the Passover is made present in its effects, as in a family Passover meal, has been regarded as the key: re-presentation makes the benefits of Jesus' cross, as well as Christ himself, to be active and effective for participants in a Eucharist. This is above all the work of the Holy Spirit (see pp. 190–91, below).

If consensus is proof, few agreements are better grounded. One is given slight pause, however, by the question of whether "remembrance" in the New Testament passages cited is Semitic or stems at least in part from Hellenistic pagan memorial meals. There are grounds for further reflection in the fact that the Spirit as vehicle of *anamnesis* seems not a Semitic emphasis but one that has grown up from the Christian practice, indeed post–New Testament practice, of invoking the Spirit in the Eucharist (*epiclesis*, pp. 190–91, below). Finally, there is the more-recent examination of the term *zkr*, "remember," in Hebraic use, and the contention that it really denotes proclamation rather than some "immanent dynamic implanted by God in the memory itself" or ancient Near Eastern cultic claim that ritual actualizes or re-presents the content of a prior myth or event (cf. pp. 29ff., above).

In spite of widespread employment of the *anamnesis*/re-presentation argument, therefore, perhaps further consideration is in order.

It may also be asked whether this focusing upon the phrase "remembrance," or "memorial of Christ," directs attention away from the original sacrificial death that took place once for all, the physical body and blood of Jesus which he said in the Upper Room was going to be given/broken/poured out—and which was—on the cross. Furthermore, should the Lima text have said more about "remission of sins" as a result in this "sacrament of pardon" (Tillard, in *Ecumenical Perspectives*, Paper No. 116, pp. 109–10)?

11. The Eucharist as *epiklesis,* or *invocation of the Spirit,* has already been mentioned as the third of the trinitarian aspects and the crucial link in the argument of how re-presentation of Christ, or *anamnesis,* occurs. The coupling of *anamnesis* and *epiclesis* takes on almost dogmatic insistence in *BEM*. It has been noted above (see pp. 155–62) how this endorsement of a contribution from Eastern theology and liturgy enriches the Latin tradition. A happy resolution has seemingly been effected between something on which the Orthodox insist (the *epiclesis)* and Western practice, and so also a link has been forged between Reformed interest in the Spirit and other (more vivid) expressions of Christ's presence.

Yet there remains a certain strand of Roman Catholic thinking still that no *epiclesis* of the Spirit is absolutely needed at the point proposed in a eucharistic prayer after the Words of Institution, since the *verba* in the canon of the Mass have already brought about the consecration (and transubstantiation) of the elements (cf. G. A. Maloney, "Epiclesis," in *New Catholic Encyclopedia* [1967], Vol. 5, p. 465; contrast the more-nuanced answer of J. H. McKenna in the 1974 *Supplement,* Vol. 16, p. 155: an epiclesis is not "absolutely necessary" or "the only means of expressing the role of the Holy Spirit in the Eucharist," but it is "a *practical* necessity").

Perhaps more serious as an obstacle to this emphasis is the dearth of evidence for invoking the Spirit in Judaism as a vehicle for "remembering" and the lack of reference to the Spirit in the New Testament in connection with the *verba* (cf. von Allmen, *Lord's Supper,* p. 31). The cry was more likely, "Our *Lord,* come." (The Faith and Order "Eucharistic Liturgy of Lima" at its second *epiclesis* uses the Aramaic *Maranatha,* but, while not dividing the phrase either as *marana tha,* "Our Lord, come!" or as *maran atha,* "Our Lord has come," glosses it with "the Lord comes"; cf. Conzelmann, *1 Corinthians,* Hermeneia [Philadelphia: Fortress Press, 1975], pp. 300–301; for the liturgy, see *Ecumenical*

Perspectives, Paper No. 116, pp. 232, 243–44.) Hence, as an alternative or parallel there exists the invocation of the Word, as in some ancient liturgies and in Reformation thought.

Karl-Hermann Kandler has called attention to the astonishing frequency with which recent ecumenical agreements, both Protestant and Roman Catholic, stress the *epiclesis* of the Holy Spirit as the vehicle for "presence," yet at the same time to the paucity of references to the Spirit in such contexts in the confessional writings of, for example, Lutherans or the dogmatic statements of Roman Catholics. (See "Abendmahl und Heiliger Geist," *Kerygma und Dogma* 28 [1982]: 215–28.) Kandler also quotes Orthodox theologians to the effect that in the New Testament there is no express connection between Eucharist and Spirit and cites the conclusion that the *epiclesis* was first of all an invocation of the Spirit upon the congregation, only later and secondarily upon the elements. After canvassing various Western theologians on the topic, Kandler concludes with a plea for further dialogue on the connection of the Spirit with the Lord's Supper; the debate has scarcely begun, and many of the assertions on the matter in recent ecumenical documents he terms "worthless" because of lack of explanation, differentiation, and evidence.

Might one suggestion be worth examining? The New Testament (for example, 1 Cor. 15:49; 2 Cor. 3:16–18) closely relates "Lord" and "Spirit." Jesus Christ has become a "life-giving spirit." "Christ" and "Spirit" are never, I would insist, identified with each other, but they are related so that "Spirit" is seen in light of Christ. John Ziesler has suggested, "Christ is now Spirit, especially in the way he comes to his people and deals with them" *(Pauline Christianity* [New York: Oxford University Press, 1983], p. 45). To this extent, there may be a biblical basis for what is later developed as invocation of the Spirit to come so as to provide the presence of the Lord Jesus Christ.

12. *Communion of the faithful* in the Eucharist has two aspects: Communion with Christ and with each other. Both have existed since New Testament times. For the Corinthians Paul stressed "participation" (or, RSV note, "communion") in the body and blood of Christ, that is, with the Lord's whole person (10:16), but also meeting together (11:18, 20) and eating and drinking together, while "discerning the body" (11:24) in the sense of the community, with concern for one another (11:33). In the history of this sacrament and its reception, there has often been an oscillation between emphasizing fellowship with Christ (at the expense of fel-

lowship with one's sisters and brothers in Christ) and at other times emphasizing communal relations (at the expense of sharing in Christ's presence). The fourth century, for example, saw "the coincidence between Eucharist and communion" begin "to dwindle," von Allmen notes (*Lord's Supper*, p. 61), while the Reformers, he allows, tried in their own way to restore the emphasis on Communion of the faithful at the Sacrament. *BEM* seeks to include both aspects of Communion: with Christ and with each other. The ARCIC *Final Report* has put all it says about sacraments, ministry, and church within a framework of *koinonia* (Communion, participation, fellowship).

Churches run a constant temptation to swing—like a pendulum—between the two, both vital, poles, emphasizing now the vertical relationship with Christ, now the horizontal with others.

Perhaps the emphasis on "the faithful" here makes this the place to assert the importance of never losing sight of the place of faith in any sacramental theology.

13. To speak of the Eucharist as *the Meal of the Kingdom* does more than raise up again aspects of the meal-nature of the sacrament already touched upon (for example, the communal aspect), for it suggests the Lord's Supper roots in the other meals of Jesus, often with the poor and with outcasts, and in his feeding of the multitudes, as well as in the Last Supper. But most important, by those connections and by reference to "the kingdom" and the imagery of the banquet to come in the last times, it reminds us of the *eschatological* dynamic in the Eucharist. Scripture references such as 1 Cor. 11:26 and Mark 14:25 plainly point to a future fulfillment. *BEM* and other statements—not unbiblically but perhaps too quickly—stress a realization of present eschatology in the eucharistic celebration, a "foretaste of the feast to come." Albert Schweitzer (and others) would lament the almost appendagelike character given to eschatology by making it the last of five aspects. What if one were to begin with it?

14. The *burning issues* posed by *BEM* can readily be pointed out. A Dutch theologian has written of the process leading to *BEM* thus:

Pedo-baptists [those who baptize infants] and believer-baptists corrected one another; churches of the West learned from churches of the East to restore the epicletic character of the eucharist; Catholics and Protestants learned from the Jews what it means to celebrate the Memorial of Christ as *zikkaron-anamnesis;* episcopal churches had to learn together with non-episcopal churches, what "episcopé" really means in both the Ancient Church and today. (Anton Houtepen, in *Ecumenical Perspectives,* Paper No. 116, p. 146)

A Lutheran participant said of *BEM:*

> The Faith and Order statement on baptism invites the Lutheran churches . . . to understand holy baptism as an action based on faith and therefore to concede a relative justification for the churches which practise believer's baptism. The Faith and Order statement on the Eucharist invites the Lutheran churches to understand Holy Communion not one-sidedly in terms of the forgiveness of sins but as a eucharistic act of the Church, and this as a basic, essential interpretation of the Lord's Supper. The statement on the Ministry invites the Lutheran churches to a new theological and spiritual office of bishop. . . . A similar list of invitations could be drawn up for other churches to whom these reports have now been transmitted. (Ulrich Kuhn, in *Ecumenical Perspectives,* Paper No. 116, p. 170).

All in all, the most burning issues posed are probably *believers' baptism* (over against infant baptism); *infant Communion* (in contrast to first Communion at age seven or so or confirmation as admission to the sacrament); and the *threefold ministry,* including *historic episcopate.*

Does all this mean, as the Moderator of Faith and Order has named the suspicion, a kind of "interconfessional syncretism" (Nikos Nissiotis, in *Ecumenical Perspectives,* Paper No. 116, p. vi)? Is it conceivable that the result could be a church so pluralistic that one might have both infant Communion (for all in "the family of God") and adult (believer's) baptism? (Who says no new sacramental models are possible?)

Others may wish to add their own examples of crucial issues that are raised by *BEM* and other ecumenical advances or crucial issues that are perhaps omitted or undervalued by them. To take a phenomenon widespread across denominational lines, *the role of the laity* is increasingly being pressed by lay people (and some clergy). Very probably, save for a nod to "the ministry of the whole people of God," all too little has been said in the dialogues and even *BEM* about that ministry. Could lay roles in eucharistic celebrations involve more than reading Scripture or assisting the ordained at certain points? At least some would press for it.

On the matter of *chrismation/confirmation,* devastating quotes can be cited from past history. About the custom that "the bishop should rush about to those who have been baptized by presbyters and deacons far from larger cities, to call down the Holy Spirit by the laying on of hands," Jerome wrote:

It is done rather for the glory of the bishop than for any pressure of necessity. If the Holy Spirit only descends at the mighty imprecation of a bishop, they are most unfortunate who live in farms or villages, or who happen to die in remote spots after being baptized by presbyters or deacons before the bishop can discover them. *(Dialogus contra Luciferianos* 9, as cited by C. Argenti, in *Ecumenical Perspectives,* Paper No. 116, p. 62)

Yet Pope Innocent I insisted that transmitting the Spirit at the hands solely of bishops

is not demonstrated by ecclesiastical custom alone, but also by the passage in the Acts of the Apostles [Acts 8: 14–17] which states that Peter and John were sent to transmit the Holy Spirit to those who had already been baptized. (DS #98; in 34th ed., #215; Argenti, in *Ecumenical Perspectives*, Paper No. 116, p. 63)

Luther once said:

I allow that confirmation be administered provided that it is known that God has said nothing about it, and what the bishops say about it is false. *(Von ehelichen Leben,* as cited by D. R. Holeton, in *Ecumenical Perspectives,* Paper No. 116, p. 83; "The Estate of Marriage," *Luther's Works,* Vol. 45 [Philadelphia: Fortress Press, 1962], pp. 24f., but cf. pp. 5 and 8; Luther was condemning not the rite of confirmation but its elevation to a sacrament.)

Perhaps what is needed is to sort out the arguments, from modern exegesis, historical developments, and theological insights, on this topic, with something of the attention given in *BEM* to its three subjects (see pp. 194–95, below).

BEM has on occasion been called "the least worst draft" the churches could expect at this point. Could it not be bettered at some points, possibly among them at some of the points noted above?

15. *Sacramental systems* enter into the equation in a way not always made clear by bilaterals or even *BEM*. In commenting on the work of Faith and Order, Lukas Vischer has contrasted churches that attach primary importance to the question of "the one faith" in a confessional approach and those that attach primary import to "the sacraments and structures of the Church." He urges the Reformation churches, which emphasize the living Word, not to "under-rate the significance of the sacramental structures of fellowship," but he also sees a challenge to churches in the "catholic" tradition to recognize the need for "common

confession," since "unity in the sacramental structures *can* be a dead unity" *(Ecumenical Perspectives,* Paper No. 116, pp. 7–8).

We have already indicated the fact that, in reality, several different sacramental structures or ways of looking at the Eucharist in a systematic context do exist (see p. 144, above, where Wagner's sequence followed a different order). These systems include at least the following, as outlined below, involving baptism, Eucharist, and chrismation/confirmation:

A. The Eastern Orthodox model: all three at first initiation;
B. The Western Latin (Process) model: infant baptism and then (at age seven, or age thirteen or fourteen) first Communion and confirmation (or vice versa);
C. The Baptist model: believer's baptism with the anointing of the Spirit, followed by participation in the Lord's Table.

Features of each, pro and con, were noted above, and the suggestion that only model B, with some sort of "confirmation," was viable for uniting all three groups. Here is not the place to argue that (or any other view) but simply to record the necessity to look at any sacrament within the systematic setting of a tradition and to caution about too readily mixing parts of one system with those of another until the whole is thought through.

16. The role of *faith* has several times been alluded to in connection with the Eucharist (see above, points 12 and 14). Involved is the relation between the subjective and the objective sides in treatment of the sacraments (or of almost anything else in religion). There has been a long history of shifting between an emphasis on the objective efficacy of the sacrament *(ex opere operato;* recitation of the *verba;* an *epiclesis;* the work of Christ) and on the subjective appropriation of its benefits (by faith; receptionism). Probably today we are in a period of emphasis on objectivity and of reaction against subjectivism (and individualism), though not in all quarters of the church. From the discourse in the Gospel of John (6:29, 30, 35, 36, 40, 47, 64, 69) on believing that Jesus is the bread of life, through the centuries, this aspect of faith/trust/belief appears often enough that it should not be overlooked—even when the scale is tipped in the other direction—nor should it be overstressed to make everything into a matter of individual subjectivity.

17. On occasion, the matter of *frequency* of Communion has surfaced, in bilateral statements and in the varied phrases of *BEM,* Eucharist ##30, 31. We have also noted the necessary distinction between celebration and

reception, and a tendency to find agreement on the idea that normally no Mass should be without communicants. While many ecumenical statements and liturgiologists state that the Eucharist should be the normal or sole Sunday service, the situation even in communions which have stated goals to that effect probably varies considerably, and, given a chance to discuss the matter, some laity (and clergy) would ask "Why weekly Communion?"

All too infrequently are the further questions honestly surfaced of "If weekly, why not daily?" and whether the effects of receiving the Eucharist (for example, Christ's presence, forgiveness, Communion, thanksgiving) cannot be present also in other ways (proclamation of the word, absolution, other types of prayer). Some of the arguments employed for weekly frequency seem less than convincing: to speak, as does *BEM* #20, of "the central event of the world's history" in this connection is a reference to Jesus' cross—of which the Eucharist is but one way to bring its benefits into the present ("to proclaim the Lord's death until he comes again" [1 Cor. 11:26] is surely but one form, though a powerful one, of "proclaiming Christ crucified" [1 Cor. 1:23; 2:2]). Or, to say "No Sunday without eucharist, no eucharist without Sunday" (Rordorf) seems overly rigid (and mechanical in denying weekday occasions; but so von Allmen, *Lord's Supper*, p. 112).

The strongest argument for regular Sunday celebrations seems to be the claim that Jesus instituted this meal and that it remains the uniquely Christian form of worship, elsewhere unparalleled. That argument will be evaluated on the degree to which one feels we can work back to words and intent of the historical Jesus and will be judged in light of what one thinks about cult meals in the history of world religions, in Hellenism or elsewhere, as an influence. A note of some import, biblically, is that on occasion the Hebrew scriptures speak guardedly of Moses and some Israelites, the seventy elders and three others, eating and drinking with God (Exod. 24:9–11) and hold out the vision of a messianic banquet in the future (Isa. 25:6–9). Does Christian worship now make regular what was for Israel rare and generally awaited?

18. Is sharing the Eucharist *a means toward or the goal of church unity?* Traditionally, many churches have regarded eucharistic fellowship as a goal to be attained upon agreement in certain basics. These required preliminary agreements might fall into the realm of doctrine or of church order, for example, recognition of ministry. At least since the Second Vatican Council the possibility has been held out that sacramental sharing

might begin even where churches are not yet in full agreement over all aspects of faith and life. Gradually there has been movement toward the position that, upon basic agreement in the gospel or in certain designated areas, fellowship at the Lord's Table can be practiced. Sharing in the sacrament thus becomes a lived experience that one hopes will help toward full(er) unity. The U.S. Lutheran-Episcopal agreement in 1982 to have interim sharing of the Eucharist is something of a breakthrough and a possible prototype. In a sense, *BEM* embodies a proposal for agreement on three traditional stickingpoints. For churches who find its statements satisfactory, sacramental sharing could follow as a step toward something more and ultimately lead to the Faith and Order goal of "one eucharistic fellowship" and "visible unity in one faith."

19. Attention has been drawn to steps toward that goal of fellowship and unity such as a new statement of Christian faith by *the year 2000*. Appropriate celebration of anniversaries—such as the sixteen hundredth of the First Council of Constantinople (381), marked in 1981, or the twelve hundredth of the seventh General or Ecumenical Council, the Second Council of Nicea in 787 (to be observed in 1987 when the Fifth World Conference on Faith and Order will be held)—also point us to the *past heritage in faith* that many churches share. We have several times called attention to the use of understandings about the Eucharist in "the building period of the church," the time of the Fathers, the creeds, the great liturgies, and the great councils, in contrast to the "normative apostolic period"—for example, with regard to the Eucharist, the developments taking place by the time of Hippolytus. Faith and Order sees later confessions and conciliar decrees as "always subject not only to the authority of Scripture but also to that of those universally received documents which concern the centre of faith and which the Church holds from this [building] period . . ." *(Ecumenical Perspectives, Paper No. 116, pp. xvi–xvii, reflecting Paper No. 100, Towards a Confession of the Common Faith* [1980], pp. 3–4).

Questions must now be raised about the exact relationship between apostolic Scripture and the documents of the church's "building period." To what extent are these third-to-fifth-century developments authoritative *jure divino* ("by divine law")? To what extent are they "reversible"? In what way do they relate to Scripture?

To raise such questions leads to at least two answers, obvious to different points of view. Some will say, "The developments of the church-building period are in fact, like Scripture, fully authoritative, for they reflect God's ongoing will for the church; to reconsider them is unthink-able." Others will say, "Of course they are subject to the biblical revela-tion. They may well accord with it, as later historical developments in the Greco-Roman world, and by human standards be quite natural outcomes in history, but they are subject to reconsideration in light of what is of greater authority and of the needs of today."

We may illustrate what is at issue with something that many would consider set and fixed—the Christology arrived at in the church-building period. In the U.S. Lutheran-Catholic dialogue the Jesuit John Courtney Murray maintained the position that Nicene dogma, especially about the Son, is—since its inception in 325 and development in 381—"immutable" or in effect "irreversible" *(The Status of the Nicene Creed as Dogma of the Church* [New York: U.S.A. National Committee of the Lutheran World Federation; Washington, D.C.: Bishops' Committee for Ecumenical Affairs, 1965], pp. 21–22; reprinted *Lutherans and Catho-lics in Dialogue I–III,* ed. Paul C. Empie and T. Austin Murphy [Minne-apolis: Augsburg Publishing House, n.d.]). Yet today, without rejecting Chalcedon, in its setting, as a legitimate christological statement, respon-sible theologians have stressed also a pre-Chalcedonian—indeed prepatristic—"Christology from below," drawing on the New Testament positions as earlier, authoritative, and more suitable for today. Cf. Edward Schillebeeckx, *Jesus: An Experiment in Christology* (New York: Crossroad, 1979), or J. Sobrino, *Christology at the Crossroads: A Latin American Approach* (Maryknoll, N.Y.: Orbis Books, 1978), among oth-ers. Such a stance, of course, though it may not be the primary aim of these theologians, offers a reopening of the case in Christology for the so-called non-Chalcedonian churches.

If such a move is occurring—to go, in effect, behind the church-building period to the New Testament in Christology—is not the same thing also or even more a possibility with (a) baptism, (b) the ministry, and (c) the Eucharist?

20. Therefore, is it possible, with regard to the Eucharist, to set our *perimeters* for ecumenical reunion in the matter of the Lord's Supper both as *broadly and as specifically as the New Testament does?* Can we not allow as much pluralism as these Scriptures do, as seen in recent interpre-tation? Can we be as broad in outlook—and as emphatic on some points—as the canonical books?

This is not an argument that the church-building centuries—the third to sixth—are unimportant or should not be factors in our thinking; but simply that, significant as they are, they are subordinate to Scripture and were subject to factors in development that sometimes moved away from, or unfolded in a one-sided way, the New Testament norms. (The latter part of the second century is too varied, too unknown to us, too lacking in unity to provide much help as a norm; it is a "caesura" in known development; cf. *TRE,* Vol. 1, pp. 59–60. The New Testament documents may, of course, in a few cases date from the first half of the second century as well as the first century.)

This is not an argument to repristinate solely and simply alleged New Testament views and practices, for often we do not know the views of New Testament Christians on certain issues. Certainly too there were post-New Testament questions that the church-building (and later) periods took up and answered, indeed, rightly. We need to respect such developments and answers, though holding them subject to further consideration.

This is an appeal to recognize that if the route of ecumenical discussion has been to transcend later doctrinal and other divisions from, say the sixteenth century, by appeal to earlier centuries, the next move is to allow appeal, as far as possible, to the biblical witness, to set as norm for us both the positive emphases and the allowable pluralism of the New Testament.

If it be objected that the early variety was much too diverse, we may answer with von Allmen's words about liturgical diversity in the early stages: it "did not compromise the unity of the Church, did not hinder a local Church from acknowledging in another local Church the grace which was the source of her own life, even if this other Church possessed a different liturgical tradition" *(Lord's Supper,* pp. 14–15).

If it be asked which stage or stages in the pluralism of New Testament development should be recognized, the answer must be, all of them that we can ascertain—Pauline, Johannine, Markan, Matthean, Lukan, and so forth, even pre-Pauline and Palestinian, and Jesus' own outlook, where we can tell. Would that not be an honest recognition of the fact that some churches today are in their tradition basically Pauline or Johannine, or whatever; and if biblical, then legitimate. Christendom can be as varied as the New Testament.

The ultimate outcome of the ecumenical motifs today should be, allowing for a variety of later chronological, geographical, cultural, and doctrinal developments, to reflect as much as possible the biblical motifs. Then one would be as catholic and as evangelical as this oldest Christian

witness to the word of God, and as free and as committed to Christ as
were these first followers in the Christian faith.

21. It would not leave a true impression of the biblical materials and
recent ecumenical statements on the Eucharist if one did not conclude by
noting—and giving thanks for—the sense found there of *joy, praise to
God,* and *passion for* the right celebration and reception among Christians of *the Lord's Supper.* One is dealing not with dry-as-dust doctrines
or mechanical practices but what for the writers brings life, peace, forgiveness, cause for rejoicing, and reconciliation. Even those groups that
seem nonsacramental, like the Friends United Meeting or the Salvation
Army (which holds, "My life must be Christ's broken bread, My love his
outpoured wine"), have spoken of "the sincerity of those whose understanding of God's Word leads them" to eucharistic fellowship employing
material signs *(Ecumenical Perspectives,* Paper No. 116, pp. 161–62). I
cannot help but be impressed again and again by the mood of doxology
and concern for the life of God's people in Christ that marks so much of
the literature that has passed in review in these pages. We are dealing with
what matters, an expression of the gospel, the greatest of God's gifts.

On the last night of his life on earth before the crucifixion Jesus spoke
to his disciples about not drinking of the fruit of the vine again until "that
day" when he would drink it new in the kingdom of God (Mark 14:25),
until the kingdom of God and fulfillment come (Luke 22:16, 18). Ever
since, Jesus' followers have joined, on repeated occasions, in eating and
drinking with him and with one another, "until he comes again" (1 Cor.
11:26). The remembrance is of Jesus. The presence is that of the crucified Christ who is their living Lord. The meaning is for them a covenanted relationship sealed with his life's blood once poured out, a new
covenant based upon his unique sacrifice. By God's word, by God's
Spirit, the Lord Jesus comes. Those who receive him thank God for all
these inestimable benefits and join their praise, confession, prayer, proclamation, and the totality of their lives in thanksgiving to God in service
for others in the world.

The biblical and ecumenical motifs will not be complete in life until the
eucharistic celebration of any and every Christian group is one with all
others "who in every place call upon the name of our Lord Jesus Christ,
both their Lord and ours" (1 Cor. 1:2). The biblical vision is that "every
one who calls upon the name of the Lord will be saved" (Rom. 10:13;
Acts 2:21; cf. Joel 2:32) and that the Lord will "bestow his riches upon
all who invoke him," all who have believed (Rom. 10:12, 14). Indeed,

one early definition of Christians is simply "all who call upon the Lord's name" (Acts 9:14). Hence the ecumenical restlessness. For the vision is that all who call upon the one Lord will be fed of God's richness at one table, with one loaf, and one cup. We cannot rest until all who name the same Lord are at one in his presence.

"Because there is *one bread,* we who are many are *one body,* for we all *partake of one bread"* (1 Cor. 10:17). The biblical argument for ecumenical oneness is as simple as that. The late John A. T. Robinson, bishop of Woolwich, once speculated, following Bishop A. E. J. Rawlinson, that the reason the church came to be called "the body of Christ" was because it partook of "the body of Christ" (1 Cor. 10:16) at the Lord's Supper. Several recent ecumenical statements suggest the church is never so much the church as when it gathers at the Lord's Table. The leap in faith would then be from "receiving" to "being" the Lord's body. The fact is, there are several other, also likely, explanations for the New Testament's description of the church as the body of Christ (J. A. T. Robinson, *The Body: A Study in Pauline Theology,* SBT 5 [London: SCM Press, 1952], pp. 55–58; cf. E. Schweizer, *"sōma," TDNT* 7, 1067–81), and the church is Christ's body likewise when it teaches, proclaims, suffers, and trusts God, as its Master did. It is a "working" body for and of Christ. But what cannot be shaken is the vision of oneness, with Christ and with each other, and how this vision cannot avoid the Lord's Supper but must come about at and through that sacrament.

Hence the abiding significance of "Holy Communion." Christians, already in the New Testament, are fond of adding the adjective "holy" to certain terms—"Holy Spirit," "holy people," "holy church." It is appropriate as a reminder that holiness belongs to and comes from a holy God. Here it is conjointed to this God's supreme revelation of self in Jesus Christ, and that climactic moment of the cross in the drama of redemption, interpreted by the resurrection. And the sacrament we call Communion is that particular means of bringing the results of the work of Christ to each believer individually, personally, in the corporate fellowship of the church. Thus we are to be in union with the Christ and with the sisters and brothers, all of them, who name that name. The benefits are ours, the gift is God's, of oneness, from the Lord.

Is not the One who stands at the door and knocks (Rev. 3:20) inviting the churches today, perhaps as not for centuries of Christian history, to hear and open up and eat with him, and with each other, at the Supper of our Lord?

Subject Index

Since in a sense the entire volume concerns topics like the church and ecumenism, not every instance of such words is indexed. As noted (pp. 1–2), terminologically Lord's Supper, Eucharist, communion, and other words are used with a certain interchangeableness, so readers should often check more than one entry for details about "the meal" as "sacrament." For "Catholics(s)" (as used in Lutherans and Catholics in Dialogue), see "Roman Catholic." In the Scripture Index where a related form occurs, not the exact one in the index entry, "cf." ("compare") is prefixed to the page reference. For abbreviations see the list on pp. ix–x; in the index the words for which the abbreviation stands are usually the basis for alphabetizing. "Bibl." denotes where full title and publishing date are given. "Paper No." = Faith and Order publications. An italicized page number indicates when the entry is defined as a term.

Scripture Index